DOABLE
DIFFERENTIATION

12 Strategies
to Meet the Needs of All Learners

Jane A. G. Kise

Solution Tree | Press
a division of
Solution Tree

555 North Morton Street
Bloomington, IN 47404
800.733.6786 (toll free) / 812.336.7700
FAX: 812.336.7790

email: info@SolutionTree.com
SolutionTree.com

Visit **go.SolutionTree.com/instruction** to download the free reproducibles in this book.

Printed in the United States of America

Library of Congress Cataloging-in-Publication Data

Names: Kise, Jane A. G., author.
Title: Doable differentiation : twelve strategies to meet the needs of
   all learners / Jane A. G. Kise.
Other titles: 12 strategies to meet the needs of all learners
Description: Bloomington, Indiana : Solution Tree Press, [2021] | Includes
   bibliographical references and index.
Identifiers: LCCN 2020051523 (print) | LCCN 2020051524 (ebook) | ISBN
   9781947604841 (Paperback) | ISBN 9781951075002 (ebook)
Subjects: LCSH: Teachers--In-service training. | Effective teaching. |
   Reflective learning.
Classification: LCC LB1731 .K5724 2021 (print) | LCC LB1731 (ebook) | DDC
   370.71/1--dc23
LC record available at https://lccn.loc.gov/2020051523
LC ebook record available at https://lccn.loc.gov/2020051524

Solution Tree
Jeffrey C. Jones, CEO
Edmund M. Ackerman, President

Solution Tree Press
President and Publisher: Douglas M. Rife
Associate Publisher: Sarah Payne-Mills
Art Director: Rian Anderson
Managing Production Editor: Kendra Slayton
Copy Chief: Jessi Finn
Senior Production Editor: Todd Brakke
Content Development Specialist: Amy Rubenstein
Copy Editor: Jessi Finn
Proofreader: Elisabeth Abrams
Text and Cover Designer: Abigail Bowen
Editorial Assistants: Sarah Ludwig and Elijah Oates

For Sue Blair, my dear colleague and great friend who does *not* think and learn as I do. Thank you for not only reading every chapter with care but also for engaging in many, many deep conversations to ensure these strategies will meet the needs of all kinds of learners.

Acknowledgments

To every teacher who has collaborated with me to plan lessons, try strategies, rethink assessments, and even take a few risks in going beyond what he or she had tried before, all in the interest of meeting the needs of more students—thank you!

To the school leaders who introduced the draft chapters of this book to their teachers, talked through which ideas might be best for their site, and gathered feedback that enriched these pages—Rachel Harms, Tim Riordan, Effey Nassis, and Moira Howard Campbell—thank you!

To Gary Anderson, who read early chapters from a secondary perspective—thank you!

To Wendy Behrens, who encouraged me to act on the feedback I received from doable differentiation workshops by getting to work on writing this book—thank you!

To school principal Beth Russell and the original collaborative team members who volunteered to take on extra professional development and action research time to establish the cognitive processing styles as their common framework for teaching and learning—Marcia Malecha, Nancy Holzer, Steve Pohlen, Libby Zuzik, Jon Kuch, Peg Mahon, Bruce Black, Karen Hollingsworth, Kim Anthenet, Kate Andrews, Chris Wernimont, Sarah Wernimont, Dan King, Joe Chan, and in memory of Jo Kunz (I know I'm forgetting some)—thank you!

To all the students who gave up their lunch hours to talk with me in focus groups about these strategies (yes, we served pizza)—thank you!

And to Todd Brakke, my editor, whose structure and certainty cognitive processing style added the consistency and clarity that I find so helpful as a vision and interpretation writer.

Solution Tree Press would like to thank the following reviewers:

Renee Clemmons
English Teacher
Quitman School District
Quitman, Arkansas

Kelly Hilliard
Math Teacher
McQueen High School
Reno, Nevada

Zachary Coats
Science Teacher
Northside High School
Fort Smith, Arkansas

Louis Lim
Vice Principal
Bayview Secondary School
Richmond Hill, Ontario, Canada

Lisa May
Literacy Coach
Country Meadows and Kildeer
Elementary Schools
Long Grove, Illinois

Bo Ryan
Principal
Greater Hartford Academy
   of the Arts Middle School
Hartford, Connecticut

Faith Short
Assistant Principal
East Pointe Elementary School
Greenwood, Arkansas

Robert Taylor
English Teacher
Northside High School
Fort Smith, Arkansas

Julie Wallace
Principal
Quitman School District
Quitman, Arkansas

Visit **go.SolutionTree.com/instruction** to download
the free reproducibles in this book.

Table of Contents

Reproducible page is in italics.

About the Author

Jane A. G. Kise, EdD, is the author of more than twenty-five books and an organizational consultant with extensive experience in leadership development and executive coaching, instructional coaching, and differentiated instruction. She is considered a worldwide expert in Jungian type and its impact on leadership and education. She works with schools and businesses, facilitating the creation of environments where everyone—leaders, teachers, and students—can flourish.

Jane trains educators around the world on coaching, collaborative practices, effective change processes, and differentiated instruction, especially in mathematics. A frequent conference keynote speaker, she has spoken at education conferences and psychological type conferences across the United States and in Europe, Saudi Arabia, Australia, and New Zealand. Jane has also written articles for several magazines and has received awards for her differentiated coaching research.

Jane teaches doctoral courses in educational leadership at the University of St. Thomas and is a past faculty member of the Center for Applications of Psychological Type. She also served as president of the Association for Psychological Type International (APTi).

Jane holds a master of business administration from the Carlson School of Management and a doctorate in educational leadership from the University of St. Thomas in St. Paul, Minnesota. She is certified in neuroscience and Jungian personality; is a certified Positive Intelligence coach; is qualified to use Myers-Briggs Type Indicator® (MBTI®) Steps I, II, and III as an MBTI Master Practitioner; and is certified in emotional intelligence instruments, Hogan assessments, and Leadership 360° tools.

To learn more about Jane's work, visit her website (www.janekise.com).

To book Jane A. G. Kise for professional development, contact pd@SolutionTree.com.

What Makes Differentiation Doable?

Step back into yourself as a teenager. You're taking an assessment on the first moon landing in July 1969. Which of the following assignments would you rather tackle? (Remember, you're choosing as a student, not as an adult educator.)

- Write an essay about the first moon landing. Be sure to cover the following learning targets for this unit: Understanding the Cold War context surrounding the goal of landing on the moon before the end of the 1960s and being able to explain the building of capacity to design and manufacture equipment, challenges in the training of astronauts and ground personnel, reactions to the televised event, and advances in scientific knowledge that directly resulted from the space program through July 1969.

- Imagine you watched the 1969 moon landing live. Choose a viewpoint: Were you an engineer or someone in another role at Mission Control? Did you watch it on television with your family? Were you related to an astronaut? Write a letter to a friend or relative about your experience. Be sure your letter demonstrates your knowledge of the learning targets for this unit. *Note: Your letter doesn't need to accurately replicate the experiences of the person you choose; rather, it should express how a person in that role or situation may have reacted to the moon landing.*

If you teach elementary students, which of the following would you have chosen when you were your students' age?

- Make a double timeline. On the top line, show the sequence of main events in the fairy tale "Cinderella." In the bottom line, write about why each event is important to the story.

- Rewrite "Cinderella" from the viewpoint of any character but Cinderella. Make sure your tale shows the same sequence of main events as the original version we read together as a class.

There—I differentiated (twice) in just two steps. In both examples, I wrote an assessment task that I would have wanted to answer as a student. I then wrote one that covers the same learning targets for students who think and reason differently than I do.

This is *doable differentiation*. It's one lesson plan that involves just a few minutes of extra effort to differentiate a learning task by providing choices so that students can use their strengths to demonstrate mastery of learning targets. When educators consider differentiated instruction, choice often comes to mind as a strategy for tapping student interests, skills, and more. Mastering choice strategies, as in these examples, is just one key way teachers can work within established definitions of differentiated instruction. There are many more. As you read the following definitions, each from a different resource about classroom differentiation, note the powerful role that giving choices can play in implementing effective instruction. And, bring to mind other differentiation strategies you've used:

> At its most basic level, differentiating instruction means "shaking up" what goes on in the classroom so that students have multiple options for taking in information, making sense of ideas, and expressing what they learn. In other words, a differentiated classroom provides different avenues to acquiring content, to processing or making sense of ideas, and to developing products so that each student can learn effectively. (Tomlinson, 2017, p. 1)

> [Differentiating instruction means] understanding where each student begins, where he or she is on the journey toward the success criteria for the lesson. (Hattie, 2012, p. 104)

> [Differentiating instruction means] adjusting instruction for individual learners' needs, styles, cultural values, and/or interests. (Kise, 2007, p. 1)

The first definition focuses on differentiating how students access content, process what they are learning, and demonstrate mastery via different products. The second definition focuses on differentiating instruction based on students' current proficiency levels. The third focuses on various differences among students. Providing choices fits within any of these definitions but will seldom be enough to help every student reach mastery. Thus the concept of differentiated instruction has grown to include all kinds of sophisticated tools and methods. But what is the track record for differentiation in this world of evidence-based reform?

In a study of over 2,000 middle school students, researchers Catherine A. Little, D. Betsy McCoach, and Sally M. Reis (2014) find that differentiating instruction based on proficiency makes little difference in learning outcomes. After reviewing the impact of professional development on classroom instruction, researchers Martin Mills, Sue Monk, Amanda Keddie, Peter Renshaw, Pam Christie, David Geelan, and Christina Gowlett (2014) conclude that differentiation is complex, yet schools and districts often require it of teachers without providing sufficient training and support. While investigating teacher attitudes toward moving to mixed-ability classrooms, researchers Karen Dunn and Ellie Darlington (2016) note an attitude of hostility toward differentiation. Teachers voiced their fear of barriers such as time constraints, class size, emotional impact on students of some differentiation strategies, and more. Writing for EdSurge, Wendy McMahon (2019) reports that 95 percent of the 600 teachers who responded to a 2019 study consider differentiation important—and difficult because of lack of time and resources. Still other voices decry, "Differentiation doesn't work!" (Delisle, 2015; Schmoker, 2010). Although many teachers have succeeded at using differentiated instruction (Bal, 2016; Lai, Zhang, & Chang, 2020), these collective findings indicate educators have jumped on the differentiation bandwagon without adequately allowing for one or more crucial factors for success, such as extensive professional development, planning time, and scaffolding for newer teachers.

These studies draw on input from teachers at every level of experience, but the struggle to implement differentiation is often most dire for those newest to the classroom. Imagine a surgical intern, fresh from medical school, being asked to perform advanced abdominal, orthopedic, cardiovascular, or plastic surgery for patients with varying degrees of acute conditions, all in the first months of practice. You wouldn't want to be one of those patients!

Yet, school systems, states, and provinces ask new teachers to facilitate multiple subjects with diverse learners in contained classrooms. They're striving to build relationships, master classroom control, plan lessons, and assess student readiness and progress. The expectation to differentiate, especially using a complex model, can overwhelm their capacity for learning. New teachers, and teachers new to differentiation, don't have resistance to differentiated instruction; rather, they react naturally to a scarcity of time, of expertise with foundational skills, and of expert coaching with deliberate practice. In particular, research shows expert coaching is essential to developing true expertise (Mielke & Frontier, 2012).

That's where this book comes in. It provides twelve valuable strategy groups you, as a K–12 teacher or leader, can use with what you are already doing in the classroom or at your school to meet the needs of four core cognitive processing styles your students have and that you will learn about in this book. Within each of the twelve strategy groups, you will find several approaches to using the strategy effectively with your students. Will these strategies solve every problem in a mixed-ability classroom? No, but for every strategy, you'll learn about the issues it *can* address, its research base, and multiple ways to use it. The teachers I've shared these differentiation strategies with—many of whom struggled with or resisted implementing differentiation in the past—say, "Wow, this is doable!"

In this introduction, you will learn the goals and key principles of doable differentiation. You will also become familiar with how I've organized this book so you can best use it based on your own cognitive processing style.

The Goal of Doable Differentiation

With an overarching mission focused on increasing learning for all students, this book's goal is to help you and your colleagues foster classrooms where all students reap the following benefits of differentiation.

- **Successfully learning:** Teachers need clear learning goals and ways to provide time and support so every student can reach them. Differentiation is at the heart of equity, ensuring students each experience the kind of academic success that fosters a growth mindset and the self-efficacy that helps them internalize the belief, *I am a learner!*

Example: A teacher team I worked with helped 100 percent of eighth-grade students complete and pass their National History Day projects, compared with failure rates as high as 30 percent on similar projects in past years. The team used pressure-prompted accommodations (chapter 6, page 87), combined with choice strategies (chapter 3, page 47).

- **Thriving as members of a learning community:** Classrooms, policies, curricula, and adult-student interactions need to reflect that the whole child comes to school. Social-emotional learning (SEL) isn't an add-on (Collaborative for Academic, Social, and Emotional Learning, n.d.). Students constantly pick up strategies, healthy and unhealthy, to meet their emotional needs. Careful implementation of many strategies in this book aids students in developing critical skills for cognitive processing, self-monitoring, understanding of differences, and more.

  Example: A teacher used a wait time strategy (chapter 4, page 63) to help her kindergartners learn to hold their thoughts until every student, including the English learners, had a response ready for discussions. These young students learned about having patience and respecting each other's ideas from this simple teacher move.

- **Engaged actively in their education:** Many strategies in this book require students to think for themselves, make choices, create their own meaning, evaluate their own work, and take charge of their study time.

  Example: A teacher used an open question strategy (chapter 9, page 137) and a student-centered discussion strategy (chapter 7, page 101) to change her mathematics students from passive learners to persistent problem solvers who enjoy open-ended tasks.

- **Agile thinking:** The agile mind is open to new ways of thinking, learning, and doing. Real-life problems seldom have textbook answers; students need to draw on past learning experiences *and* comfortably explore new options.

  Example: A teacher introduced her students to the four cognitive processing styles that underlie doable differentiation (chapter 1, page 15). She encouraged students to make choices in assignments that were different from what they'd normally choose. Several students commented, "I had to work hard, but you gave me strategies that helped me stretch. I think I learned more than if I'd done the usual."

- **Maturing decision makers:** Creating lifelong learners can't be a meaningless generality. Students need to learn how to learn for their own sake. If teachers tell them what and how to learn, how will they learn to define their own learning targets, narrow down the information that will be most helpful, and plan for mastery? If teachers make all their decisions, how will they learn to make decisions themselves?

Example: As students worked with the planned movement strategy Knowledge Stations (chapter 13, page 201), which combines several approaches in this book, they learned to plan their work time, work independently, work well with a partner, examine primary documents, and evaluate the quality of their work— all skills they would need as they left school.

If you overlap the traits I just listed—*successful, thriving, engaged, agile,* and *maturing*—with the conventional STEAM content areas of *science, technology, engineering, arts,* and *mathematics* education, it makes for what I call *STEAM²* (not to be confused with similar designations you might encounter online). Figure I.1 illustrates how these traits align with each other.

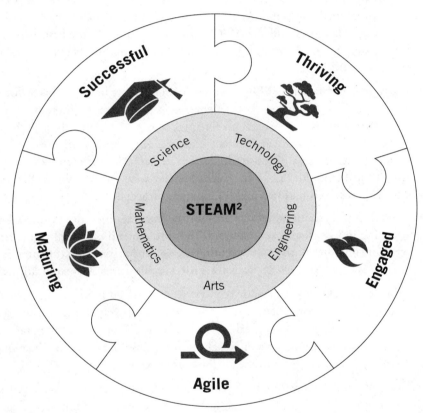

Figure I.1: *The elements of STEAM².*

You might think of these new components as aligned with a whole-child approach (Rea & Zinskie, 2017) or one focused on social-emotional components (Collaborative for Academic, Social, and Emotional Learning, n.d.). Although no one referred to it as *STEAM²* at the time, I experienced this vision of STEAM² a *long* time ago, before anyone actually coined *STEAM.* Yes, from lived experience, I know that overlapping all these traits together into doable differentiation is possible. You see, as a student, I experienced differentiation in a public school that had no textbooks for science, social studies, or language arts; we learned concepts through exploring multiple texts, a mix of direct instruction and high-level discussions, and hands-on activities. Consider how this experience helped me develop the second set of STEAM[2] traits.

- **Successful?** Yep, we students were well prepared for college classes. When a group of us gathered during Thanksgiving break our freshman year, while we were attending different universities, we discovered our high school's blend of instructional methods had cemented our foundational knowledge of science, mathematics, and composition. Content other freshmen were struggling with was review for us.

- **Thriving?** Yes, we thrived as the school's "All students can do this" approach led to a growth mindset (Dweck, 2016). As technology tools exploded, every student learned computer programming skills in grades 7–8 mathematics (utilizing a language called *BASIC*). That set us up to be the first district in the state to test a computer terminal bank, giving us access to hours of programming time.

- **Engaged?** Even eventual English and finance majors like me looked forward to the hands-on STEAM classes, centered as they were in differentiation strategies such as open questions (chapter 9, page 137) and choice (chapter 3, page 47). We experienced differentiation via our interests when each student completed a ninth-grade science research project focused on using the scientific method to solve a problem they were curious about. Several students received national awards for their projects.

- **Agile?** Our district embraced new ways of learning, including project-based learning in just about every subject. Through a blend of what I call curiosity creators (chapter 8, page 119) and unambiguous instruction (chapter 5, page 75), they gave us methods for varied applications and explorations.

- **Maturing?** During our senior year, we were involved in planning our own curriculum for world literature and world history even as our teachers guided us through the structure of calculus and physics. Can you see the gradual release of responsibility by the teachers, increasing our stake in what we were learning? We were ready to be set loose at university.

Why relate my own education? It's because my schoolmates and I weren't like the students from other schools who, for example, told me they were taking college-level courses so they never had to take a mathematics or literature or history class in college. Our STEAM classes (and humanities classes as well) left us open to learning more. All students deserve school experiences that allow them to be successful, thriving, engaged, agile, and maturing, from their first day of kindergarten to the final day of their final year.

Of course, not every student goes on to major in the same subject you, as a teacher, majored in. Likewise, not every student will declare your class the most interesting one they ever took. However, when teachers truly try to create lifelong learners, isn't part of that mission to leave them wanting more or at least feel like they grew from what they learned? Doable differentiation helps accomplish that mission.

Key Doable Differentiation Principles

Before we dig in, let's be clear about a few big ideas in this book. At a foundational level, this book defines the following four core cognitive processing styles that all students fit into.

1. **Structure and certainty:** This style defines students who prefer clear guidance on learning tasks so they know what to do.

2. **Vision and interpretation:** This style defines students who crave demonstrating uniqueness and prefer to follow their own lead.

3. **Experience and movement:** This style defines students who prefer to learn by doing—moving, talking, experimenting, touching objects— rather than passively.

4. **Question and connection:** This style defines students who prefer to collaborate and lead as they learn.

You'll learn much more about these in chapter 1 (page 15), but for now, the following guidance will answer your big questions regarding the doable differentiation approach and why you should give it a try. This guidance also establishes what separates this book from other books on differentiation that you may have read.

- **Take two steps:** To keep the differentiation process doable, once you've identified clear learning targets, you'll be using a two-step process to choose which of this book's strategies to use as part of a lesson plan. (You'll find full-unit examples that illustrate these two steps in chapter 15, page 233).

  a. Plan for how *you* like to teach and learn *or* how the curriculum presents the materials, observing which cognitive processes your plan most aligns with.

  b. Adjust that plan for students whose needs are different from those the current learning plan most supports. Meeting those needs is embedded in the twelve strategies.

- **Let content drive instruction:** Perhaps you've seen research that teaching to learning styles doesn't improve student achievement (Hattie, 2012). That's true. However, doable differentiation isn't about catering every aspect of every lesson to every student. Instead of matching students with strategies that meet their cognitive processing styles, you'll consider the best style for the course content while ensuring that, *over time*, your classroom activities involve all the styles.

  Think about the following examples of how content often drives the style in which *all* students will learn best.

  ‣ You can't learn science lab techniques without hands-on learning— the experience-and-movement cognitive process.

- At some point, reading has to involve independent silent reading—the vision-and-interpretation cognitive process.

- Some content requires mastery through practice and even memorization—the structure-and-certainty cognitive process.

- Some content works best with collaborative, rigorous group activities—the question-and-connection cognitive process.

In other words, to be successful, students need to develop agility with *all* learning styles. Consider the difference between the following two student attitudes.

- "This is hard; I can't do it" or "This is stupid, and I don't want to do it."

- "This makes me uncomfortable because it's out of my style. I need to develop strategies, and my teacher can help me."

Doable differentiation fosters the second attitude in students.

- **Concentrate on honoring rather than identifying students' processing styles:** You don't have to know each student's processing style; in a classroom of twenty to thirty students, you're almost guaranteed to have students with every style. Trying to observe which students are which might quickly become overwhelming. You'll see examples of reflection activities in chapter 1 (page 15) that can help students understand which styles are more natural for them and where they need to develop skills, but it's OK for them to remain undecided. In contrast, you *do* need to know where students are on the journey to proficiency with learning standards. You may find your current assessments work well for this purpose, but I think you'll find many of this book's strategies will improve those assessments.

- **Don't differentiate every minute of the day:** Sometimes, every student does need to be doing the same thing at the same time. Be sure to keep an eye out, though, for whether you're defaulting too much to your own style or the style your curriculum favors. Even though all students must learn to adapt to all learning styles, they need opportunities to learn in the style they favor, and your lessons should reflect that.

As you plan for instruction, deliberately decide when and how you will incorporate differentiation strategies. Perhaps you'll include activities for every style over the course of a unit or rotate the final project format for each unit. Perhaps you'll work to change up activities throughout the day. Or you might find yourself constantly incorporating the strategies that take little or no planning, such as the following.

- Using a choice strategy (chapter 3, page 47) that provides students with the motivation that autonomy fosters yet requires minimal teacher planning time

‣ Using a wait time strategy (chapter 4, page 63) to ensure all students can ready their thoughts before a discussion begins

‣ Using a planned movement strategy (chapter 13, page 201) to ensure students move and interact when you want them to and not when you need them to sit still

- **Be mindful of those who are resistant to school as they know it:** Imagine if you spent your days writing, dribbling a ball, and brushing your teeth with your nondominant hand—or think of how difficult using right-handed scissors is for a left-handed student. Using a neutral framework helps ensure that no student is spending too much time learning with his or her metaphorical off hand. The cognitive processing styles introduced at the start of this section and detailed in chapter 1 have nothing to do with intelligence; yet in school after school, patterns emerge where students with certain styles perform better than those with others because classroom activities favor them.

By understanding these principles and adjusting your instruction based on them, you will be amazed at what you can accomplish through doable differentiation. Here are some things I've experienced when schools implement this book's strategies.

- Students in an intervention session say, "Guys, we've been doing math for three hours and didn't know it!"

- Teacher comments change from "These students can't do it" to "Oh, these students need a different strategy to do it."

- Students come to class on time, sit up front, and ask questions because they've learned how to learn, instead of assuming that once again, they won't measure up.

- The student responsible for the most disruptions is never again sent to the principal's office.

- Students become more patient with and kind to each other.

- Teachers, instead of being defensive, ask for help in differentiating lessons after receiving feedback from students that didn't have to work very hard to get good grades.

- Students beg to do more than one final assessment project because so many look interesting.

These experiences highlight how doable differentiation makes it possible for educators to use their strengths *and* quickly adjust lessons for students who have different strengths. It targets not just academic success but STEAM[2], a whole-child approach that includes social-emotional aspects of learning. It provides a toolkit that lets you improve many of the lessons and strategies you love.

About This Book

This book is divided into three parts. Part 1 provides foundational knowledge about learning styles, differentiation, and instruction. Chapter 1 examines the different cognitive processes all teachers and students have and how knowledge of them leads to effective differentiation. Chapter 2 highlights the importance of having clear learning goals and expectations before employing differentiation strategies. Part 2 covers chapters 3–14 and constitutes the twelve differentiation strategies. Each of these chapters explains the strategy concept, provides a series of strategic approaches to using it in the classroom, explains essentials for success, provides answers to common concerns about using it, and highlights the research that supports the strategy's effectiveness. Finally, part 3 explains the two critical steps teachers should use when designing differentiated lessons (chapter 15) and provides closing guidance as you move forward in your journey toward doable differentiation (the epilogue).

Note that I've structured this book to model the differentiation principles I've outlined in this introduction. This means that, although I've set up this book to follow a logical progression, you don't need to read the chapters in order or the content of any chapter in order. Your brain doesn't necessarily favor the cognitive process my brain does, and the choice of how to proceed is yours.

DOING DIFFERENTIATION

This book differentiates by giving readers choices. In my experience, many teachers prefer obtaining hands-on, concrete experiences *before* they read about theories and frameworks. This is a *do-think* mentality best represented by the structure-and-certainty (let me know what to do) and experience-and-movement (let me do something) cognitive processing styles. If that's you, proceed to part 2. In particular, chapters 3 and 4 demonstrate multiple high-reward, low-planning ways of using differentiation for choice and wait time. It won't be long before you find that you're using these strategies constantly and unconsciously.

I also know many educators who prefer to know the big picture before they jump into hands-on mode. This is a *think-do* mentality best represented by the vision-and-interpretation (let me follow my own lead) and question-and-connection (let me lead as I learn) cognitive processes. If that describes you, proceed to part 1 first, which explains the four cognitive processing styles students use for taking in information, helps you identify your own style, and provides essential understanding of how to teach around all students' styles to allow for effective differentiation.

Regardless of your initial approach, you'll ultimately use the full set of strategy-focused chapters in part 2 as you might use a cookbook—learning about the strategy (recipe) that best aligns with the instructional meal you want to plan. Table I.1 shows the twelve doable differentiation strategies, along with the problems they might solve. Which do you need now? Skip around; see what works!

Table I.1: *The Doable Differentiation Strategies*

Chapter	Strategy Group	Uses for Doable Differentiation
3	Choice	Increase student engagement and creativity while differentiating for ability.
4	Wait time	Increase participation levels and quality of thinking while decreasing classroom management issues.
5	Unambiguous instruction	Improve student mastery and retention of concrete information and processes.
6	Pressure-prompted accommodations	Provide new ways of planning projects and managing time that work better for students whose creativity and focus thrive under the pressure that deadlines create.
7	Student-centered discussions	Engage all students in higher-level thinking that increases the level of content and products they can work with and produce.
8	Curiosity creators	Engage students in complex texts and tasks, increase knowledge retention, activate prior knowledge, and develop thinking skills such as inference, justification, prediction, and logical reasoning.
9	Open questions	Engage all students in higher-level thinking, allowing access to complex content and tasks while maintaining the cognitive demands of tasks.
10	Concept maps	Improve higher-level-thinking skills and develop common tools and skills needed for good discourse.
11	Big notes	Increase student collaboration during group work, simplify task management, and increase teacher feedback opportunities.
12	Moveable organizers	Improve student ability to organize and revise thoughts, processes, and arguments.
13	Planned movement	Improve classroom climate, student engagement, and classroom management.
14	Talking to write	Deepen student understanding of topics and ideas while creating energy for writing.

Sound like a plan? Great! Proceed to part 1 to understand the doable differentiation framework, *or* skip ahead to part 2 and dive into the first strategy, choice, with the goal of finding a way to immediately increase the choices your students have to guide their learning. As you read, remember that you're differentiating not just for academic success but for STEAM[2]—helping students become successful, thriving, engaged, agile, and mature.

VIRTUAL CLASSROOMS

Finalizing *Doable Differentiation* during the school and university closures due to COVID-19 gave me firsthand experience with using the strategies in this book online, both synchronously and asynchronously. The key principles I share are as valid for distance learning as for the classroom. In every chapter, you'll see tips or adjustments in feature boxes like this one that show how to use a strategy to enhance distance learning and other online student experiences.

Reflection Activity

Consider the following questions as you reflect on this introduction's content.

1. What are your experiences with differentiation? What problems with differentiation, or with instruction in your classroom, are you hoping to solve? Write down your thoughts so that you can reflect back on them as you gain experience with the twelve groups of strategies in this book.

2. Look back at the moon landing and Cinderella examples on page 1. Show them to your colleagues, family members, and friends, and ask a few questions.

    ‣ Which options would they have chosen and why?

    ‣ Do any of the options resemble assignments they loved or hated when they were in school?

    ‣ What does and doesn't surprise you about their answers?

PART 1

THE FOUNDATION

CHAPTER 1

Cognitive Processes and Effective Differentiation

Think back to your student days. How would you have ranked the following four activities, all with the same goal of demonstrating your mastery of key concepts regarding the eighty-year struggle for women's voting rights in the United States? (Assume each of these would include further instruction and a rubric to ensure the assignments are equal in rigor and requirements.)

1. Write a first-person magazine article from the viewpoint of a historical figure in the women's voting rights movement. Include information on at least eight significant events.

2. With a partner, write and perform a dialogue between two leaders in the women's voting rights movement as they vote for the first time. They should recall at least eight significant events that led to this historic moment. Turn in your script.

3. List at least eight key events from during the struggle for women's voting rights, explaining why they were significant. You may write an essay or use presentation software to convey the information.

4. With a partner, create a *Jeopardy!*-style game using JeopardyLabs (https://jeopardylabs.com) that demonstrates your understanding of the significance of at least eight key events from the women's voting rights movement.

Now, think of a colleague who regularly engages students in classroom activities very different from the ones you prefer. Perhaps you've observed or shared lesson plans and wondered, *Would I have thrived in this teacher's classroom or even enjoyed having this teacher?* Consider—or ask!—how this person would rank the same choices.

When I run a similar exercise in workshops, I ask, "Who ranked the first option the highest?" At least a few hands always go up. I then ask, "Who looked at the first one and thought, *I'd rather clean my classroom floor with a toothbrush than do this?*" Again, at least a few hands go up. The point is made: what some teachers see as the best option, others view as the worst. What if you were a student in your colleague's classroom and spent the majority of class time on assignments misaligned with your learning style?

An alarm bell might be ringing in your head, "But students can't just do what they want to do!" This is absolutely true. However, as teachers, if we lack a framework for understanding how our own learning experiences and preferences drive our educational beliefs and practices, we can accidentally leave out some students. In fact, schools do just that. From the 1940s onward, researchers find patterns in dropouts, Merit Scholars, and more (Macdaid, McCaulley, & Kainz, 1987; Myers & Myers, 1995; Myers, McCaulley, Quenk, & Hammer, 1998). To consider how this research holds up to a modern context, my colleague Maryanne Sutherland, a retired special education teacher, tracked student cognitive processing styles at the alternative high school where she taught for thirty-five years. Year after year, the dominant cognitive processing style of her students was the experience-and-movement style (Sutherland, 2014). Further, my colleague and coauthor on *Creating a Coaching Culture for Professional Learning Communities* (Kise & Russell, 2010), Beth Russell, and I worked with students who were at risk of academic failure in the schools where she served as principal and saw the same patterns. While all students can be at risk of academic failure in certain learning environments, most students in the alternative schools that colleagues or I have worked with would choose the fourth option from the list on page 15, yet they are more often required to complete tasks that have more in common with options 1, 2, and 3. That isn't fair or equitable.

With an eye firmly on learning equity, this chapter provides a neutral framework that describes how people process information, affecting how they learn best. Neutral frameworks allow discussion of teaching and learning in nonjudgmental ways, emphasizing strengths rather than limits on what individuals can do; they are also useful in describing which learning styles a practice will reach and apply across cultures and to both adults and students (Kise, 2017). For example, note that in contrast to a neutral framework, strengths-based multiple intelligences suggest that some students will do better in certain content areas—or at least their language evokes this thinking in both adults and students. Without a neutral framework for understanding differentiation, teachers' own biases and curricular biases show up in what and how they teach.

This chapter also details how the neutral framework that underlies doable differentiation helps teachers meet more students' needs and how it helps students successfully engage with assignments that are outside their hardwired cognitive processes. From it, you'll learn about how students' innate tendencies are categorized into four specific cognitive processing styles (those I established in this book's introduction, page 1) as well as how you can arrange classroom instruction to appeal to each style as part of a lesson or unit plan.

Whether you use this book on your own or as part of a collaborative team, this neutral framework provides insights into not just your practices but also those of other teachers. You'll find yourself thinking, "No wonder my colleague implemented that strategy well when it was so difficult for me." Or, "So that's why that works in my classroom. Now I know how to explain it to other teachers." If you're a coach or administrator, you'll have a vocabulary for understanding your reactions to teacher practices and an easier way to help teachers adjust those practices, when necessary, to meet the needs of more students.

DOING DIFFERENTIATION

Unless you plan to invest significant time in helping students understand the processing styles described in this chapter, I encourage you not to use any existing free tools for students to self-asses their style or personality type. None of the free quizzes you might find on the internet provide reliable or valid data, and accurate commercially available tools require certification. Students are more likely to accurately identify their cognitive processes through the activities included in this chapter. Instead, consider three levels for using the processing styles detailed in this chapter.

1. Understanding your own processing style and—knowing that you are bound to have students of every style—differentiating so that no student is constantly at a disadvantage for learning and engagement

2. Understanding your own style and using reflection activities to build classroom relationships and norms while helping students recognize when activities use their strengths and when they need strategies to stretch

3. Investing in a type-tool certification for at least one member of a collaborative team so that all team members might benefit from using identification tools for both adults and students; this has applications for collaboration, leadership, coaching, instruction, classroom management, stress management, career development, and more. The only certification designed specifically for educators (for which I am the course leader) is available from Type Pro (www.type-pro.com).

The Doable Differentiation Framework and School

I picked the example assignment choices at the start of this chapter to appeal to students who process information in the four different ways that I introduced in this book's introduction. Figure 1.1 (page 18) describes each of these cognitive processing styles. While you read information about each one, consider which style best describes how you approached learning as a student. As with the assignment choices, more than one may resonate, but one probably seems very *unlike* you.

When I ask differentiation workshop attendees, or students, to reflect on figure 1.1, most agree that the cognitive processing style diagonally opposite the one most like theirs is the one *least* like them. Students who prefer to follow their own lead (vision and interpretation) typically aren't all that fond of using hands-on manipulatives because they can already see things in their heads. Students who want to act (experience and movement) often struggle to sit still for independent reading. Students who want to lead as they learn (question and connection) dislike repetitive tasks. And students who just want to know what to do (structure and certainty) typically aren't comfortable with open-ended tasks.

Structure and Certainty
(Let Me Know What to Do)

At their best, these students seek clarity on what is to be learned and the best way to learn it. Their motivation may be efficiency ("Let's not waste time guessing if there's a good way to do it"), a desire to please adults, or a healthy love of getting the right answer.

What they want:

1. Set clear expectations and goals.
2. Show me examples.
3. Provide the steps in writing.
4. Answer my questions as I have them.
5. Give me time to think.
6. Let me work with and memorize facts.
7. Avoid too many surprises.
8. Build on what I already know.
9. Let me know along the way if I'm doing things right.
10. Connect content with past efforts and experiences.

 Vision and Interpretation
(Let Me Follow My Own Lead)

At their best, these students seek answers to their own questions, use their imaginations, and express in unique ways what they have learned. Their motivation may be curiosity, a desire to solve a problem they've identified, or a desire to follow up on the connections, imaginings, and hunches their brains create.

What they want:

1. Let me delve deeply into things that interest me.
2. Avoid repetition and routine.
3. Let me figure out for myself how to do things.
4. Give me choices.
5. Listen to my ideas.
6. Let me learn independently.
7. Let me start with my imagination.
8. Help me bring what I envision into reality.
9. Give free rein to my creativity and curiosity.
10. Provide references for me to build my own knowledge base.

 Experience and Movement
(Let Me Do Something)

At their best, these students use acute observations of the real world to solve problems. They think by touching, manipulating, and experimenting, often through purposeful trial and error. Their motivations involve making, solving, or fixing things, often to help others one on one.

What they want:

1. Start with hands-on activities.
2. Give me steps to follow.
3. Build on what I already know.
4. Tell me why I'm learning something.
5. Give me chances to talk, move, and work in groups.
6. Set a realistic deadline.
7. Give me examples.
8. Provide clear expectations.
9. Go light on theory.
10. Let me apply it immediately.

 Question and Connection
(Let Me Lead as I Learn)

At their best, these students move quickly from what is taught to what could be. They think by collaborating, discussing, or debating to generate ideas or plans that get others excited. Their motivations include influencing others and using theoretical or imaginative approaches to create new ideas.

What they want:

1. Start with the big picture, not the details.
2. Let me dream big without penalties.
3. Let me find a new way to do it.
4. Let me experiment.
5. Give me choices.
6. Keep changing what we do.
7. Let me teach or tell someone what I've learned.
8. Let me be in charge of something.
9. Let me talk or work in groups.
10. Let me come up with my own ideas.

Figure 1.1: The cognitive processing styles.

Visit **go.SolutionTree.com/instruction** *for a free reproducible version of this figure.*

Understanding these four basic ways students process information lets teachers add scaffolding for individual students or groups most out of their comfort zone on an assignment, thereby helping them access all four styles as necessary. Note that this framework also provides a different way of examining equity and inclusion issues. As mentioned, when educators teach predominantly to their own cognitive processing style (as is most natural to them), the result is instruction that meets the needs of some students more than others. Consider the data in table 1.1, which compare cognitive processing styles in the 130 teachers at an alternative high school of nearly 2,000 students with those of students deemed at risk due to psychological or emotional concerns and students who drop out of school. These data are from a one-year sample from years of data collection by special education teacher and colleague Mary Anne Sutherland (2014); many schools and programs have shown similar results.

Table 1.1: *Cognitive Processing Styles in Educators and Students at Risk*

Structure and Certainty (Let Me Know What to Do)	Vision and Interpretation (Let Me Follow My Own Lead)
U.S. representative sample: 47 percent Teachers in the school: 58 percent Students at risk: 4 percent Dropouts: 8 percent	U.S. representative sample: 8 percent Teachers: 20 percent Students at risk: 4 percent Dropouts: 1 percent
Experience and Movement (Let Me Do Something)	**Question and Connection (Let Me Lead as I Learn)**
U.S. representative sample: 25 percent Teachers: 4 percent Students at risk: 41 percent Dropouts: 59 percent	U.S. representative sample: 18 percent Teachers: 18 percent Students at risk: 50 percent Dropouts: 31 percent

Source: Adapted from Myers et al., 2018; Sutherland, 2014.

It's fair to ask, What does table 1.1 really show? Because these cognitive processes do not describe differences in ability, if there were no biases against any of the styles, the percentage of students at risk or who have dropped out would be close to the numbers given for the general population. Instead, we see the experience-and-movement and question-and-connection students seem far less likely to succeed in schools as most educators know them. These are the students whose cognitive styles are least like the majority of their teachers, and the patterns reflected in these data exist across the diverse schools and school cultures with which I have worked. There are overlaps between these ways of looking at information processing and the values of various cultures, meaning that this framework can provide insights into culturally responsive and equitable teaching. This invisible form of diversity is only a starting place, yet it can also be a bridge between other crucial ways to look at diversity and inclusion.

In the following sections, you'll examine ways of energizing instruction through extraversion and introversion and allowing students to take in information through sensing and intuition. These four characteristics are the building blocks for the four cognitive processing styles detailed in figure 1.1 (page 18).

Extraversion and Introversion

While extraversion and introversion are hardly new concepts, note first that I use the spelling extra*v*ersion to indicate the context of Swiss psychologist Carl Jung's (1921/1923) work on psychological types. Jung (1921/1923) developed the framework of psychological types through his clinical observations, and his concepts have since been confirmed in multiple ways, most recently through the neuroimaging work of Dario Nardi (2020) and other highly regarded and well-researched personality frameworks (Myers et al., 2018). Jung (1921/1923) observes two patterns in how patients gain energy: (1) through the outer world of action and interaction or (2) through the inner world of solitude and reflection.

The concepts of extraversion and introversion have nothing to do with sociability—who is shy or who has the most friends—but instead describe a person's preference, whether the inner or outer world has the most pull on an individual. If you're skeptical about accommodating these differences in your instruction, consider these implications.

- Just as you need energy to teach, students need energy to learn. The right blend of interaction and reflection can keep everyone energized.

- If you don't plan for movement and interaction, students who prefer extraversion will move and interact when you least want them to.

- If you don't plan for engaging introverted students, they can easily get lost in thought in their fascinating inner worlds and fail to pay attention.

- By definition, children, and thus your students, are immature. They need help to make wise choices. For example, think about how the Retrieve-Pair-Share approach (page 66) helps extraverted students think instead of blurt and gives introverted students a chance to form their thoughts before bringing them to the external world.

- Meeting the needs of both extraverted and introverted students decreases classroom-management issues, increases the depth of student thinking, and, as discussed in Why Wait Time Works (page 73), is essential to helping students improve their ability to take in information and make decisions. This is the essence of executive function (Murphy, 2013).

As you look at the lists in table 1.2, consider how the listed characteristics might affect student engagement and success with various classroom activities.

I've asked groups of extraverted and introverted adults, teens, and children from around the world to draw pictures of their ideal classrooms or office environments, always with starkly contrasting results. What might a floor plan look like? Who would be in the classroom? Where would they read and write? What else might be in the room?

Table 1.2: *Extraversion and Introversion in Students*

Extraverted students tend to:	Introverted students tend to:
• Think out loud (Sometimes, their answers might sound as if they're changing their minds, but they often make sense of information as they speak.) • Gain energy by moving (They may fidget or look for reasons to move, such as seeking out bathroom breaks, sharpening pencils, asking for help, and so on.) • Say what they're thinking (Primary grade students, especially, are prone to blurt out answers or thoughts better not voiced.) • Do, reflect, do (They prefer trying a hands-on activity and then subsequently learning necessary background information.) • Show less interest in independent reading because it requires sitting still • Work more efficiently when quietly chatting, standing at a windowsill, or working at the classroom whiteboard is allowed • Forget answers if too much time passes in between raising a hand and being called on • Enjoy being interrupted when they are concentrating (It's an energy booster.) • Grow more energized as the day continues—more specifically, as activities continue	• Think before speaking (They prefer to have full answers ready before participating in discussion, but they may be very talkative if reflection or assignments allow them to form their thoughts.) • Gain energy by staying still (They often find it easy to finish engaging tasks without taking breaks.) • Keep thoughts to themselves unless asked to share (This may include thoughts they should voice.) • Reflect, do, reflect (They prefer reading background information before trying an activity so that they can anticipate what will happen.) • Enjoy independent reading from an early age • Work more efficiently in silence where background noise is a steady hum • Hesitate and hedge if they are called on before they are ready to answer • Dislike being interrupted when they are concentrating (They were lost in thought and have to recapture the threads of their ideas.) • Become more tired and more irritable as the day continues—more specifically, as activities continue

Figure 1.2 (page 22) is representative of students' vision of the ideal extraverted classroom. This classroom welcomes students with a red carpet. Student chairs are mounted on balls so they can bounce away their energy without getting in trouble. There is a fast-food outlet, a candy store, and a maze with snacks hidden throughout. Sports areas include a basketball court, track, wrestling mat, swimming pool, and dance floor. In one corner is a couch where the students' more introverted friends can get away from the noise.

Figure 1.3 (page 22) is representative of students' vision of the ideal introverted classroom, one focused on comfort and convenience. The middle of the room has a comfortable rug where they can sprawl out and read one of the countless books from the shelves that surround it. A circle of couches, with two students per couch, is substituted for desks. In front of each couch is a table holding individual laptops. The teacher

Figure 1.2: *Drawing to show personality—Extraversion example.*

Figure 1.3: *Drawing to show personality—Introversion example.*

has a separate couch. Instead of lectures or discussions, assignments are emailed to students. Refrigerators are within reach of all students so they don't have to leave for snacks or beverages.

Drawings like these are hardly the most extreme examples I've seen. One group of extraverted students I worked with placed their classroom within the Mall of America for hands-on learning. A group of introverts drew their own personal classrooms in their bedrooms at home—and this was long before the COVID-19 pandemic.

As you reflect on these images, consider what they communicate about learning preferences based on extraversion and introversion. Also, reflect on the following examples of what research says about learning environments' impact on the success of extraverted and introverted learners.

- Research involving ten schools in four states and over 2,500 students looked at student attitudes and academic performance (McPeek et al., 2013). The researchers concluded that while students who prefer extraversion show more academic progress and are more comfortable in elementary classrooms, the reverse is true by middle school.

- British educational consultant David Hodgson (2018) works extensively with teachers and students to increase student engagement and academic success using the cognitive process concepts. He finds that teacher-student differences in extraversion and introversion are the main drivers of student boredom and disengagement and are frequent factors in the deterioration of teacher-student relationships.

- Richard Felder and Rebecca Brent (2005) are, respectively, a professor emeritus of chemical engineering at North Carolina State University and president of Education Designs, who used cognitive-process concepts to differentiate instruction for several cohorts of freshman engineering students. They find that when instruction balances extraverted and introverted needs, differences in academic performance disappear (Felder & Brent, 2005). Further, while extraverted students initially express more interest in group work, introverted students are equally satisfied with group work by the end of a course.

The common thread through this research reveals that paying attention to the needs of both extraverted and introverted students as you plan for instruction not only ensures that everyone has energy for the work, including you, but can improve academic performance. Of the four cognitive processing styles, two are more extraverted, and two are more introverted. The next section adds two more preferences for how students (and all people) take in information.

Sensing and Intuition

In addition to extraversion and introversion, people naturally pay attention to different information and process the world around them in two different ways (Jung, 1921/1923; Lai et al., 2019; Majors, 2016).

1. *Sensing* types start with *what is*. The information they note first and trust most comes from what their five senses can observe and from past experiences or proven ideas.

2. *Intuitive* types start with hunches, connections, and analogies. They largely skip by *what is* as they engage with *what could be*.

Have you ever given what you thought were clear directions, yet some student responses made you think those students didn't listen at all? This even occurs among adult educators. Take a look at the adult writing samples in figure 1.4, which shows sensing versus intuitive responses to specific prompts. The two response sets represent one sensing and one intuitive response to a prompt, respectively. Chances are, you've seen these differences play out in your classroom. Perhaps students interpret your instructions in a to-the-letter literal way you didn't anticipate; or maybe they applied their imagination in ways you never intended.

Whether I ask adults or students to write about coffee cups, Salvador Dalí paintings, apples, tea bags, or beaches, the results are the same as what you see in figure 1.4. The sensing responses are grounded in reality, while the intuitive responses encompass connections and what could be. As people compare responses, laughter often abounds. For example, two mathematics teachers on the same team wrote the M&M responses. They shared with their colleagues, "This explains our different approaches to getting students to master basic algorithms. No wonder we sometimes drive each other nuts!"

When conducting these writing exercises, I debrief by asking, "If I had asked you to describe the object [snowman, candy packet, or holiday table] in detail, could you have done it?" The answer from sensing and intuitive types is always, "Of course!" I then ask, "If I'd asked you to write a fictional tale about the object, could you have done it?" Again, the answer is, "Of course!" The difference between sensing and intuitive types isn't the quality of response to the different writing prompts; the difference is where your and your students' minds go *first*. Jung (1921/1923) believed that sensing and intuition are irrational processes; that is, people can't control their first response. However, with conscious effort, they can go back and fill in what they missed.

Consider the examples in table 1.3 (page 26). Which sound more like your approach to learning when you were your students' age? Consider how these characteristics might affect student engagement and success with various classroom activities.

Why does this difference in how we process information matter in the classroom? Information is the heart of education, isn't it? And while a student's preference for sensing or intuition shouldn't have any correlation to academic performance, it often does (Blair & Sutherland, 2018; Myers et al., 2018). How successful and motivated can *you* be if information seldom appears in ways that naturally fit your needs?

Writing Prompt	Sensing Response	Intuitive Response
Write about a snowman.	White Coal eyes and mouth Red scarf Carrot nose Three levels (big to small) Stick arms 1. Start with wet snow; roll three balls, each a little smaller than the first. 2. Stack the medium ball on the large ball and the small on the medium. 3. Place the coal eyes and coal mouth on the front of the small ball, then add the scarf and carrot nose and stick arms.	Snowmen are constant reminders of youth; school being canceled and playing in the snow remind me of snowmen. I have made a snowman, but that's not my favorite snow activity. Snowball fights in snow forts are the best use of a snow day off from school. The best feeling is waiting for your school's number to call, signaling a day off from school and a day of freedom.
Write about a packet of M&M's.	The bag is approximately two and a half by three inches. It is brown. The wrapper crinkles when you handle it. There's a hotline number to call. This may contain peanuts. There are two M&M's on the front, red and blue. Other people's packets have different-colored ones. On the back is a picture of many M&M's. Inside are twenty-two M&M's: four blue, three red, nine orange, two brown, two yellow, and two green.	One day in the land of M, seventeen to twenty M&M's were playing a friendly game of Frisbee outside when, all of a sudden, the dreaded bag master swooped down from the sky, took the M&M's, and put them in the fun-size bag. Later that night, the M&M's found themselves in a high school vending machine along with their good friends Reese's Pieces. They knew they had to escape. Together, they . . .
Write about your holiday table.	Duck Turkey Dressing Potato salad Cranberry sauce Candied yams Mustard greens Macaroni and cheese Smoked ham Cornbread Dinner rolls Sweet potato pie	Huge. A mass of family members. Everyone's talking, trying to catch up on what's been going on. Great smiles. Lots of food. Eating too much. Kids everywhere.

Figure 1.4: *Sample sensing and intuitive responses to identical writing prompts.*

Table 1.3: *Sensing and Intuitive Students*

Sensing Students Tend to	Intuitive Students Tend to
• Prefer clear assignments with requirements spelled out (They don't want to waste time if there's a "right" way to do an assignment.) • Enjoy learning factual information or proven methods • See practice as a route to improvement, although some need more breaks than others during practice sessions • Ask questions to clarify expectations, understand examples, and make real-world connections • May interrupt as you give directions, often asking questions your directions will answer in just a moment • May hesitate to make inferences and connections, mistrusting their hunches (They need scaffolding to guess.) • Read at one speed, word for word (They need support for skimming when appropriate.) • Thrive when building on past experiences and successes • Start with finding facts and use them to support the big picture	• Prefer open-ended assignments that give them freedom to put their own spin on things • Enjoy exploring hunches, connections, analogies, and possible ways to proceed • See practice as a route to boredom, potentially becoming careless if assignments seem repetitive • Ask what-if questions or questions that make connections with themes or information outside the assignment • May not read directions but work from their own hunches as to what is expected (Or, they may ask to alter the assignment to make it uniquely theirs.) • May make mistakes as they rush through material they believe they know (They need scaffolding to notice the details.) • Read complex texts word for word but take in chunks of text at a time when reading for pleasure (They need support to slow down, note details, and read directions.) • Thrive when they can be innovative, creative, and unique • Start with grasping the big picture and find facts to support it

Think of it this way: The primary grades are about facts, proven methods, and mastery of basic processes—mathematics facts and algorithms, phonics and reading, and so on. The higher the grade level, the more teachers expect students to move beyond what is known; they ask students to apply the information by innovating, creating, and, hopefully, thinking for themselves. The sensing cognitive processing styles (the left half of figure 1.1, page 18) correlate with field-dependent learners who prefer sequential information and tasks. If sensing students don't receive proper scaffolding when they are uncertain of the way forward, they underperform on tasks that allow for productive struggle, such as creating, analyzing, synthesizing, questioning, and hypothesizing (Blair & Sutherland, 2018). The result? These learners become dependent on their teachers, unable to tackle new kinds of learning without teacher direction, scaffolding, or direct help (Hammond, 2015).

In contrast, the learning preferences of intuitive students more closely resemble those of field-independent learners, who significantly outperform field-dependent learners in tasks involving complex problem solving (Angeli & Valanides, 2013). During the primary years, if intuitive students don't receive room to roam or are given too many tasks that involve repetition or set procedures, they may not show their potential. The higher the level of creativity, innovation, or independent thought required, the more engaged and successful they become. Yet, school also requires paying attention to directions and mastering basics in ways that better align with a sensing student's approach to thinking.

Remember that one of the key doable differentiation principles is allowing content to drive instruction while helping students develop the STEAM[2] component of agility. As educators, we want those who prefer sensing to gain confidence in their hunches, connections, and inferences. We want those who prefer intuition to incorporate details, use key procedures and heuristics, and follow directions as needed. Think of how much easier it is to develop a growth mindset if your early years in school allow you to use your strengths and provide scaffolding when tasks require you to stretch and grow.

As a teacher, regardless of instructional level, you can use the four cognitive processing styles both to engage students and to help them stretch by developing skills for tasks that don't fit their natural preferences. Here are a couple of other classroom considerations that will help you support learners of both sensing and intuiting inclinations.

- Think about assignments designed to help students practice new skills. Beth Russell and I find that sensing and intuitive students have different attitudes toward practice (Kise & Russell, 2010). Sensing students, especially those who also prefer introversion, often continue to practice processes or concepts they have mastered. Intuitive students do not seek extra practice once they understand a concept. Repetitive practice makes them feel bored, and they often rush through assignments that involve practice and drills. This results in their making careless mistakes or refusing to do the work altogether.

- People who prefer sensing report using different memorization strategies than those who prefer intuition (Kise, 2009). Intuitive students frequently come up with their own sound strategies, such as finding major themes and organizing information to be memorized under each theme, developing mnemonics, or otherwise linking the information to structures or big ideas that make it easier to commit to memory. Sensing students report that they struggle to limit what to memorize and they don't trust their ability to determine what is most important (Kise, 2009). They seem to think knowing the facts is the most important thing to be tested. They need to memorize information from start to finish; if they break it into chunks, they often leave out a whole chunk. They also report that while they initially struggle to come up with mnemonic devices, they appreciate being provided with effective ones (Kise, 2009). Further, once they find effective ones, they frequently make up mnemonics. (See Direct Instruction, page 79, for more information on memorization.)

These differences in learning needs (extraversion and introversion *and* sensing and intuition) are real, and they matter for student motivation and success. Again, school success requires that students be able to learn in combinations of all four of the cognitive processing styles: (1) structure and certainty, (2) vision and interpretation, (3) experience and movement, and (4) question and connection.

Cognitive Processing Styles in the Classroom

If you're familiar with personality type, you might be wondering about the other well-known personality preferences from the Myers-Briggs Type Indicator (Myers et al., 2018). I explain and detail *thinking* and *feeling*, which describe the criteria we use for decision making, in chapter 14 (page 215). *Judging* and *perceiving* describe how people approach the outer world, and you'll learn more about them in the context of accommodating pressure-prompted students (chapter 6, page 87). Separating out these personality components to their relevant chapters allows this chapter to focus specifically on this book's differentiation model, as described in figure 1.1 (page 18).

To help you use this chapter's framework in your classroom, I designed figure 1.5 to help you easily plan instruction that teaches around the cycle of the cognitive processes—that is, to choose a balanced set of instructional strategies to ensure that students of all styles are comfortable in your classroom.

Structure and Certainty (Let Me Know What to Do)
Words that motivate these students to engage in learning:
Read, identify, list, label, name, notice, observe, apply, analyze, graph, examine, work, prepare, do, organize, complete, answer, listen

Education content and processes that require *all* students to access this style:	Best-fit doable differentiation instructional strategies for this style:
• Practice for mastering mathematics facts and algorithms • Spelling, grammar, and other conventions • Assignments with specific directions • Structured writing assignments, such as lab reports • Content knowledge building • Lectures • Memorization • Tasks that require repetition, including practicing musical instruments, developing automaticity in writing chemical formulas, and so on	• Assignment Menus (page 55) • Discussion Protocols for Wait Time (page 69) • Discussion Protocols (page 108) • Direct Instruction (page 79) • Self-Monitoring for Progress (page 81) • The World in Numbers (page 144) • Student-Centered Discussion Roles (page 150) • Thinking Maps (page 160) • Graphic Organizers (page 162) • Advance Organizers and Learning Maps (page 165) • Learning Progression Study Guides (page 166) • Segmented Notes (page 189) • Essential Question Priming (page 217) • Worked Examples (page 78)

Experience and Movement (Let Me Do Something)
Words that motivate these students to engage in learning:
Build, show, assemble, tell, discover, make, demonstrate, figure out, touch, design, suggest, solve, choose, construct, examine, explore, discuss

Education content and processes that require *all* students to access this style:	Best-fit doable differentiation instructional strategies for this style:
• Skills, such as titration, from structured science labs and other experiments • Chorus and instrument practice and ensemble play in music • Physical education • Fine motor skills such as keyboarding, using tools like compasses and rulers, and handwriting • Work with manipulatives (such as in mathematics) • Makerspace activities • Simulations	• Places (page 51) • Mystery Draws (page 120) • Bug Lists (page 131) • Spiderweb Discussions (page 146) • Group Whiteboards (page 177) • Big Manipulatives (page 178) • Personal Manipulatives (page 191) • Story Aids (page 191) • Card Sorts (page 192) • Standing Room, Wiggle Room (page 202) • Forced Choice (page 203) • Question Hunts (page 204) • Task Fetch (page 204) • Knowledge Stations (page 206) • Talking to write (all strategies; page 216)

Vision and Interpretation (Let Me Follow My Own Lead)
Words that motivate these students to engage in learning:
Read, think, consider, design, evaluate, clarify, speculate, dream, envision, paraphrase, brainstorm, create, elaborate, illustrate, write, reflect, chew on, make connections, compare, contrast, compose

Education content and processes that require *all* students to access this style:	Best-fit doable differentiation instructional strategies for this style:
• Individual, open-ended tasks • Silent reading • Unstructured art projects • Complex problem solving • Creative writing (narrative, poetic, persuasive, or fictional) • Independent study • Individual inquiry-based assignments and research projects	• Task Order (page 48) • Reading Materials (page 53) • Key-Word Prediction (page 122) • Stop the Story (page 125) • Visual Entry Points (page 127) • Student-Generated Open Questions (page 140) • Open Questions for Applying and Critiquing Text (page 140) • Catalysts (page 141) • Freeform Organizers (page 165) • Graphic Recording (page 167) • Knowledge Stations (page 206) • Imaginative Dialogue Pairs (page 219)

Figure 1.5: *The cognitive processes and doable differentiation strategies.*   continued →

Question and Connection (Let Me Lead as I Learn)
Words that motivate these students to engage in learning:
Create, discover, pretend, design, develop, discuss, synthesize, collaborate, find a new . . ., generate, visualize, evaluate, problem solve, experiment, invent, hypothesize

Education content and processes that require *all* students to access this style:	Best-fit doable differentiation instructional strategies for this style:
• Collaborative problem solving • Student-centered discussions • Debates • Simulations • Role play • Group inquiry-based science labs • Outdoor environmental learning • Student-designed project-based learning • Drama	• Task Order (page 48) • Anticipation Guides (page 123) • Stop the Story (page 125) • Tea Party (page 129) • Open Questions for Applying and Critiquing Text (page 140) • Posthole Questions (page 143) • Multiple Right Answers (page 145) • Freeform Organizers (page 165) • Graphic Recording (page 167) • Concept Map Manipulatives (page 193) • All-Class Brainstorming (page 196) • Pocket Problems (page 209) • Yes-And Improvisation (page 218) • Simulations and Role Plays (page 223)

*Visit **go.SolutionTree.com/instruction** for a free reproducible version of this figure.*

As you study figure 1.5, consider how you distribute time in your class. Some content areas require more of one of these styles than the others. In such cases, the chart becomes useful in understanding the adjustments you can make so that students who prefer other styles develop necessary skills and mindsets. Remember, it's not necessary for every lesson to offer learning in every style, but it is important that you offer balance over time. Choosing various activities from different cognitive processing styles over the course of a lesson, day, or unit should sound doable. You'll not only be helping more students succeed academically, but also thrive, engage, become more agile, and mature—our STEAM[2].

DOING DIFFERENTIATION

Set out an object—a tea bag, a Styrofoam cup, a whiteboard eraser, an apple, a peanut, or a two-liter plastic bottle. Ask students to write about the object. Don't say, "Describe," or else you'll get all sensing responses. You might also display Salvador Dalí's *The Enigma of Hitler* (Dali, 1939) or *The Discovery of America by Christopher Columbus*, (Dali, 1958), available online.

As students write, read over their shoulders. Sensing students might write a list of characteristics of the apple, such as *red*, *shiny*, *black stem*, *wider at top*, *crunchy*, and so on. Intuitive students might write a fictional story about the apple or list connections such as *Apple Records*, *cooks up for sauce or pies*, *Johnny Appleseed*, *pioneers*, *trees for climbing*, and so on. Find the three or four clearest examples that will help all students see the difference in approaches. Have the sensing students you selected read their writing first. Then, have the intuitive students read. Ask students what differences they notice between the two groups.

Read or display the definitions of *sensing* and *intuition* found in the Sensing and Intuition section (page 23). Emphasize that all students can do a good job of writing either a sensing or an intuitive response, but usually, one comes more naturally.

As an extension, break students into pairs. Have them examine the object again and list twenty sensing responses (facts about the object) and twenty intuitive responses (what the object reminds them of, or other uses for the object). Students in grades 3–5 might list ten responses for each. As they prepare their lists, ask them to think about which list is harder to complete. Most students discover that they *prefer* working on one list more than the other. This works particularly well with two-liter club soda bottles, as students are already familiar with them. If they struggle to come up with twenty facts, ask them to consider what each of their five senses would tell them and what they already know about where they are found or how they are used. If they struggle to come up with new uses, ask them to picture how they might use one in each room of the place where they live or what uses come to mind if they think about cutting it into different pieces.

Reflection Activity

Consider the following questions as you reflect on this chapter's content.

1. Look back on your own school days. Do you see overlap between your favorite learning experiences and the cognitive processing style you favor as a teacher? Note that some learning experiences are memorable because of the content or the teacher, or because we met an engaging challenge put before us.

2. You don't need to know the learning type of each of your students to successfully use this chapter's model. Rest assured, you have all types in your classroom. How can you use the Doing Differentiation activity on page 17 with students to develop a common language around extraversion and introversion and to help students reflect on which processing style energizes them naturally? How can you use the writing-prompt approach depicted in figure 1.6 (page 32) to discuss sensing and intuition with students?

3. Discuss with your collaborative team the sample activities students might choose in figure 1.6 to demonstrate understanding of a novel. Which styles are easiest for you to accommodate given your style and the content you teach? Which would you naturally avoid as a student and as a teacher? Why?

Structure and Certainty	Vision and Interpretation
• Prepare a flow map of about ten key events in the book. By each event, write your reaction to that event or why you think it was important to the story. • As you read, keep a list of events in the book that remind you of events in your own life.	• Think of three to five questions you would like to ask a character in your book. Imagine that you are the character, and answer the questions. • What key messages do you think this book conveys? Choose one and write about it, using events in the story as evidence of that message.
Experience and Movement	**Question and Connection**
• Make a tree map of two or three major themes of your book and the events that explore those themes. Use the map to tell your group what you learned from the book. • Make a Hall of Fame and Hall of Shame poster of characters in the book, using your own drawings, clip art, or magazine photos. Under each picture, write why the character deserves his or her placing.	• Collaborate with a partner to act out a dialogue based on a scene in the book. However, change the ending to reflect a better choice a character could have made. • Design your own method to communicate to others your reactions to or learnings from the novel you read.

Figure 1.6: *Sample activity choices for the four cognitive processing styles.*

CHAPTER 2

Clear Learning Goals and Expectations

Almost every thorough process for creating lessons or units, including the use of the differentiation strategies in this book, emphasizes the importance of having clear goals and expectations (DuFour, DuFour, Eaker, Many, & Mattos, 2016). For example, in a professional learning community (PLC), there are four critical questions:

1. What do students need to know and be able to do?
2. How will we know when they have learned it?
3. What will we do when they haven't learned it?
4. What will we do when they already know it? (DuFour et al., 2016, p. 251)

Notice the first two questions focus on having clear goals (determining what students are to learn) and expectations (determining how teachers will know that learning took place). When teachers answer these questions and combine them with clear examples that demonstrate what success looks like, students have the supports they need to succeed with any of the differentiation strategies you'll find in this book.

As this chapter explains, to succeed in this effort requires understanding the concept of success criteria, knowing how to clarify the big ideas of a unit, developing learning progressions for achieving standards, and developing learning maps.

Clear Success Criteria

I like to think of the collective effort to establish clear goals and expectations as fulfilling John Hattie's (2012) vision for *success criteria*, which he defines as the standards by which teachers assess a project or assignment to determine whether it's successful. These criteria usually are brief, use student-friendly language, and aim to remind students what they need to focus their learning efforts on. Having clear goals and expectations before choosing differentiation strategies is essential so that, regardless of whether students use the same processes, create the same products, or work with the same information, they all reach the established success criteria. This ensures goals and expectations remain intact after differentiation.

How might differentiation fall short of ensuring all students meet learning goals and expectations? One common aim of differentiated lesson planning is to adjust content to accommodate students with different levels of reading or other skills. Consider a planned reading of *Hamlet* (Shakespeare, 1603/2019) with the following differentiations.

- One group reads the full original text.
- A second group reads a paraphrase of the text in modern English.
- A third group reads a graphic novelization of the play.

Let's place this in the context of the following paraphrases of Common Core State Standards that could serve as a focus for the reading (National Governors Association Center for Best Practices & Council of Chief State School Officers, 2010).

1. Understand craft and structure and how an author's ideas or claims are developed and refined by particular sentences, paragraphs, stanzas, chapters, or scenes.

2. Determine a central idea of a text and its development over the course of a text.

Can you see how using any of the three proposed versions of *Hamlet* might meet the second goal but not the first? Each of them is fine if the goal is to familiarize students with the story. However, only reading Shakespeare's words (or watching the play) can meet the learning target's success criteria of understanding craft and structure, let alone convey the development of the themes of revenge, loyalty, inaction versus action, and so on, over the five acts of the play.

Crafting clear goals before you plan is only the beginning, of course. Students must also understand your expectations of them, which includes communicating what success looks like through a rubric, an example of student work, or a worked example (see Worked Examples, page 78). The remaining sections in this chapter will help you ensure that the success criteria you set (the goals and expectations) are clear for students as you use this book's strategies to differentiate for all students' preferred learning styles.

Clarification of the Big Ideas

Are you clear on the *enduring understandings* from a unit—the important ideas and concepts that allow students to make connections across curricula and to real life (Wiggins & McTighe, 2005)? Enduring understandings are a unit's *big ideas*.

With so many lessons to teach day in and day out, it's easy for teachers to default to a state or provincial standard, a textbook chapter title, or another source to determine the big ideas underpinning a lesson. Clarifying the big ideas is useful for communicating to students what their learning goals are, especially when teachers use the big ideas to restate learning standards using student-friendly language. The challenge for teachers is that sometimes, the sources for learning standards disguise more useful concepts or a lesson's real point. For example, a literal interpretation of a standard focused on asking and answering questions regarding a text (referring only to that text) to demonstrate under-standing could keep teachers from also encouraging students to compare and contrast what they are reading with other sources, their own experiences, or events they have read about. Stepping back from the standards to contemplate longer-term goals can ensure students don't, for example, master the five-paragraph essay and internalize that anything with more or less than five paragraphs can't be an essay (Warner, 2018). Here are two examples of ways to establish useful, enduring understandings.

1. **Teach an enduring habit of mind:** A team of secondary mathematics teachers had committed to using richer, more open-ended problems for group work. They saw how the *habits of mind*—practiced dispositions of how to confront challenges (Costa, n.d.)—associated with these problems were different from the lists of standards they were responsible for teaching—*and* how they aligned with the thriving and maturing markers of STEAM[2]. After much discussion, the team members decided that the enduring understanding for the group tasks was, "Persistence results in solved problems"—an understanding needed in science, politics, teaching, engineering, and so on. Stating this as the goal for these group tasks changed how the teachers interacted with students. They also created a rubric that students could use to assess how well they persisted.

2. **Clarify a lesson's focus:** Identifying learning targets in language arts, science, and social studies can be tricky as teachers balance ongoing skills (such as those related to grammar, experimentation principles, and the tools of anthropology, geography, and history) and content (such as specific novels, laws of motion, genres of writing, the Great Migration, and the U.S. Constitution). Huge units on topics such as persuasive writing or forms of energy might have multiple enduring understandings, and trying to teach them all at once can easily result in not enough time spent on any of them. Thus, a science teacher might decide the focus of a lesson that involves experimentation will be on accurate measurement—an enduring understanding in science related to producing replicable, valid research. The teacher might provide students with lab instructions rather than engaging in a more open-ended inquiry so that small groups can concentrate on determining, for example, how they will know they are dropping various balls from exactly the same height as they record data on the height of each ball's bounce. While hypothesizing is also a key enduring part of science, the only nod to it in this lesson is a quick thumbs up or down from students to the question of whether all balls will bounce equally high.

Let's take the U.S. Civil War as a further example that combines these ideas. A content standard in Virginia says that students will be able to discuss the causes, major events, and effects of the war by "describing the roles of Abraham Lincoln, Jefferson Davis, Ulysses S. Grant, Robert E. Lee, Thomas 'Stonewall' Jackson, and Frederick Douglass in events leading to and during the war" (Virginia Board of Education, 2008, p. 13).

Here are three possible goals and potential differentiation strategies that show clear expectations and provide opportunities to show students clear examples of the work they must produce.

1. Students will master the facts about these individuals as well as their ongoing influence. Options to accomplish this goal might include the following, which each aligns to an individual cognitive processing style.

    ‣ *Experience and movement*—Engaging in a card sort activity (see Card Sorts, page 192)

    ‣ *Structure and certainty*—Constructing parallel timelines for all the figures and the actions they took that had a lasting impact

    ‣ *Vision and interpretation*—Searching for important quotes from each individual and providing short descriptions of how they represent the person

    ‣ *Question and connection*—Creating a group presentation that conveys the roles these individuals played in history and their lasting influence

2. Students will learn how gaining multiple points of view on the same historical figures can enlarge their understanding of an issue. Options to accomplish this goal might include the following.

    ‣ *Structure and certainty*—Recording observations of how each person viewed major events leading up to the war using four corners notes, expanded to six points (See the four corners notes activity in Graphic Organizers, page 162.)

    ‣ *Question and connection*—Searching primary texts for how other historical figures viewed each of these individuals, and sharing findings via student-centered discussions (chapter 7, page 101)

    ‣ *Vision and interpretation*—Analyzing various forms of nonfiction regarding these figures, including narrative texts, persuasive texts, primary-source letters and speeches by them, and so on

    ‣ *Experience and movement*—Using primary sources while working in pairs to construct a poster about an assigned historical figure; the class then engages in a poster walk, comparing the different posters on the same figures and engaging in a student-centered discussion to identify similarities and differences in how the various sources viewed the individuals.

3. Students will write a high-quality compare-and-contrast essay about the same historical figures. Options to accomplish this goal might include the following, both of which provide the sensing cognitive process learners (structure and certainty, and experience and movement) with a process to follow before they engage in the more intuitive process of composing an open-ended essay.

> ‣ Using a moveable organizer (chapter 12, page 187) to record facts about all the figures, with a final essay comparing and contrasting two of the historical figures

> ‣ Using a moveable organizer to record facts about all the historical figures, with a final essay that discusses the figures' impact on current civil rights issues

Knowing how to extract the enduring understandings of a lesson or unit ensures you can clarify for students the big ideas they need to know. Consider the following example of a team of first-grade teachers who asked me for help with their first common assessment of the year. This assessment featured the following question.

I have eleven balls. Some are tennis balls, some are basketballs, and some are soccer balls. How many of each might I have?

The teachers assigned several practice problems they hoped provided differentiation on this learning, changing the objects to stuffed animals, cars, fruit, and more. The students seemed to do well on this assessment right after completing the practice problems, but they didn't retain the strategies they'd used for more than a few days.

I commented, "Wow, that's a tough problem for early first grade. It contains so many big mathematics ideas."

"It does?" said one of the teachers.

I could tell from the teachers' faces they had been thinking not about the big ideas, like conservation of quantity and combinations of ten, but rather in terms of algorithms. I provided them with a tool similar to the "Big Ideas in Early Mathematics" reproducible at the end of this chapter (page 42). Once the teachers realized they were teaching these big concepts, rather than *How many balls?*, they could design differentiated instruction that helped students master the learning goals and expectations for the assessment.

Learning Progressions

Learning progressions lay out how knowledge, skills, and concepts build on each other, or the sequence in which students will learn content to meet an overarching learning standard (learning goal), such as a Common Core standard. For example, when teaching kindergarten, first-grade, and second-grade students how to write sentences, elementary educators begin with simple sentences that contain subject and object, gradually adding more parts of speech and punctuation. Secondary social studies teachers know that a learning goal based on understanding democracy as a form of government requires comprehending where power resides, the nature of decision making in various forms of government, the conditions necessary for a healthy democracy, and so on. Learning progressions make these pathways visible to students. For teachers, learning progressions can act as a tool for planning to meet the needs of the four cognitive processes over the course of a unit, using select doable differentiation strategies at various points to ensure work within the unit aligns with each cognitive process at some point. For example, a teacher might ask, "For this lesson in a long unit, would accommodating the pressure-prompted ensure more students are successful? Or, might choice or wait time increase engagement?" Teachers can also use learning progressions to plan the integration of STEAM[2] components into a unit.

You'll find predetermined learning progressions designed for countless subjects online, but they may have too much or too little detail for your students. Or, these learning progressions may include concepts, knowledge, or strategies that you cover elsewhere. They might also assume you've already covered something that you haven't. Therefore, learning progressions work best when teachers work as part of a collaborative team to construct them or specifically adapt existing learning progressions to better align with their essential questions and success criteria.

The following list features some of my favorite resources for constructing effective learning progressions. Applying the knowledge they offer will help you craft progressions that provide opportunities for using differentiation strategies.

- *The Teacher Clarity Playbook: A Hands-On Guide to Creating Learning Intentions and Success Criteria for Organized, Effective Instruction* by Douglas Fisher, Nancy Frey, Olivia Amador, and Joseph Assof (2019)
- *Transformative Assessment in Action: An Inside Look at Applying the Process* by W. James Popham (2011)
- *Essential Questions: Opening Doors to Student Understanding* by Jay McTighe and Grant Wiggins (2013)

Figure 2.1 shows an example learning progression for English language arts. Consider how you might expand or adapt this progression to include semicolons, adjectives, dependent and independent clauses, other punctuation rules, and so on, depending on your students' needs. The goal is to create a progression appropriate for your students— one that isn't so detailed that it gives students too many targets to absorb as they monitor their own progress.

My Paragraphs Include Good Complex Sentences

1. I can list words that are prepositions. If you give me a list of words, I can identify the prepositions.
2. If given several sentences, I can accurately underline prepositional phrases.
3. I can write good sentences with prepositional phrases at the beginning, in the middle, or at the end.
4. I know how to use a colon before a list in a sentence.
5. I know how to use a colon to introduce a definition, an example, or a series.

Figure 2.1: Sample learning progression—Writing complex sentences in ELA.

Figure 2.2 highlights a mathematics-based example for adding fractions. I helped develop this progression with a team of teachers who realized that several steps for adding fractions weren't separated in their curriculum (represented here as steps 3–5); the

---

I Can Add Fractions

1. I can add two fractions that have the same denominator.
2. I understand how to factor numbers.
3. I understand how to use factoring to add two fractions where one denominator is a factor of the other denominator.
4. I understand how to use factoring to find the least common denominator when adding two fractions whose denominators are not factors of each other.
5. I can add three fractions that have three different denominators.

Figure 2.2: Sample learning progression—Adding fractions in mathematics.

curriculum-provided problem set, which introduced fractions with unlike denominators, included examples of three kinds of problems without an adequate learning progression. Analysis of student work showed that students struggled to make the conceptual leaps the curriculum assumed. So, the teachers expanded the progression and taught each step separately, assigning new problems accordingly. They also provided students with extra practice problems and watched as student understanding grew.

Note that thoughtfully constructing a learning progression is helpful in avoiding what Chip Heath and Dan Heath (2007) call "the curse of knowledge." This phrase refers to the fact that teachers' familiarity and ease with the content they teach can blind them from seeing the assumptions they make about what others know or need in order to learn. Think of how a mathematics teacher might assume that students who can add ¼ + ½ should also be able to add ¼ + ⅓, even though that requires additional knowledge about fractions-based computations. Consider: If your preferred cognitive process is vision and interpretation or question and connection, what intuitive leaps might you be assuming students can make when some students might actually require increased modeling or other scaffolds?

Learning Maps

Learning maps are another useful tool, particularly for content teachers who organize around big ideas. Jim Knight (2013), a veteran researcher and expert on instructional coaching, describes learning maps as:

> Two-dimensional depictions of information that usually include (a) a core idea, often the name of the unit; (b) subtopics (usually surrounded by shapes such as ovals, rectangles, squares, or stars); (c) details; (d) lines that show the relationship between the different parts of the map; and (e) line labels that explain the relationship between the core idea and the subtopics. (p. 89)

Knight (2013) suggests that teachers might organize good maps around a unit's essential questions. Teachers should limit the content to one page, giving students a concise view of a lesson's flow. They should further organize learning maps to match the lesson or unit progression, labeling it with words, lines, and arrows to show topic connections.

At the start of the unit, show students a big-picture map with just the main topics so that students understand the scope of what they will be learning throughout the unit. While learners who favor structure and certainty might prefer a complete map, having them complete the map as the unit progresses will increase their knowledge retention. Thus, a teacher might provide the major big ideas on a map handout but leave plenty of room for students to add to the map as the unit progresses.

Consider a social studies unit, such as one on the expansion of ancient empires. A learning map might depict topics such as leaders, cultural influences, geographic territories, and ongoing influences, which all intertwine throughout the unit's lessons. Under ongoing influences, for example, students might learn about the influence of ancient Roman highways on modern-day routes, as well as themes in Greek mythology that influence modern thought, such as *Oedipus complex*. A learning map allows students to group these under influences, even though they may learn about them in lessons that are days apart. Learning maps allow for this sort of grouping more easily than linear lists of objectives, especially when students can use connecting lines or arrows to show relationships among topics.

Or, consider what a learning map might look like for a marketplace simulation in a foreign language class designed to show students how they will master vocabulary for shopping in a country where people speak the language they are studying. The map might include distinct topics on currency, clothing items, food, and bargaining vocabulary, intertwined with common customs or etiquette.

Remember that understanding where students are on the learning journey begins with defining what that journey looks like. The *S* for success in STEAM^2 starts here, with teachers knowing what they want students to learn and certainty about how they'll know if students have learned. Once teachers have answers to these questions, they can add doable differentiation strategies to help every student thrive, stay engaged, become more agile with different learning activities, and mature as they take ownership of their learning.

Reflection Activity

Consider the following actions and questions as you reflect on this chapter's content.

1. Create a learning progression for a unit you'll be teaching; *or*, find a learning progression on the web for a unit you will be teaching. Print it off. Cut it apart based on its individual steps or components. Which steps work for you? What do you want to add? What might you reword so that your students understand it and can use it to self-assess? Share your created or revised learning progression with a teacher who doesn't think like you. How can you use the feedback you receive to make the learning progression more useful to your students?

2. With your collaborative team, use a moveable outline (chapter 12, page 187) to brainstorm the enduring understandings and learning progressions for

an upcoming unit. Start with the related standards or curriculum goals. Have the team members each write their own versions of the enduring understandings on a large piece of paper (perhaps one-sixth of a sheet of chart paper), big enough for everyone to see when standing around a table. Discuss and agree on your team's wording, answering the question: Will it make sense to students?

Record the team's final version on a new sheet of paper or a wall whiteboard. Then, have the team members write out the steps in the learning progression, each on a separate sheet of paper. Organize the steps by clustering ideas and placing them in the order in which students might master them. Work together to identify the steps for which students need to reach mastery.

3. Make a learning map for an upcoming unit so that you have Worked Examples (page 78) to share with students. Consider whether a Thinking Map, such as a tree map (page 160), graphic organizer (page 162), or some other concept map (chapter 10, page 159) might be most useful. Where appropriate, use highlighters and colored arrows to show connections or to emphasize important ideas. As you look at the map, consider how you might enhance it to answer the ubiquitous student question: Why are we learning this?

Big Ideas in Early Mathematics

Use this chart to identify specific big ideas in the lesson you are teaching. For later grades, identify the big ideas students need. There are far fewer of these than there are standards, but they are often the building blocks for students to master more standards. Whether or not these big ideas are specifically assessed on accountability tests, they are essential to students' being able to master more and more complex ideas in mathematics. These ideas often spiral, or instruction loops back, with a new, deeper level of understanding. They are thus listed in alphabetical order rather than an order for mastery.

Associative property: An operation is associative if you can group the numbers in any way without changing the answer.

- Work with fifteen counters. Ask a student, "Could you arrange them so that you have a group of eight and a group of seven? How many are there? Now make groups of eleven and four. How many markers do you have?" If they recount after rearranging, ask them why they did that.
- Use related equations in number talks, leaving the answer to the first equation on the board so that students who remember the associative property can use it as a strategy and help the rest of the class learn it. For example:
  - **Problem 1:** (2 x 3) x 5 (mental math)
  - **Problem 2:** 2 x (3 x 5) (mental math)

Cardinality: Cardinality is an understanding that the name of a number relates to a specific quantity of objects. "How many?"

- Ask a student to hold up three fingers. Ask the student, "Where's the three?" If the student points to the last finger, rather than to the three total fingers, the student is still thinking of numbers as names, not quantities.
- Use matching games, such as matching numbers and the numbers of objects in a picture.

Combinations that make five and ten: This refers to the use of automaticity with combinations of numbers that make five and ten.

- Talk about using these combinations. "We know that 4 + 1 is 5. So, to add 4 and 2, we can apply that combination of 5: 5 + 1 = 6. Who can draw this for the class?"
- Play the memory game (also known as pairs or concentration) with just cards for numbers one to five or for numbers one to nine. Students keep cards when they draw a pair that adds to five or ten.

Commutative property: An operation is commutative if you can change the order of the numbers involved without changing the value of the equation.

- Use triangle fact cards (both commercial sets and reproducible masters are widely available) where, for example, 5, 3, and 8 are placed in the points. Note that these cards also embed the relationships between addition and subtraction and between multiplication and division, demystifying the latter operations.
- Use number talks where changing the order of numbers makes a problem easier to solve. (The problem 8 + 3 + 2 is one example.) When students use the commutative property, name it, or ask them, "What's that called again?"

page 1 of 3

Compensation: In addition and subtraction, if you add to or subtract from one addend (or subtrahend) to make a friendlier number, that quantity must be subtracted from or added to the other addend (or subtrahend) to maintain equivalency, such as 8 + 6 = (8 + 2) + (6 − 2) = 10 + 4.

- Ask questions such as, "I'd like you to add 8 and 3, but is there a way you can use one of our friendly numbers to do that? Why does that work?"
- Practice mathematics facts in families that demonstrate compensation (such as 5 + 1, 4 + 2, and so on, or 75 + 28, 74 + 29, and so on).

Conservation: The number of objects remains the same no matter how the objects are arranged.

- Line up twelve counters in two rows of six. Ask a student how many counters there are. Then ask the student to place the counters in four equal rows. Ask how many counters there are now. What if they're in one row? How many are there?
- Find different trays that students can count objects into—egg cartons, mancala boards, muffin tins, strips of paper with six boxes marked off, and so on. Number the bottom of each tray with places for numbers 1–6. Have them drop six counters, one by one, into each tray. Does each tray have six? How can they tell? Does six look the same in each one?

Counting on: This is the ability to continue in counting, as opposed to starting from zero, when adding more to a sum.

- Place six counters in front of a student, and ask the student to count them. Add three more, and ask the student, "Now how many are there?" The student understands counting on if the student simply says, "Seven, eight, nine," rather than starting over.
- Play "Captain, May I?" with counting. Students line up at the starting line. Teacher lines might be, "Take three steps. Who can tell me how many steps you'll have taken in total if you add two more steps?"

Hierarchical inclusion: Numbers build exactly one by one, and they nest within each other by this amount (five, four, three, two, and one nest in six).

- Using counters, ask, "If I add one more, how many counters will I have? If I take one away, how many will I have?" With the same counters, emphasize, "How many do I need to make five? Ten?" to demonstrate combinations of five and ten as well as how the numbers nest the combinations.
- Play 7 Ate 9 (a commercial card game). You might start with the simplest cards in the deck.

Magnitude: This means understanding, without counting, which group of objects has more parts (an easier concept to grasp than cardinality).

- Show student groups two sets of objects side by side, one with five objects and one with seven objects. Make sure that one group's objects aren't spread so far apart that the students might be misled. Ask, "Without counting, can you tell which is the bigger group? How do you know?"
- Lay out between one and seven counters. Ask students to make a group of counters that is larger (or smaller) than your group. Or, draw a number of circles

page 2 of 3

(faces) and, separately, set out a number of buttons for eyes. Ask students whether they think there are enough eyes for the faces and how they can find out. Repeat this activity for mouths, noses, and so on. Speak in terms of more than, less than, as many as, and How can we find out?

One-to-one correspondence: Counting means one number per object.
- Make counting part of class—counting people on the cover of a book, trees in a picture, dice in a bag, and so on.
- Show a row of five grapefruit and a row of five oranges (or show rows of two other objects that are similar yet different in size), and ask whether there is the same number of objects in each row.

Subitizing: This involves immediately recognizing a collection of two, three, or four objects as a single unit.
- Using dot cards and five frames, check whether a student can recognize the quantities without having to count each dot.
- Play memory games with cards that feature one, two, three, and four objects, encouraging students to practice letting their eyes recognize how many objects there are rather than counting each object.

Unitizing: This refers to the ability to understand the units a numeral represents. For example, the number 2 always represents two units, but it means two tens in 21 and two ones in 12.
- Ask questions such as, "In 1,624, the one is worth one thousand. What is the two worth?" and "What is ten less than 4,000?"
- Utilize quick whiteboard problems such as, "Write a three-digit number where the two is worth twenty and one where it is worth two thousand." Have students place their numbers on small whiteboards at the front of the room, or compare their numbers in small groups, and work together to see whether all their answers are correct.

PART 2

THE STRATEGIES

CHAPTER 3

Choice

Providing choice is a quick way to differentiate for skills, interests, culture, or the cognitive processes via the content students will work with, the processes they will experience while learning, and the products that will show their learning, including assessments. Choice differentiates learning by increasing autonomy, a significant motivator and core human need (Beymer & Thomson, 2015; Chamine, 2012). Here are some easy-to-implement examples of providing choice.

- "Instead of writing a report, can I pretend I'm the first explorer ever to visit Louisiana and write a letter home to my mom about what I discovered?" a fifth grader asks. "As long as your letter meets the success criteria, sure," his teacher replies, thinking to herself, "At least I know this student won't plagiarize."

- A first-grade teacher avoids an argument with a young student by saying, "Would you like to put away your book first or your calculator first?"

- A tenth-grade mathematics teacher says, "Complete the first two problems and your choice of three of the remaining five problems."

For all the interest many teachers have in differentiating instruction, genuine choice, let alone choice based on students' cognitive processing styles, is rare in classrooms. For example, writing for the Education Trust, Joan Dabrowski and Tanji Reed Marshall (2018) find that only 10 percent of middle school English language arts (ELA), social studies, and science assignments offer choices to students. The percentage drops to 3 percent in mathematics classes. Often, a lack of choices suitable for different cognitive processes isn't even a conscious decision teachers make. No doubt you've given students choices, but consider whether they met the needs of the four cognitive processes in chapter 1 (page 15). Countless teachers have told me, "Now that I understand these four ways of processing information, I see that I was only suggesting activities that motivated or intrigued students who think like me. No wonder some students remained

Choice Strategies
(From quickest to deepest)

- ✔ Task Order, page 48
- ✔ Motivating Word Pairs, page 49
- ✔ Places, page 51
- ✔ Solo or Partner, page 51
- ✔ Reading Materials, page 53
- ✔ Objective and Subjective, page 54
- ✔ Assignment Menus, page 55

apathetic no matter what choices I offered!" Or, teachers realize that the choices they provided didn't assess the same success criteria, resulting in some students mastering more of the learning targets than others.

In this chapter, you'll read about choice strategies you can implement with only a few moments of planning. Other strategies in this chapter go much deeper, resulting in a unit plan that meets the needs of students at different proficiency levels. You'll also find two big essentials for success with these strategies and review common concerns teachers have about trying choice strategies.

If you're a learner who says, "Give me an experience first, so I have firsthand knowledge of what we're talking about," try one of the choice strategies, and use it a few times so that you and your students become comfortable and skilled with it. If you're a learner who wants the *why* first, skip ahead to Why Choice Works (page 60). Then, come back and read through the strategies. See, I've differentiated by giving you a choice with regard to the order in which you read chapter sections. Not that hard, is it? You'll have this choice for every chapter in part 2.

DOING DIFFERENTIATION

What will you be doing in your classroom tomorrow? Think through where you'd like to increase motivation or cooperation or student success with a task. Then, choose one of the choice strategies and incorporate it into your plans.

The Choice Strategies

This section presents seven activities for facilitating choice in your classroom: (1) Task Order, (2) Motivating Word Pairs, (3) Places, (4) Solo or Partner, (5) Reading Materials, (6) Objective and Subjective, and (7) Assignment Menus. These choice strategies are designed to provide students with more intrinsic motivation by permitting them some autonomy in how they conduct their learning, building on their interests, allowing them to choose an approach that uses their strengths, or allowing them to stretch beyond the learning goals if they wish. Note that I present these approaches in order based on ease of implementation. This gives you options to use for anything from a quick nudge to motivate students to a highly differentiated major project.

Task Order

This approach, which gives students flexibility in how they complete assignments, may be the simplest of any of the doable differentiation strategies to implement, and it appeals to all cognitive processing styles. Some students like to start at the beginning of a multistep assignment and work sequentially. Some work best if they can start with the task, question, or step they feel most confident about. Note that students who prefer structure and certainty may not give themselves permission to start with what they know unless you explicitly give them permission. Their confidence then rises as they tally up completed work. Students who prefer experience and movement often prefer starting with anything that allows for action or interaction. Vision-and-interpretation and question-and-connection students thrive on looking for less-conventional approaches; for example, one of my nieces always constructs the border of a jigsaw puzzle *last*, starting with a random middle piece and working from there.

Here are some ideas that facilitate flexibility in how students approach tasks. While you might think students don't need your permission for some of these, those who believe they must strictly follow all rules will welcome your say-so.

- "For this assignment, you can answer the questions in any order you want. There's no need to go in order."

- "If you'd like to read about the ideas behind this experiment before performing it, come over to these tables. If you'd like to try the experiment and then read about it, go right to your lab station."

- "You can work alone first, jotting down some ideas for this writing assignment, and then discuss the ideas with a partner. Or, you can pair up and discuss the assignment first, and then get your general ideas down on paper."

When thinking about what choices to offer students, do so with an awareness of the four cognitive styles, and try to offer choices that appeal to each.

Motivating Word Pairs

Think about this for a moment: Are you more motivated when you're asked to *explain* or *imagine*, or when you're asked to *make* or *create*? Further, what words or phrases might *de*motivate you? *Role-play*? *Don't touch*? *Memorize*? *Follow the directions*?

The words teachers use in explaining assignments and setting success criteria can actually draw some students in while pushing others away. Table 3.1 (page 50) provides several pairs of words or phrases. Within each pair, research shows that students are either more motivated by those on the left, which tend to convey objectivity or concreteness, or more motivated by those on the right, which tend to convey multiple approaches or room for individuality (Murphy, 2013; Payne & VanSant, 2009). When using a word from one of the two columns, try pairing it with the other word from the same row.

Here are some ways you might use these word pairs.

- Add or substitute words in specific directions and tasks. Examples include "Make or create a T-chart that shows . . ." and "Answer or solve the following problems."

- Tell students, "Show your work" or "Think about how you got your answer, and write down enough information so that someone else can understand your process." Do this for verbal and written directions.

Table 3.1: *Motivating Word Pairs*

Words That Convey Objective, Concrete Approaches (Structure and Certainty, and Experience and Movement)	Words That Convey Multiple or Individual Approaches (Vision and Interpretation, and Question and Connection)
Make	Create
Find	Discover
Suggest	Brainstorm or generate
Explain	Evaluate
Fix	Find a new . . .
Organize	Develop
Assemble	Design
Apply	Make connections
Complete	Expand
Answer	Solve
Build	Dream
Experience	Imagine
See	Visualize
Show	Write
Observe	Discuss
Work	Analyze
Watch	Reflect
Recall	Pretend
Put together	Categorize

*Visit **go.SolutionTree.com/instruction** for a free reproducible version of this table.*

- For lengthier assignment directions, try equally embedding words from both lists. In the following example, locate the words that appear in table 3.1.

  Read through the directions for this science experiment. Make a list of the equipment and supplies you will need. Develop a plan for organizing your workspace and recording your results. Complete your preparation by writing down your hypothesis of the results you will see. Then work through the experiment, analyze what happened, and evaluate your hypothesis.

When planning to use the Motivating Word Pairs approach, consider printing the online version of table 3.1. Some teachers I've worked with also use the planning template I introduce in A Primary-Grade Example (page 238 in chapter 15). Using such a template keeps word choices handy so teachers can quickly change out words to increase engagement.

Places

While structured seating arrangements may seem like, and often are, an effective approach to classroom management, how long could you sit still when you were six years old? Or twelve? Or even eighteen? In the adult workshops I facilitate, participants frequently choose to stand for a bit, move so that they can see the screen more easily, or otherwise change where they position themselves. People accept this in the adult learning environment. Try allowing for small changes in place for students as well. Some students will engage better or pay more attention if they can do one of the following (Kercood & Banda, 2012; Sousa & Tomlinson, 2018).

- Sit on the floor for a bit.
- Stand while using a windowsill or the top of a low bookcase as their desk for a while.
- Sit back-to-back with a classmate during sustained silent reading.
- Work quietly in the hallway, just outside the classroom door.
- Work a problem while standing at a whiteboard rather than while sitting and writing on a sheet of paper.

What other places might you offer students that could either add variety to the day or let them get their wiggles out without disrupting the class? See chapter 13 (page 201) for more ways to incorporate physical movement and interaction in your lessons.

VIRTUAL CLASSROOMS

Note that much of the advice parents and guardians receive about distance learning involves setting up a quiet study space with perhaps a desk for learning. Consider changing this emphasis by encouraging families to have a place for students to sit and a place to stand. For standing, students might simply put a sturdy box on their desk to set up their tablet or laptop at a standing height. If students have windows in their work area but no whiteboard, perhaps encourage parents to let them use wet-erase markers on the windows. How else might you give your virtual students some choice in their learning environment?

Solo or Partner

Students can perform many, many tasks equally well whether they complete them alone or with a partner. By nature, people are social creatures; for millennia, most learning took place in social environments, such as within the family, tribe, or village. In *Cultivating Genius: An Equity Framework for Culturally and Historically Responsive Literacy*, Gholdy Muhammad (2018) describes the norms and aspirations of Black literacy societies from the 1800s and their modern implications:

> To keep knowledge to one's self was seen as a selfish act, and each person therefore was responsible to elevate others through education in the immediate

and larger community. This ideal of collectivism is in direct conflict with schools today, as schools are largely grounded in competition and individualism. This is perhaps one major reason why students of color often do not reach their full potential in schools—because schools are in disharmony with their histories and identities. (p. 26)

As you plan lessons, think about when you can offer students the choice to work solo or with others. In physical education, students might choose between individual and team free-throw or goal-kicking contests. In calculus, students might work alone or with a partner on a problem, with each student being responsible for explaining their solutions. In other classes, students might read silently or take turns reading out loud with a partner.

Consider helping students understand how sometimes working alone and sometimes working with a partner or group benefits *everyone*, whether they prefer the more introverted cognitive processes (structure and certainty, and vision and interpretation) or the more extraverted ones (experience and movement, and question and connection). Set up six simple tasks, perhaps using a planned movement strategy such as Task Fetch (page 204). Ask students to complete three tasks alone and three with a partner and then reflect on how they felt each approach helped or hindered them. Here are some sample reflections I've collected from sixth graders using this strategy.

When I work by myself . . .

- "I sometimes have trouble paying attention and space out."
- "I work faster; I did twice as much work alone as when I worked with the group. I can think better and come up with really good ideas."
- "I don't get very far; I need to help people and get help from people."

When I work with a group . . .

- "I don't work as fast as I work by myself; I don't think as fast as other people. For example, my partner was going faster than me on one task, and I didn't understand what we were doing."
- "I work better; for example, while working with two classmates, I didn't get one of the questions and they helped me understand it."
- "I have a hard time staying on task; for example, we were working on a project, but mostly we talked."

As you can tell from these responses, students may need help learning how to work productively with others, but many are more successful and engaged (the *S* and *E* in STEAM²). Note that other doable differentiation strategies, such as the big notes strategies in chapter 11 (page 175) and Group Work That Works (page 110), help you monitor progress and help students mature in their ability to collaborate (the *M* in STEAM²).

VIRTUAL CLASSROOMS

Allow students the choice of whether to work alone or with others in a virtual classroom by saying, "If you'd like to work with someone [or discuss this topic or try out this idea], leave your camera on, and I'll assign you to breakout rooms. If you'd rather tackle this by yourself, turn off your camera and come back to the large group in _____ minutes."

Reading Materials

Consider for a moment how choosing an *all-class text* or *anchor text* that students refer back to throughout a semester or school year might be a sacred task. While anchor texts can be magical and often provide connections with culture or crucial common knowledge, these texts also have great power to quickly disengage students if they dislike, find irrelevant, or struggle to comprehend them.

Having choice in reading materials is not only motivating for many students but also tied to growth in reading proficiency equal to or better than growth due to other reading instruction strategies (Allen-Lyall & Davis, 2020; Miller, 2013). Teachers have many ways to provide choice with regard to reading materials. Consider the following, which work at all grade levels.

- To ensure students read different genres, designate one genre per month. Students choose a text within that genre to read that month. Biography, historical fiction, science fiction, informational text, realistic fiction, history, poetry, short story anthology, and so on—What might you add?

- Designate one novel with a specific theme for all-class instruction and discussion but allow students to choose another novel with the same theme (with approval). These students create their own study questions and final project, and they share book talks about their novels with the class. This approach requires no extra work for the teacher but provides more learning for students who may have already devoured the all-class novel. Theme possibilities include dystopia, historical events from a specific time period, coming-of-age stories, friendship, bullying, epic journeys, fantasy, and more.

- In some cases, providing a choice between fiction and nonfiction texts may enrich class discussions. Consider the following.

  ‣ At the high school level, *Maus* by Art Spiegelman (2011), a Pulitzer Prize–winning graphic nonfiction account of the author's discussions with his Holocaust-survivor father, would pair well with fiction titles involving genocide.

  ‣ For middle-grade students, try pairing *Hana's Suitcase* (Levine, 2002) with a Holocaust fiction title.

> ‣ Primary-grade teachers might pair two picture books, such as *Hedy Lamarr's Double Life* (Wallmark, 2019) and *The Most Magnificent Thing* (Spires, 2014). The first book highlights how movie star Hedy Lamarr developed and held the patent on the frequency-hopping technology still used for encoding mobile devices. The second book tells the story of a girl who hesitates but finally takes a risk. Both books involve females going beyond prescribed gender roles and taking risks.

- Literature circles—in which students meet in small groups to discuss books—are an obvious method of providing choice since not all groups need to be reading the same title. For example, teachers might provide a short list of titles that cover the same theme, are from the same genre, or otherwise fit with a curriculum goal. Literature circles are effective not just in ELA but in foreign language, social studies, and science classes, as long as students are choosing from among a menu of texts and aren't being assigned texts based on ability. (The latter may also result in sound differentiation but doesn't provide autonomy.)

- Many students fare better with even a small bit of autonomy—for example, by having a choice between two short stories with similar themes. Perhaps one is in the class anthology and another is freely available on the internet or via a library. The same is true of articles in other disciplines; provide choice and organize group presentations to increase everyone's knowledge of a topic.

Although providing choice in reading materials is usually easy to implement and provides students with a beneficial measure of autonomy, offering choice in reading materials is not always possible. Sometimes a specific text is so powerful and central to a unit or course that every student needs to read it. If so, delve into differentiation strategies other than choice in reading materials to ensure everyone stays engaged and thrives.

Objective and Subjective

Adults and students tend to have a natural preference for either objective assignments that have clear processes to follow or clear answers, or subjective ones they can accomplish in multiple ways and may be graded with rubric criteria rather than with an eye to simply right or wrong answers. In general, teachers and students who favor structure and certainty or experience and movement favor more objective assignments. Others prefer more subjective and open-ended tasks (those who crave vision and interpretation or question and connection). In this case, try creating two assignments for students to choose between, one objective and one subjective, that both measure student progress toward the same learning targets.

Providing students with this kind of choice is likely to increase their engagement and the quality of their products, which leads to fairer assessments of their learning. Psychologist and type expert Elizabeth Murphy (2013) asked over one hundred groups of teachers to design test questions they believed would best allow students to demonstrate content knowledge on a summative assessment. In every group, teachers wrote questions that worked best for students whose preference for either the objective or the subjective matched their own. Without awareness of this blind spot, it's easy for teachers to accidentally create assessments that favor students whose preferred cognitive process matches theirs over other students. Simply focusing on creating objective and subjective tasks and assessments can help you avoid this blind spot.

Assignment Menus

Assignment menus provide students with multiple opportunities to make choices as they proceed through a major assignment or unit. Just as you make choices at a restaurant based on what soups, salads, entrées, sides and so on are on the menu, you offer students menu options for acquiring learning about core content, practicing a new procedure, displaying mastery of a new skill, applying what they've learned, and so on.

Kathie F. Nunley (2014) describes *Layered Curriculum* as a teaching model that divides the learning process into three layers based on the complexity of thought process required. The following explains what all students are doing at each layer (Nunley, 2014).

- **C layer:** Students can demonstrate a basic understanding of the topic by gathering information through the activities they choose from this layer. Successful completion results in a letter grade on the assignment no lower than a C, but not a B or A.

- **B layer:** Activity choices from this layer have students applying or manipulating that information. Satisfactory completion of tasks from this level, in addition to the C layer tasks, results in a letter grade no lower than a B, but not an A.

- **A layer:** Activity choices involve critical thinking such as evaluating an issue, researching multiple points of view to develop an argument, and so on. Successful completion of all three layers results in a letter grade of A.

This approach works as a menu because students select the ways in which they will gather C-layer information, apply that knowledge through the B-layer choices, and use it for critical evaluation in their choice of an A-layer task. For example, for a one hundred–point assignment, menu ideas that offer students choices might include the following.

1. **C layer, basic understanding (sixty-five points maximum):** Create eight to ten activity choices, such as listening to lectures or accessing online programs, reading a textbook, answering worksheet questions, or researching basic concepts. Determine a point value for each activity based on its complexity.

   Alternatively, design a tic-tac-toe board as a form or rubric to clarify for students what traits their work must demonstrate. This can work well to ensure all students cover essential content. For example, repeat a required task in three boxes on a diagonal. Then, with the instruction that their horizontal, vertical, or diagonal choice of three tasks can't include a repeat, all students will have a row with this task in it. (See figure 3.1, page 56.) Note that all three items in a row include one activity for background information, one for practice, and the same final assessment.

Directions: Choose three activities to form a horizontal, vertical, or diagonal row without repeating an activity.		
Read and study the "Rules of Basketball" handout.	Study for the quiz in any way you choose.	Take the basketball rules quiz.
With a partner, practice demonstrating common referee calls and resulting plays found on the study guide.	Take the basketball rules quiz.	Use one of the basketball rules flashcard sets to study the rules with a partner.
Take the basketball rules quiz.	Watch the YouTube video "Rules of Basketball Explained" linked from our class website.	Watch the "Rules practice" video on our class website, pausing to answer the questions embedded in the video.

Figure 3.1: *An assignment menu of C layer items.*

2. **B layer, application of the information to previous learning (fifteen points):** Provide students with options "to manipulate or apply the information they learned in the C layer" (Nunley, 2014). Usually, this layer provides fewer choices but involves some variation on building, applying, problem solving, creating, brainstorming, and so on (Nunley, 2014). These might include doing an experiment, analyzing a real-life example of the principles involved, or using the information to write a story, design a game, or create an art project.

3. **A layer, evaluation (twenty points):** These high-level tasks ask students to use what they have learned to investigate problems with no right or wrong answers, such as current events or leadership decisions.

Reflecting on her use of this layered approach, Nunley (2006) summarizes, "Now a letter grade earned in my class had some consistent meaning: A student who earned an A was one who could gather information, manipulate that information, and critically evaluate the topic with some level of proficiency and accountability" (p. 28). Note that this differs from tiered assignments, where choices are arranged by ability level. In a Layered Curriculum, all students engage in all three task levels, can see how the first and second layers provide a foundation for the third, and can see the path to success.

Using assignment menus, teachers ask *all* students to perform each layer of the assignment. The C layer provides scaffolding so that all students have the information they need to go on to the B and A layers and provides the path that structure and certainty, and experience-and-movement students crave. In turn, vision-and-interpretation and question-and-connection students feel motivated by knowing the big-picture purpose for an assignment (by previewing A-layer tasks) before they gather information about it. Further, *all* students can see from the point distribution for each layer that they can meet standards on the assignment even if they might struggle with the A-layer portion.

VIRTUAL CLASSROOMS

Especially for the C layer, be mindful of how, during distance learning, you can allow student autonomy by offering one option for information gathering (such as watching a video or working in a group to fill in a learning map using assigned resources) as a synchronous option. Students could choose other options and work on their own, rejoining the class as directed. This provides autonomy not just in the learning tasks but autonomy in place, some flexibility in timing, and an energy boost for those who find online interactions more draining.

Two Big Success Essentials

Choice is a wonderful motivator and differentiation tool leading to more student engagement, the E in the STEAM^2 framework. However, as you've seen, some of the choice strategies take planning or attention to certain details, such as which cognitive processes a choice may favor. What follows are lessons learned and summaries of how to make choice work from teachers who have successfully used these strategies.

Establish Clear Learning Targets

As discussed in chapter 2 (page 33), clear goals and expectations come before using differentiation strategies. No matter what choices you provide or what choices students make, you and they need to know what you expect them to learn.

Establishing clear learning targets or success criteria may seem obvious, but teachers who have been newly empowered to provide choices commonly hand me lesson plans where the choices they've come up with simply won't lead to the same learning outcomes. Consider the choices you would give for the different learning goals in the following examples. Might the choices you design be different depending on whether you focus on the first goal or the second goal in each of the following?

- Understanding the purpose of finding common denominators *versus* being able to find common denominators; observe how a worksheet asking students to practice finding common denominators, where students can choose ten of twelve problems, will meet the second learning goal but not the first.

- Sequencing key events in a story *versus* identifying how key events tie to an important theme in a story; observe how a choice of making a timeline of story events or illustrating main events in the story will meet the first learning goal but not the second.

- Writing a persuasive essay *versus* writing an opinion piece; observe how students might choose between an essay on their opinion of a current event or a book they've read for the second option, but the instructions for the essay or book report would need to change to fulfill the first.

- Understanding the plot of Shakespeare's (1603/2019) *Hamlet versus* gaining skills with reading a Shakespearean play independently; observe how students might be able to read a plot summary of the play for the first goal and how, for the second goal, they might work alone or in a group, or just read or read and watch a film version of the play.

- Understanding the effects of exercise on blood pressure *versus* being able to design and conduct an experiment that provides data on exercise's effects on an easily measured indicator of a human system; observe how students might choose between reading about exercise or experimenting for the first goal but will need to experiment for the second goal.

Clarify your learning target and then figure out the choices that support it. Use chapter 2 (page 33) and its focus on setting clear learning goals and success criteria to guide you in this work.

Have a Plan for Grading

Another common oversight teachers make is providing choices on wonderful projects without first planning how to grade them fairly. This may be why one of my colleagues complained about crafts assignments for ELA that used up lots of poster board and glue but didn't seem to further learning about the literature they had read. Traditional rubrics may or may not be helpful in such cases. Will all students be taking the same assessment, no matter how they access the information? Will they be turning in different projects? What decisions might you make up front that will save you work in the long run by structuring certain hard-to-grade choices before you give them? Simple checklists that allow for a variety of products, such as the rubric in figure 3.2, often help.

Success Criteria	Value
☐ Does your project demonstrate understanding of the plot?	10 points
☐ Does your project include a clear description of the novel's theme, with supporting evidence from the text?	10 points
☐ Did your three-minute book talk (a) provide a teaser and (b) avoid spoilers (five points each)?	10 points

Figure 3.2: *Final project rubric—Dystopian novels.*

Common Concerns About Choice

The following statements represent common concerns I hear from educators as they consider using choice strategies. Beside each statement, you'll find text on how you might address any resistance you encounter (by yourself or with colleagues) because of such concerns.

- **"Students won't choose wisely!"** Choice does not equate to saying, "Anything goes." Keep the choices you provide to students within the parameters that meet the learning targets, the grading criteria, and— as a stretch for you—the very outer boundaries of your comfort level. Remember, choice is about pushing a bit on what is comfortable for you in the interest of meeting students' cognitive processing styles, some of which are quite unlike yours. Further, remember that students learn to make good decisions only through the experience of making decisions. They can't mature without some autonomy.

- **"Students will stick to favorites when they need to expand their horizons."** You determine the choices available to students so you can provide options that *do* expand students' horizons. Examples from this chapter include giving genre requirements for choices in reading materials, asking students to sometimes work solo and sometimes work with others, and more. Name your fears, and plan so they don't come to be. For example, one of my colleagues teaches students three different note-taking formats. All students are required to use each one when it is introduced. Once they understand and have used each approach, they have the autonomy to use the format that works best for them or to make up their own if they can demonstrate success with it.

- **"But all students have to _____."** Think of anything you want to fill in this blank: "Memorize their multiplication tables," "Learn to give a demonstration speech," "Master content about the laws of energy and thermodynamics," "Work cooperatively," and so on. Providing choice isn't necessary at all times. None of the strategies in this book apply to every situation. Choice is simply one of the easiest differentiation strategies.

- **"Students will just do what takes the least time or what their friends are doing."** Some students may do this. They may need more encouragement and experience with true engagement before they begin to believe that engaging with what interests them results in delight while learning. Consider engaging students in the exercises in Extraversion and Introversion (page 20 of chapter 1) and Sensing and Intuition (page 23 of chapter 1) and sharing figure 1.1 (page 18) so they can identify which style is the one they enjoy using most. Then, if they understand that a choice matches the cognitive process they resonate with, they just might be more enthusiastic about trying related choices.

Why Choice Works

Choice is both simple and powerful. Here are three research-based reasons for its inclusion as a solid differentiation strategy.

1. **Executive function:** You've probably heard that social-emotional learning includes helping students develop better executive functioning.
   The prefrontal cortex is key to this capacity, and it doesn't fully develop until around age twenty-five (Arain et al., 2013; Davidow et al., 2019). Executive function includes working memory, reasoning, information processing and filtering (which lies at the heart of making choices), task flexibility, problem solving, planning, and execution. Students don't learn to plan by following what others tell them. They don't figure out how to solve problems if the steps in the solution are spelled out for them. They learn to process information and make decisions by processing information and making decisions. Giving students choices allows them to practice these skills. One study shows that imaginative play (not controlled by adults) increases executive function (Berk & Meyers, 2013). This is one of the purest forms of choice.

2. **Motivation:** Daniel Pink (2009) compiled research on what motivates human beings, young and old, to learn, to persevere, and to step out of their comfort zones. Three main factors turned out to be key: (1) autonomy, (2) mastery, and (3) purpose. It's not pizza parties or stickers or other extrinsic rewards that motivate students. Choice provides that autonomy and increases intrinsic motivation (Patall, Cooper, & Robinson, 2008; Ulstad, Halvari, Sørebø, & Deci, 2018; Wallace & Sung, 2017). For example, a study on learner-centered teaching and student choice shows that students who received choices completed 36 percent more assignments than they were required to do (Hanewicz, Platt, & Arendt, 2017). Mike Miller (2018) summarizes research showing that giving genre choices in writing assignments increases student writing skills. Angela Duckworth (2016) points out that perseverance isn't enough for success; students need perseverance and passion—and passion often comes from a combination of self-efficacy and autonomy to pursue one's interests or self-set goals.

3. **Reading research:** Think of all the reading strategies used in your school or district. Allowing students to read materials of their own choosing during the school day is consistently as effective as or even more effective than using those strategies (Miller, 2013). It's also far more cost-effective and less time-consuming than many intricate reading strategies. In *Reading in the Wild: The Book Whisperer's Keys to Cultivating Lifelong Reading Habits*, Donalyn Miller (2013) points out that students who receive time to read for pleasure are more likely to become lifelong readers. The case for providing choice for reading materials is strong.

Note that students with *every* cognitive processing style benefit from choices *if* you design the choices to include each of the styles, at least some of the time.

Reflection Activity

Consider the following actions and questions as you reflect on this chapter's content.

1. How might you explain the power of choice to a teacher who asks, "Why give choices? I'm preparing students for the real world, where they'll need to do lots of things they don't want to do!"

2. Choose one of the choice strategies in this chapter. Commit to a small action-research project (taking action on an initiative and then reflecting critically on the outcomes) that will help you improve how you use the strategy—and perhaps provide some data to convince others to use it. If the strategy is working, what might you observe: Increased student motivation? Fewer groans and less eye-rolling? Higher-quality work? You might observe the impact of the strategy on just a few students who aren't working up to their potential, who seem content to do no more than they are asked to do, or who seem disengaged in your class.

    Use any of the following forms of data to reflect on the outcomes that your use of the strategy achieved.

    ‣   Assessments or other measures of progress toward proficiency

    ‣   Student reflection exercises or exit tickets

    ‣   Observation data such as time on task or the number of times you need to help students refocus

3. How might teachers be given choice during professional development using these strategies? What might you suggest?

CHAPTER 4

Wait Time

Wait time, where students receive time to think, form answers, or challenge themselves to come up with more than one answer, differentiates learning by helping all students develop the following essential social-emotional learning skills: sharing thoughts, holding thoughts, collaborating, working independently, thinking before they speak, speaking up even if they're unsure they have a fully correct answer, and listening to and building on the ideas of others. It increases the number of students who participate and thus contributes to equity (Ingram & Elliott, 2016). Consider the following everyday classroom interactions.

- "By the time I'm ready to talk, all the good answers are taken."
- "Other students blurt out the answers so fast we don't have a chance."

These statements came from middle school students who were struggling in regular classrooms as they chatted with me about their frustrations with classroom discussions. They wanted more time to think, and isn't thinking exactly what teachers want students to do?

It isn't a new idea or finding that teachers tend to ask questions in rapid succession and wait on average only a second before asking again, rephrasing, or adding more information. Mary Budd Rowe (1974a, 1974b), who conducted the original research into wait time strategies, finds when teachers learn to wait three more seconds, the average number of words in a student's response and the frequency of inferences and speculations more than triple. Discipline issues decrease. Further, teachers in Rowe's (1974a, 1974b) study realized that they'd been providing more wait time for high-performing students than for others when calling on individuals. With this simple change in practice of using wait time, the students who struggled most provided better answers.

In teacher workshops, I often cite Rowe's initial research into this strategy and then demonstrate how long three or four seconds are by counting silently on

> **Wait Time Strategies**
> *(From quickest to deepest)*
>
> ✓ One One Thousand, Two One Thousand . . ., page 64
> ✓ Hold That Thought, page 65
> ✓ Ten Hands Up, page 66
> ✓ Retrieve-Pair-Share, page 66
> ✓ Wait-Go Cards, page 67
> ✓ Discussion Protocols for Wait Time, page 69

my fingers. Invariably, I barely get to the third finger before at least one teacher blurts out, "Dang, that's a long silence!"

In this chapter, I detail six strategies to include wait time as part of your instruction. You'll also find three big essentials for success with these strategies as well as answers to common concerns about trying the strategies. If you'd like to explore more research on wait time before experimenting in your classroom, see Why Wait Time Works (page 73). Or, first try a few of the wait time strategies in this chapter to see for yourself how providing wait time affects your students.

DOING DIFFERENTIATION

Try a very simple strategy with your students (or colleagues). Display a picture that you've taken and ask who has a question about it with an immediate show of hands. Respond to a few questions, and then tell students you're going to ask them to come up with a question they can ask about a different picture. However, you won't be calling on anyone until you can see that just about everyone has a question ready by putting a thumb up. Display the photo you've taken, and wait for everyone's thumbs up. When everyone, or just about everyone, has done so, let them share questions and answer the ones you can.

After you're done, ask for comments on whether it was easier to form a question when the wait time was provided. Who struggled to remember what they meant to ask? Comment on question quality and anything else you notice, and take comments on how wait time might become a helpful discussion norm. You can extend the learning with students by including information from the Extraversion and Introversion section (page 20). Have them do a quick write or exit ticket on which of these traits has the strongest pull for them and how they reacted to the wait time in this exercise.

The Wait Time Strategies

This section presents six strategies for wait time: (1) One One Thousand, Two One Thousand . . ., (2) Hold That Thought, (3) Ten Hands Up, (4) Retrieve-Pair-Share, (5) Wait-Go Cards, and (6) Discussion Protocols for Wait Time. These strategies are designed to foster more participation, give students who are more introverted a chance to think, give extraverted students a chance to rethink or practice listening, and help all students engage in critical thinking and problem solving.

One One Thousand, Two One Thousand . . .

Yes, count in this way to four—or five. Whether I'm working with kindergartners, middle schoolers, college students, school leaders, or retirees, I've learned to ask a question and wait: one one thousand, two one thousand, three one thousand, four one thousand, five one thousand. The length of the pause should reflect the dynamics of the discussion.

Two great results flow from this simple technique.

1. Students and adults ask more questions, provide more relevant examples, unearth important topic connections, and deepen the conversation.

2. The entire room becomes more aware of how many participants raise hands or voice thoughts at the last second and becomes more patient with pauses.

More participation, better answers, no planning—what more can you ask for? Your more introverted students will thank you, and your extraverted students will mature (the M in STEAM[2]) as they practice taking turns and listening.

VIRTUAL CLASSROOMS

Wait time strategies are crucial for virtual environments, where streaming speeds may differ and monitoring your students' faces for engagement, no matter how big your screen, can be difficult. Experiment with using the hand-raising function on your platform, having students literally raise a hand onscreen, or having them respond through the chat function but not hit Send until you give a signal. Or, have everyone turn their camera off, form a question, and turn their camera back on as soon as they're ready to respond.

For online discussions, counting to as high as ten may be necessary to achieve effective results using this approach. This was the case with my doctoral students as we migrated to the Zoom platform during the COVID-19 pandemic. Experiment, perhaps using the hand-raising function on your platform. If you count to five, seven, or ten, do you receive more responses and questions, as I experienced?

Hold That Thought

It's rather a cosmic joke that some students—and adults—do their best thinking while talking (showing extraversion), and some students do their best thinking when it's quiet (showing introversion)—and both have more energy for learning when their needs are met (Blair & Sutherland, 2018). You've probably seen extraverted students nearly bounce out of their chairs as they put up a hand, anxious to answer a question. Then, when you call on them, they say, "Um . . . I forgot." They really did forget because they need to talk to think. This approach helps them remember what they want to say.

For this approach, have students capture the gist of their thoughts on paper or their mobile devices—a few quick words, bullet points, a diagram, or anything else that will help them recall their thoughts. Clarify that you aren't looking for formal sentences. Tell them, "This is for *you*. Don't you hate it when you think of a good answer and then lose track of it while you're listening to others?" While helping extraverts hold their thoughts, this quick-note approach also appeals to introverted learners because it can keep their minds from wandering off into their own tangential ideas. It's a win-win strategy that students of all cognitive processes can use for a lifetime.

Encourage students to use this strategy when they're preparing for all-class discussions using Wait-Go Cards (page 67) and when they're listening to classmate responses.

Ten Hands Up

This approach both allows introverted students to form their thoughts and, by setting a threshold participation level before a teacher will listen to responses, sets high expectations for contributions from all students. Announce, "I'll call on someone when I see ten hands up," or whatever number of hands you wish to see. Because most students get a bit impatient when nothing is happening, the hands often go up pretty fast.

Time and again, with adults and students, I find that when the content is rigorous, changing up the signal you ask for can increase engagement, simply because you've activated the part of the brain that pays attention to novelty (see Why Curiosity Creators work, page 135). I've asked for elbows on the table, arms crossed, fingers on the nose, and other rather crazy signals with students. In fact, when content is complex, adult workshop participants also enjoy this approach.

I once watched a ninth-grade teacher struggling to keep her students engaged one sunny afternoon in an overly warm classroom. She posed a question, and when too few students raised hands, she said, "OK, I need ten feet up." Several students said, "What?" She repeated, "When you have an answer, put up a foot. Get those feet up—I want ten of them before I call on anyone." Amid student laughter, for subsequent questions, she continued by asking for hands on heads and so on. The students shook off their lethargy and participated.

Retrieve-Pair-Share

Most teachers are familiar with Think-Pair-Share, in which students think about a teacher-assigned question for a text, pair with a partner or small group, and then share their thinking with each other. If you already use this approach, keep using it, perhaps pairing it with the Hold That Thought approach (page 65). Besides providing wait time for your more introverted students, being able to test out an answer or idea with a partner before sharing it with the whole class can provide emotional safety and build confidence and classroom trust. It's also been shown to increase critical thinking (Kaddoura, 2013; Petruţa, 2017).

Retrieve-Pair-Share is similar, but instead of having students simply think about a topic or potential answer, it places emphasis on drawing out of students' brains the information that you've helped them learn. While Think-Pair-Share is often an instant strategy to help more students share responses with confidence, the applications of Retrieve-Pair-Share are often a bit more planful, with the emphasis on revisiting prior learning, often with the intention of connecting it to new ideas. Pooja K. Agarwal (2020), cognitive scientist, educator, and founder of RetrievalPractice.org, states:

> Too often, we teach, students learn, they take a test, and we move on. But if you want your students to remember what they've learned (and you can stop re-teaching), students can't just take what they've learned and leave it. They have to retrieve it. (p. 1)

To use this strategy, post a question such as the following on the board or a screen.

- "What do you remember about _____, which we recently talked about in class?"

- "Bring to mind a feminine German noun. Use it in a sentence that incorporates the proper article, pronoun, and verb conjugation."

- "Jot down a few notes about a way you've seen _____ used in real life."

- "Before you sight-read this song, what do you want to think about and check for?"

- "List what you remember about _____. List questions about things that you think we may have covered but that you can't quite recall."

- "Write down your summary of the text you just read."

Then, pair up students to compare their answers and expand their notes before facilitating an all-class discussion that will serve as a review or provide students with multiple examples of applications.

This is one of the strategies that has something for everyone. Structure-and-certainty students enjoy working with knowledge they've mastered to prepare for discussion, and experience-and-movement students like the practical review and a chance to talk. Vision-and-interpretation students enjoy the chance to synthesize ideas, especially if they're interested in the topic and have more to add to what was learned in class, and question-and-connection students enjoy the chance to share what they know and make connections among ideas.

Wait-Go Cards

Wait-Go Cards are an idea that comes from child psychologist Elizabeth Murphy (2013), who suggests making cards that are red on one side and green on the other for students to use to indicate whether they are ready to contribute to a class discussion. In addition to using red and green, add contrasting patterns or shapes associated with each color to ensure that students who are color-blind aren't confused. For example, you might print a red hexagon on one side and a green circle on the other side.

Sherry Parrish (2010), an author and educational consultant who specializes in mathematics, points out that if students are used to their teacher calling on one of the first classmates to put up a hand, they often stop thinking once they realize that others are ready to answer—or they never really start thinking since someone else will give them the answer. Wait-Go Cards set the expectations that everyone needs to be ready to participate and that speed isn't as important as engaging with the learning.

Before beginning a large-group discussion, give students each a card. Ask them to place their card Wait (red) side up, in front of them where you can see it. Pose a question, and ask them to turn the Go (green) side up when they are ready to add to the discussion. Two steps help establish the norm that you expect all students to be ready to respond.

1. Start with questions that you know everyone can answer. For example, every student will have some sort of opinion about a story character, video clip, or school rule.

2. Scaffold thinking in students who generally take a passive approach to class discussions by posting at the front of the room a list of potential response stems such as the following.

   ‣ *Ask a question*—"I don't understand why . . ." or "Why did the character . . . ?"

   ‣ *Make a connection*—"This reminds me of . . ." or "_____ is making the same kind of mistake as _____."

   ‣ *Give an opinion*—"I don't think this rule is fair because . . ." or "That event in the story isn't realistic because . . ."

   ‣ *Clarify something*—"I've made a little diagram of this word problem and . . ." or "At first, I thought _____, but now, I think _____."

   ‣ *Make a prediction*—"If we agree on _____, I think _____" or "If this character _____, I think _____."

   ‣ *Add on*—"I'd like to add to what _____ said . . ." or "In addition to that, _____." Allow students to agree with someone else's response, encouraging them to add their reasoning or otherwise enrich the answer.

The cards you use for this approach don't have to be huge. Some teachers laminate them. Students can make their own, coloring a red hexagon on one side of an index card and a green circle on the other. They might make their own designs as long as you can tell which side is which. Wait-Go Cards are also useful for small-group discussions. See Group Work That Works (page 110) for ideas.

Teachers can use Wait-Go Cards in several other ways.

• For discussions, have students start with the Go side up. Once they've spoken, the Wait side goes up, and they need to wait to speak again until others have taken a turn. You may note that students who prefer introversion speak up more quickly this way, either to ensure their answer doesn't get taken or to get speaking over with.

• Signal all-class thinking time by posting a large Wait card at the front of the room. Set expectations by saying, for example, "We're all going to take two minutes of wait time to think this through. Then you'll have five minutes of go time to work with a partner on it." Flip to the Go side at the end of two minutes.

• When students are working individually on an assignment, have them place the cards Go side up where you can see them as you walk by. They can turn the cards to the Wait side if they finish their work, have a question, wish to share a comment with you, or need feedback before continuing.

- Ask students to work up to a certain point in an assignment (a step, for example, for which you want to ensure students have approached correctly before they proceed to the next step) and then turn their card Wait side up. This lets you provide individual feedback on quality or correctness before they proceed, which motivates structure-and-certainty and experience-and-movement students because they know they are on track, not wasting effort. It also helps vision-and-interpretation and question-and-connection students by ensuring that their tendency to follow their own ideas hasn't taken them off track from the success criteria. You can also count Go cards to gauge class readiness for moving on, to spot who needs enrichment, or to identify which students need targeted instruction.

- When students are sitting together at a table but working independently, have them each work behind a screen, such as an open, upright binder. Have them place a card on top and turn it to Wait when they have their final answer or need help. Students feel safe when their mistakes or attempts are private. Plus, you know they are thinking for themselves.

Think of Wait-Go Cards as similar to traffic lights for both teacher-student and student-student interactions. You're providing a visual rather than auditory reminder of designated thinking time. Whether students are more extraverted or introverted, they can literally see when it's time to engage with the outer world.

Discussion Protocols for Wait Time

Many discussion protocols favor either extraverts or introverts. For example, one protocol I've experienced asks participants to write down an answer to a specific question and then compare their answer with as many other participants in the room as they can. The extraverted participants often love the chance to wander all over and meet multiple people. The introverts would rather have deeper discussions with just a few people and often ignore the directions by staying with one or two partners. I've also experienced *silent* gallery walks, where every participant moves from poster to poster, either writing comments on adjacent paper or taking notes for later discussions. The extraverted participants are usually ready to start discussing the posters long before the silent walk is up.

So that no one is uncomfortable for too long, look for protocols that provide some wait time yet also allow chances for everyone to speak up. One of my favorite discussion protocols is the Last Word protocol. Here is how it works.

1. Students silently read a text and mark passages they would like to discuss.

2. One student reads a passage *without* commenting on it. In a round-robin fashion, each student makes a comment about that passage, poses a question, shares a connected idea or example, or provides a contrasting idea.

3. After each group member has commented, the student who chose the quote explains why he or she chose it.

4. The process continues until each group member has shared a quote.

Can you see how everyone gets to prepare, knowing they will get to speak? And everyone has time to gather their thoughts since they've all read the entire article?

Look through the discussion protocols you already use in your classroom. Do they allow for wait time? How might you adjust them so all students have a chance to both think and participate?

Three Big Success Essentials

Wait time strategies help students succeed by allowing them to think through answers, thrive as they become more confident, stay engaged as they no longer wait for others to answer, increase agility as they learn to both speak up and hold thoughts, and mature as they build more SEL skills—all five components of STEAM[2] with relatively little teacher planning! While you can quickly implement many of the wait time strategies in this chapter, students can become frustrated if they don't see the point or if a lesson drags on too long. What follows are lessons learned and summaries of how to make wait time work.

Teach Fairness

Students of every age are pretty good at noting whether they feel rules and processes are fair or unfair. When using wait time strategies, take a few moments for social-emotional learning. Demonstrate the inherent fairness of the strategies to increase empathy and patience among students as they begin to recognize each other's needs for think time and talk time.

To help students understand, you might use the Doing Differentiation strategy from the start of this chapter (page 64). Or, first, ask a question such as, "I'm going to ask you to bring to mind a menu item you wish our cafeteria would serve—something the cafeteria workers would make from scratch or even something they'd have delivered from your favorite restaurant. When you've thought of that menu item and are ready to begin talking about it with someone, quietly show me a thumbs-up so I can see who is ready."

Usually, some thumbs are up within two seconds. These students will often stay silent but will start fidgeting, glancing around to see who else is ready, or looking at you as if to say, "Come *on*, can't we start talking?" Other students will calmly reflect for much longer. Observe as closely as you can how many seconds pass before all thumbs are up, and ask for a show of hands: "Who thought that was a really long time to think alone? Who found the time to think refreshing?" Tell the class how many seconds elapsed between the first and last thumbs' going up. Give the students a few minutes to pair up and share their responses to the initial question you asked. Then, debrief with a few of the following questions.

- "For those of you who enjoyed the time to think, was this experience any different from usual class discussions? How? What happens to your thoughts if questions come really rapidly during class?"

- "For those of you who were ready to talk right away, what was it like to hold your thoughts? Did anyone forget what they really wanted to say?"

- "Think for a moment. Do you tend to be hesitant about sharing in class? I'm going to count to twenty silently and then ask you to share thoughts about how wait time might help you find it easier to participate."

- "If you struggled to wait, what might make it easier to wait and to remember what you want to say?"

- "Let's share some answers to my question. For me, I'd love it if . . . !"

Then, set up norms that will lead to fairness, respect, and patience so all students become comfortable with wait time. Everyone needs to participate. If there are reluctant students, emphasize that the whole class benefits from everyone's ideas, creativity, and questions. Also, everyone needs to be able to hold their thoughts since not everyone can go at the same time. Tell students, "We're going to be using some strategies to ensure that both talk time and wait time work for everyone."

Reframe Behavior

Reframing behaviors such as quickly blurting out answers, in your own mind and for students, can be helpful in building classroom trust and respect. First, remember that faster really isn't smarter. Carol S. Dweck (2016) points out how damaging this misconception is to all students. Some assume that they must not be very smart because they're slower to answer than others, but fast students begin doubting their abilities when tasks become more complex and they, too, need more time. Wait time strategies take the emphasis off fast, correct answers, and allow you to push everyone to entertain multiple ideas, justifications, and deeper reasoning.

Second, reframe students' blurting out answers in your mind. Tell yourself, *I bet this is an extraverted student who hasn't learned to hold thoughts.* Remind students about fairness. Suggest, "If you know you'll be tempted to blurt out an answer, please place a finger over your mouth"—demonstrating the "Shh" gesture—"so you remember to wait." Occasionally, you may need to go a step further, perhaps providing a student with three speaking tokens, such as chips or cards, and saying, "Once you've used these up this hour, you'll need to be quiet for the rest of class to allow your classmates a turn." Usually, the student hoards the chips or cards rather than run out of chances to talk.

Third, picture a quieter student's attempts to enter an all-class discussion as similar to the moves one might make trying to enter double-Dutch jump roping. If you've ever tried this, think back to how you almost rock on the balls of your feet trying to get the rhythm, looking for that entry. Of course, the two ropes can't stop, or else the game is over, but in the classroom, you can slow down the ropes of a discussion so every student can find a comfortable entry point. This makes wait time an equity-focused strategy, ensuring everyone can enter the discussion game.

Wait for Students' Light Bulbs to Light Up

Too often, in a rush to get through the curriculum or with the goal of being helpful, teachers cut off students' thinking before they're done. Wait time strategies allow for productive struggle that leads to long-term learning retention. For instance, I filmed students completing mathematics tasks for a research project, providing them with materials that allowed them to tackle the tasks in very different ways. One student engaged in what I would call *purposeful trial and error*. He drew a diagram, compared it to the written problem, realized it wasn't right, and tried another idea. On the third try, he not only got it right but *knew* it was right.

After watching the film with other teachers as part of a workshop, a participant said, "I would have jumped in after his second mistake. And that wouldn't have helped, would it?" Another teacher said, "But we don't have time for students to try things three times." And a third spoke up slowly: "So we don't have time for students like this boy to learn?"

In an era of too much content and too little time, waiting is difficult. However, giving space for the light bulb to light is a low-cost, high-impact, evidence-based approach.

Common Concerns About Wait Time

The following statements represent common concerns I hear from educators as they consider using wait time strategies. Beside each statement, you'll find text on how you might address any resistance you encounter (by yourself or with colleagues) because of such concerns.

- **"Won't students just stall?"** If one or two students seem to be testing you while using Wait-Go Cards, consider saying, "I'll be looking for just about all the cards to turn to the Go side. At that point, I'll assume I can call on anyone because you'll all have had plenty of time." If one of the "laggers" doesn't have an answer, use the *restate* component in the Use Teacher Moves section (page 111) to signal your high expectations.

  Often, I see teachers surprised to learn the amount of time students need to think through a problem or concept. One teacher had her eighth graders watch a film on George Washington and then asked students to retrieve knowledge by writing down information they recalled from the film. She reported, "I couldn't believe that some of them took a full ten minutes before they turned their cards to the Go side. But then it was amazing. I could call on any student, and they all had quality responses ready."

- **"There's never enough class time."** This is probably true, but what other strategy takes almost no planning, brings results in as little as five seconds, and increases quality responses? Wait time is a short-term strategy with long-term results, turning all students into active rather than passive learners and creating higher expectations for participation, deep thinking, and cooperation and listening.

- **"Students will resent writing things down when they could just say them."** As long as you aren't requiring full sentences and allow students to use diagrams, doodles, or emojis or pictures, students are likely to realize that recording their thoughts prevents the frustration of forgetting their brilliant ideas and that it helps pass what may seem like a long wait until they can talk.

- **"Doesn't this pressure the quiet students or those still learning English?"** If you're worried about this, it's important to reframe this approach as providing students with the strategies they will need to be heard, to be valued, and to be successful. I've worked with teachers who, when introducing the use of Wait-Go Cards, give quiet students the option of writing down their thoughts and handing them to a friend to read aloud. And what do the students do? Because this would mean writing out complete sentences, most of them choose to share their ideas aloud and learn that, since they had time to think of something worthwhile to say, saying it wasn't so hard to do.

Why Wait Time Works

Think of wait time as a multipurpose tool. I present several more discussion protocols in chapter 7 (page 101), which focuses on student-centered discussions. All of them incorporate wait time. Education researchers Jenni Ingram and Victoria Elliott (2016) investigated the effectiveness of different uses of wait time, finding evidence that activities that incorporate it lead to the following outcomes.

- Wait time improves equity regarding who is heard and establishes healthy classroom norms such as turn taking (see Wait-Go Cards, page 67).

- Wait time increases participation as well as encourages all students to think (see One One Thousand, Two One Thousand . . ., page 64; Ten Hands Up, page 66).

- When used with higher-level questioning, wait time is most effective if teachers encourage students to use the time to enhance the quality of their responses by improving thought coherence, reasoning, and justification (see Hold That Thought, page 65; Retrieve-Pair-Share, page 66).

- Wait time allows students to be more confident in their answers (see Retrieve-Pair-Share; Wait-Go Cards; and Discussion Protocols for Wait Time, page 69).

I've interspersed other research findings on wait time throughout this chapter, but one major finding remains. Executive function—proper use of the brain's prefrontal cortex—involves two processes: (1) taking in information and (2) drawing conclusions. Carl Jung (1921/1923) postulates that each of us uses one of these processes in the external world and the other in our internal world. More recently, brain scans have shown evidence of these introverted and extraverted processes (Nardi, 2020). Wait time, paired with discussion, ensures that students learn to use both processes. My use of this strategy also indicates that wait time assists in developing maturity, the *M* in STEAM[2].

Reflection Activity

Consider the following actions and questions as you reflect on this chapter's content.

1. Reflect on your own learning experiences. Do you need to talk to think? How far in advance do you like to know what you'll be talking about?

2. Talk with colleagues about shyness versus the need to have time to think. Have they experienced the difference? Do they see it in students?

3. Find at least one discussion protocol, and analyze it in terms of the human need for wait time, similar to the analysis provided for the Last Word protocol example (page 69). How might you modify it to better incorporate wait time or in other ways to meet the needs of more learners?

CHAPTER 5

Unambiguous Instruction

During professional development with elementary and middle school teachers, I often introduce them to the Singapore mathematics bar-model drawing strategy, a technique I favor for teaching students to solve word problems (Cavendish & Clark, n.d.). Teachers like it so much, they often invite me into their classrooms so I can work with them to coteach it to students. These sessions, for both adults and students, involve unambiguous, direct instruction using an eight-step model to solve problems.

Through a gradual release of responsibility instructional framework (*I do, we do, you do*; Fisher & Frey, 2014; Mooney, 1988), they learn how to use this wonderful heuristic approach that works for about 80 percent of the word problems that so many people dread. However, the model is worthless unless you use it as intended. Figure 5.1 (page 76) shows an example.

Educators sometimes dismiss instruction that tells adults and students exactly how to approach a learning task or rests on one correct solution as boring, dumbing down, or even insulting. However, some instruction must be done with fidelity to rules, procedures, learning targets, and so on. For example, my high school writing instructor made it clear that her students needed to understand and use the rules of grammar before we could willy-nilly break them, such as by starting sentences with *because*. Because we needed to know when we shouldn't.

Unambiguous instruction strategies are an important tool in your instructional toolbox for several purposes, including the following.

> **Unambiguous Instruction Strategies**
> *(From quickest to deepest)*
> ✓ Worked Examples, page 78
> ✓ Direct Instruction, page 79
> ✓ Self-Monitoring for Progress, page 81

- To introduce procedures that only benefit students if used as designed, such as using the Singapore bar-model drawing, learning the best way to insert a zipper into a garment, or using a framework for understanding geography

- To provide students with clear examples of quality work or successful completion of learning targets or tasks

- To increase student success by modeling a method they might use to tackle similar tasks

- To quickly convey background or essential knowledge to students

1. Read the following problem.

   There were 240 students attending the STEAM² School. Two-thirds of the students rode a school bus to school. Three-quarters of the remaining students walked. The rest were driven to school by parents. How many students walked to school?

2. State what the problem is asking (leave space for an answer):

   _____ students walked to school.

3. Identify who or what is in the problem.

   Students who rode the bus, students who walked, students whose parents drove them

4. Draw the unit bars.

   Students at STEAM² School

5. Reread the problem, and label the unit bar to reflect the information.

   Students at STEAM² School   240

   Students who rode bus (2/3)

6. Place the question mark in the diagram. What part shows the answer to the question?

   Students who rode with parents

   ?

   Students who walked

7. Work the computations, guided by the bar model.

   240 / 3 = 80
   80 / 4 = 20
   20 * 3 = 60

   | 80 | 80 | 80 | 240 |

   80

   60

8. Restate the answer in a complete sentence.

   Sixty children walked to school.

Figure 5.1: Sample Singapore eight-step bar-model problem.

This chapter covers the strategies of unambiguous instruction so that students know what success looks like and the processes that will bring them success. If your students have asked questions such as the following, know that the strategies in this chapter will embed the answers in your lessons.

- "How long does this journal entry have to be?"

- "What do you mean, show my work? I just *know* the answer."

- "What if I've thought of another way to do this?"
- "Can you show me another example?"

You will also learn about two big essentials for success and suggestions that address common concerns teachers have about using these strategies. Note that two of the cognitive processes (structure and certainty, and experience and movement) gravitate toward unambiguous instruction, while those who prefer the other processes may feel constricted if they don't understand why they are using a strategy to master specific skills or knowledge or meet specific criteria. If you, like many teachers, worry that unambiguous instruction is the polar opposite of student-centered learning, you might want to first read the Why Unambiguous Instruction Works section (page 84) before looking at the strategies.

DOING DIFFERENTIATION

There is a fun way to introduce the importance of unambiguous instruction. Participants need a blank sheet of paper and a writing utensil; a finger on a tablet or smartphone also works. Tell students you'll be giving directions for making a drawing and that they are to follow the directions as best they can. Working from a simple drawing, give step-by-step oral directions for students to follow. Don't tell them what the object is or name parts by saying, for example, "Draw two eyes. . . ." Instead, use phrases such as, "Draw an upside-down teardrop about an inch in length in the middle of your paper. Now, draw a circle about the size of a quarter." After you've finished giving the directions, show the image. Let students compare their work. Whose drawing came closest? Usually, there is a good deal of laughter. Debrief by discussing the following.

- How would the task be different if you could have seen the original drawing while following the oral directions?

- When do you like having clear directions? When is it difficult for you to complete assignments exactly as directed and why?

- When have you put in a lot of effort on something at school only to realize you hadn't followed directions or didn't understand what a teacher was expecting?

Finish by talking about how these unambiguous instruction strategies ensure that when students are putting in the effort, they know what to do to be successful. If you have time, pair students up, hand out new drawings, and have the student pairs give unambiguous drawing directions to each other in the same way as you did for the whole class. Students (and adults!) often gain insights into their own strengths and struggles with crafting directions as they engage in this task.

The Unambiguous Instruction Strategies

This section presents three strategies for unambiguous instruction: (1) Worked Examples, (2) Direct Instruction, and (3) Self-Monitoring for Progress. Each of these strategies is designed to bring clarity to how to do a task, illustrate what success looks like, or make specific the knowledge students need to master.

Worked Examples

Worked examples support teachers in setting high expectations by providing students with models of exemplary work. Students can use these to check whether they are completing a task correctly, answer their own questions about a process, or gauge the quality of their own work. Helping students meet your high expectations, and raising their expectations for themselves, is key in making expectations useful rather than meaningless jargon to be invoked and soon forgotten. Worked examples, also called *exemplars*, play a role in providing unambiguous guidance by modeling high-level work in anything from writing, speaking, and problem solving to basketball. Authors and education experts Gavin Grift and Clare Major (2020) write on the usefulness of exemplars:

> Exemplars usually involve the sharing of a work sample or finished product. Sometimes referred to as worked examples, they demonstrate the expected learning in relation to the criteria for that standard and ensure students get the opportunity to see what proficiency would look like if they were to be successful. Students know the steps required to achieve success through the teacher's explanation of how they relate to the exemplar being shared. An exemplar will only be powerful when it is modeled by the teacher effectively. (pp. 61–62)

For example, one teacher found that when she provided writing prompts for journaling, a majority of her students wrote entries of only one or two sentences. She created three sample entries and labeled them *Good*, *Better*, and *Best* and discussed them with students. The quality of journal entries increased immediately. You can make sharing work of varying quality even more powerful by leading a classroom discussion to identify the traits of high-quality work for the particular task. You might even involve the students in constructing a rubric for quality work, based on the exemplars.

The possibilities for using worked examples in any content area are limitless. In mathematics, begin saving examples of student work, or locate sets of high-level work on the internet. This is also a content area where students often over explain their answers, muddling their work. Other students under explain their answers, making their thinking hard to interpret. Have students use a rubric to self-evaluate whether they have given a correct answer and explained their thinking well. For writing work in any content area, show exemplars of opening sentences and paragraphs, character descriptions, scientific analysis, supporting details for making a point in a persuasive paper, descriptions that make scenes and emotions come alive, and so on. In an arts class, display an exemplary project and explain why it meets necessary criteria. If you have high-quality learning maps (see page 165) from past students, show them to students while explaining the traits that made the maps successful. In a physical education class, you could demonstrate the difference between a sloppy and well-executed cartwheel. To involve students in setting success criteria, have different students concentrate on watching your feet, knees, arms, face, and head as you demonstrate more than once.

Ultimately, your purpose is to ensure students understand what good work looks like for a particular task.

Direct Instruction

Explicit, direct instruction, where teachers provide content or processes via lecture, demonstration, reading, and other teacher-directed activities, is an important part of teaching and learning. Remember that content drives the preferred method of instruction. Learners who just want to know what to do (structure and certainty) usually like direct instruction, and although direct instruction is contrary to the preferences of learners who like to do things their own way (vision and interpretation) or who prefer to lead as they learn (question and connection), *all* students benefit when teachers use direct instruction for the right purposes.

Direct instruction works best when all students understand *why* they are being asked to master certain content and processes and they grasp what mastery will look like. Consider the following examples of effective ways to use direct instruction.

- **Teaching learning processes when there is a proven method to master:** Here, a teacher walks students through a specific process they will be using. For example, a secondary mathematics teacher I coached signaled her students with, "What I write, you write," to indicate that what followed would be direct instruction, giving them a worked example they could revisit to self-monitor whether they were using the new process correctly. Excellent applications of direct instruction include mathematics basic algorithms; how to write sonnets, haiku, limericks, narrative poems, and other set forms of poetry; using a pottery wheel; and so on.

- **Teaching heuristics:** Heuristic instruction involves methods that assist students in thinking as opposed to following procedures. When students learn to use heuristics well, they can use these learned shortcuts to concentrate their thinking on the immediate problem rather than search for a way to approach it. Think of the *who, what, when, where,* and *why* of news reporting as a heuristic that students can apply to analyzing events, outlining a story, summarizing a story, and more. The Singapore mathematics model-drawing technique, the bar model you saw an example of at the start of this chapter, is a heuristic for solving word problems. The step-by-step scientific method is a heuristic for investigation. Many concept maps are heuristics. (See chapter 10, page 159.)

- **Teaching foundational content:** Direct instruction is often the quickest way to provide students with facts, rules, or processes either essential to a content area or to an upcoming learning task. For example, the German language is much easier to master if you take the time to memorize the genders of nouns: *das buch, die universität, der garten.* Note that teachers need not deliver all such content via lecture, but the drills, worksheets, games, online activities, and so on that they select need to appropriately emphasize right-answer thinking.

- **Teaching mnemonics for memorization:** A *mnemonic* is a pattern of letters, ideas, or some other device that assists in memorization. Do you remember the colors of the rainbow via ROY G. BIV? How about telling your left hand from your right by holding out your hands, palms down, fingers together, thumbs outstretched? These are all mnemonics.

Direct instruction often requires memorization, which is why mnemonics can be handy. In 2009, I facilitated differentiated instruction workshops in Saudi Arabia, and my host asked me to include information on what might help students successfully memorize information. I surveyed colleagues who use the cognitive processes framework for a few key memorization strategies connected with each cognitive process (Kise, 2009). Table 5.1 describes a few of them. Note that people in every group mentioned setting information to music as helpful, as well as strong mnemonics.

Table 5.1: Memorization Strategies

Structure and Certainty (Let Me Know What to Do)	Vision and Interpretation (Let Me Follow My Own Lead)
• Use mnemonic devices, either self-created or proven devices. • Write out, over and over, the information to be memorized.	• Create mental word pictures of the content to memorize. • Say the information out loud while studying independently but as if talking to an audience.
Experience and Movement (Let Me Do Something)	**Question and Connection (Let Me Lead as I Learn)**
• Memorize long passages in their entirety by adding one line (and only one line) at a time and then reciting the whole piece from the start. • Work with a friend, using flashcards or stating information out loud and quizzing each other.	• Walk about while saying the information out loud. • Develop a structure—key words or ideas around which to memorize information, put the information in order of importance to the student, or use a self-created or well-established mnemonic.

Sometimes, teachers see direct instruction as the polar opposite of student-centered learning. As a result, they see it as an inferior instructional strategy. In many ways, direct instruction and student-centered learning are interdependent. Students often need basic content or processes to engage in guided discovery, and they may need direct instruction at the end of guided discovery to cement what they learned. Think of how elementary ELA teachers explicitly teach phonemic awareness; they don't have students arbitrarily discover these sounds. It'd be just as inappropriate to have students experiment to define safe science lab procedures, even though they may design explorations while following designated procedures.

VIRTUAL CLASSROOMS

Direct instruction can easily become the default mode in virtual classrooms. Enliven instruction for virtual environments by reframing with flipped-classroom ideas, where homework involves recorded direct instruction or individual study of foundational information, and class time involves interactive learning tasks. For example, consider a lesson on field notes to ready secondary students for a research project. You might assign homework of watching a YouTube video (or one you record) on taking good field notes. In class, you might then have all students practice taking field notes while watching a high-interest movie scene related to a topic they are researching. Then, use direct instruction to present two Worked Examples (page 78) of good field notes and walk the class through the rubric or success criteria you've established for field notes. Students work alone or in pairs to self-monitor their progress and note how they can improve their note-taking techniques.

Self-Monitoring for Progress

With self-monitoring for progress, students check their work against rubrics, quiz themselves, look at exemplars to improve their own efforts, record their progress on a learning progression—anything that has them asking themselves instead of a teacher, "Am I doing this right? Am I holding myself to a high standard?" What John Hattie defines as *self-reported grading* encompasses the purpose of self-monitoring of progress:

> [Self-reported grading is] a practice by which students assess the quality of their own work or their level of mastery over a given subject domain. The validity of such self-grading is often assessed by comparing a student's "self-reported" grade with that provided by an instructor. (Corwin Visible Learning+, n.d.b)

Consider how you might use clear learning goals and expectations to help students monitor their own progress. By helping students set high expectations for themselves and take charge of reaching learning goals, they begin to meet the successful and maturing components of STEAM[2]. Additionally, when students course-correct while they work, they may stay more engaged and thrive as they see that their hard work is paying off.

How do you do it? Grift and Major (2020) suggest reversing the process teachers typically use. Usually, a teacher grades students' completed assignment and provides feedback to students. Instead, have students self-assess using success criteria you established as part of your work in chapter 2 (page 33). These self-assessments provide teachers with feedback on how students think they did. Then, teachers review the students' work and self-assessment. Here are four factors for implementing this well.

1. Ensure that learning goals and expectations use language students can understand and apply.

2. Model for students how to self-assess. Teach this process using real examples.

3. Set aside time to conference with students about their self-assessments. You don't need to do this for every student in every assignment, but do so enough to support students in improving their self-assessment skills.

4. Provide students with a graphic organizer with reflection questions to help them organize their thoughts.

Besides helping students take ownership in the quality of their work, developing student ability to self-monitor eventually leads to more agility among the cognitive processes, the *A* in STEAM[2]. Student self-monitoring of progress at their own pace, as questions arise or when they think they've got it, provides confidence-building scaffolding when tasks ask students to stretch from their preferred learning methods.

Two Big Success Essentials

Unambiguous instruction can accidentally become *too* structured (after all, with enough steps, a six-year-old can do a calculus problem) or not be structured enough (especially if, as one teacher I know put it, "I don't read directions, so I really struggle to write them clearly"). What follows are lessons learned and summaries of how to make unambiguous instruction work from teachers who have successfully used the strategies.

Test Your Clarity

Reflect back on the Doing Differentiation exercise at the start of this chapter (page 77). How clear are your directions, definitions, examples, and lectures? Find a colleague who doesn't think like you—you might pair up with your opposite with regard to preferences for sensing and intuition, as described in table 1.3 (page 26). Recall that sensing types tend to overstructure tasks and intuitive types tend to understructure tasks. Your partner doesn't even have to teach the same content area to be a resource for checking your clarity. Does your colleague find that your learning goals and expectations demonstrate clarity or confusion?

Allow For Individuality in Student Work

No matter how clear your expectations, some students chafe, sometimes unconsciously, at any attempt to get them to conform or to do exactly as you instruct. Remember the chapter 3 introduction (page 47) example of the student who wanted to write a letter to show his knowledge of Louisiana? The teacher could have insisted on a formal report. Instead, because the success criteria were clear regarding content being conveyed rather than the genre of writing to be used, the teacher flexed with the student's creativity. Have you seen students who go out of their way to come up with unusual methods of completing assignments? Ensure their creativity isn't constantly squelched by learning goals and expectations that are so clear that these students have no room to roam.

Another way to liven up students who aren't connecting with your unambiguous instruction is to add curiosity creators (page 119), such as Visual Entry Points (page 127) or throw in an additional engagement component such as a student-centered discussion (page 101).

Common Concerns About Unambiguous Instruction

The following statements represent common concerns I hear from educators as they consider using unambiguous instruction strategies. Beside each statement, you'll find text on how you might address any resistance you encounter (by yourself or with colleagues) because of such concerns.

- **"Direct instruction is boring."** It can be. In fact, all instruction can be boring if learners don't have the background knowledge, if tasks aren't clear enough for students to gauge progress, if too much time is allotted, and so on. Good instruction with any strategy takes a bit of planning, but consider how strategies such as curiosity creators (chapter 8, page 119) or the Mistake Modeling approach to student-centered discussion (page 105) might increase interest in the materials covered via direct instruction. Or, think of how learning maps might keep students engaged via the clear understanding they provide about the scope of the unambiguous learning that will occur before they can apply or get creative with their new knowledge and skills.

  If you are a fan of inquiry-based learning, as I am, there are two important considerations you should keep in mind. First, the effect size for guided inquiry is only 0.46 (as opposed to 0.59 for direct instruction), meaning students make just slightly over a year's growth via inquiry-based instruction (Corwin Visible Learning+, n.d.a). Second, teachers who prefer the vision-and-interpretation and question-and-connection cognitive processes usually *love* inquiry-based learning. A majority of your students, though, prefers the other two styles (Myers et al., 2018). Further, high-level inquiry-based instruction often requires more, not less, structure than direct instruction. Yes, students have autonomy to question, experiment, research, and more, but without careful planning, not all students reach the learning targets.

  Note that chapter 7 (page 101), on student-centered discussions, and chapter 9 (page 137), on open questions, both contain inquiry-based differentiation strategies with guidelines for solid planning. Chapter 11 (page 175) contains strategies that allow you to monitor and guide inquiry-based group work using big notes. Robert J. Marzano (2011) coined the term *guided inquiry* to describe this kind of open but structured path to successful inquiry-based tasks.

- **"What if our shared standards and learning progressions aren't very student friendly?"** Although your existing standards and progressions may be adequate, consider whether they are useful for self-monitoring, useful for explaining the quality of worked examples, or whether some revisions to them would help support your use of this chapter's strategies.

Why Unambiguous Instruction Works

The best evidence for the strategies in this chapter comes from John Hattie's meta-analyses of teaching and learning strategies, as recorded in the Corwin Visible Learning+ (n.d.a) Global Research Database (www.visiblelearningmetax.com/Influences). This database lists an enormous number of teaching strategies along with multiple criteria, such as the number of studies and students involved, and indicates the strategies' overall effect size (a numerical measure of the effect a new learning initiative has relative to making no changes at all). An effect size of 0.4 is the equivalent of students' achieving a year's growth, so any action that results in a larger number indicates an improvement in learning. Consider the effect sizes for the strategies related to this chapter, given in order of their impact on student learning.

- **Self-reported grades (effect size 1.33):** The practice of having students assess their own work against success criteria, then comparing their evaluation with a teacher's assessment, ranks third highest out of 276 strategies in the Visible Learning MetaX database.

- **Success criteria (effect size 0.88):** An effect size of 0.88 indicates that learning more than doubles when teachers convey in terms students can understand or even helped construct the criteria by which their work will be assessed. Note that as powerful as success criteria can be, teachers sometimes implement them in a token fashion (Crichton & MacDaid, 2016). To make them truly useful, students need direct instruction and worked examples of using success criteria for self-monitoring.

- **Mnemonics (effect size 0.8):** Providing tools for memorization clearly fosters student success in mastering knowledge. Jacqueline Lubin and Edward Polloway (2016) summarize the effectiveness of mnemonics for students with learning disabilities and provide strategies and tips for incorporating them into instruction.

- **Teacher clarity (effect size 0.76):** When teachers are organized, give clear directions, provide good examples, and communicate success criteria, student learning nearly doubles. For example, John Almarode, Doug Fisher, and Nancy Frey (2019) point out that clarity during science labs and demonstrations ensures that students are not only engaged via whiz-bang experiments but gain the content knowledge they need.

- **Direct instruction (effect size 0.59):** As you've observed throughout this chapter, effective direct instruction involves far more than teacher lecture. Student success comes from clear directions and success criteria, engaging students by providing modeling and guided practice. Research continues to demonstrate its effectiveness, even in more creative tasks such as creative writing (Humphrey & Feez, 2016; Main, Blackhouse, Jackson, & Hill, 2020).

As you saw in chapter 2 (page 33), successful differentiation builds on a platform of clear learning goals and expectations for students. In this chapter, you've seen the power of continuing with clear success criteria, clear directions, clear examples, and clear processes for students to assess the quality of their work. Remember that the learning journey is more engaging and more likely to get students to the right destination if they know where they're going and have a map of how to get there. Once those elements are in place, all kinds of differentiated instruction strategies are doable.

Reflection Activity

Consider the following actions and questions as you reflect on this chapter's content.

1. What are the norms and beliefs around unambiguous instruction versus more student-directed learning tasks in your learning community? I've worked with school leaders who are staunch opponents of any kind of memorization, others who evaluate teachers based on whether or not students are quietly working at the direction of a teacher, others who insist on fidelity to a scripted curriculum, and still others who push for real-life project-based inquiry. How do these norms affect your use of unambiguous instruction? (You might ask colleagues the same question to understand the influence of your school culture.)

2. Note that some people easily understand the Singapore mathematics bar model while others need more practice before they grasp its magic for solving common word problems. Can you see how it is a flexible heuristic, not a structured algorithm? What are the heuristics in your discipline that facilitate student thinking rather than telling students exactly what to do?

    To learn more about mathematics heuristics, visit https://mathsnoproblem .com/en/approach/bar-modelling or download one of the grade-level apps under the title Singapore Math Bar Models. How might the app specifically meet your needs for unambiguous instruction? How would you supplement it to use in your classroom? What can you learn from these examples of direct instruction and worked examples?

3. Reflect on past assignments where students were very successful and on ones where student results were not what you hoped for. When did you employ unambiguous instruction strategies, and what were the results? Where they didn't meet expectations, how might you use curiosity creators (chapter 8, page 119) or planned movement (chapter 13, page 201) to increase engagement? Similarly, when did you employ more inquiry-based tasks with more and less success? How might adding unambiguous instruction to those experiences have increased student success?

CHAPTER 6

Pressure-Prompted Accommodations

Perhaps you've noticed that not everyone takes the same approach to work, to assignments, to chores, to vacations, and to life in general. Do you, like me, tend to plan your work and work your plan? Or do you prefer to keep options open for as long as possible, making choices as situations unfold and the pressure for resolution builds?

When I try to build awareness in educators or students about their tendency to plan or to wait for the pressure to build, I start with a planned movement exercise (chapter 13, page 201) where participants organize themselves along a continuum, based on when they finish major projects. On one end are those who feel most comfortable with a done-by-midterm mentality; on the other, those who are comfortable with being late to class because they literally just finished their work. I have the participants at the extremes answer the question, "What's it like to try to do the opposite?" The pressure-prompted say that if they start early, they can't think, or they end up changing their topics and starting over anyway. They also say, when they know they're under no pressure to be done immediately, they waste time daydreaming. The early starters say, when the pressure is on, they make more mistakes, can't think, and their work quality goes down.

I once consulted at a school where teachers asked me to work directly with a group of students they deemed most at risk academically, and a preponderance of the students gathered at the late-for-class end of the spectrum. As the discussion went on, two boys who had started at the done-by-midterm end quietly edged along the back of the line until they stood at the opposite end. They told the group, "We thought this was going to be another lecture on being responsible. But this is spot on. We need to learn when the last minute realistically starts!"

Research shows that students who truly do their best work under pressure make up a high percentage of students who drop out of school or otherwise fail to thrive (Blair & Sutherland, 2018). Pressure-prompted

---

Pressure-Prompted Accommodation Strategies
(From quickest to deepest)

✓ Reframing, page 90

✓ Backward Planning, page 91

✓ Pressure-Prompted Project Planning, page 92

students can align with each of the four cognitive processing types, but many self-identify as experience-and-movement or question-and-connection types. A philosophy of *start early, work steadily* doesn't work for them. The differentiation strategies in this chapter do.

Look at figure 6.1. Can you see how both planning and reacting in the moment are valuable approaches to life? Can you picture how either one, if overused, can lead to problems? These approaches are actually interdependent. Useful, enduring, successful plans usually include plans for potentially changing direction!

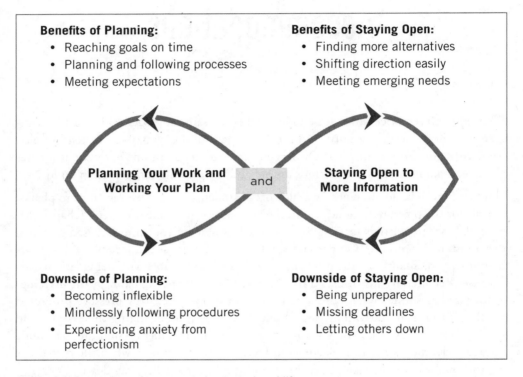

Figure 6.1: *Comparison of two approaches to work and life.*

Note that education in many regions is very much oriented to the left side of figure 6.1. Students who miss deadlines are considered immature, irresponsible, lazy, or all three. We forget that students who meet deadlines may rush through their work, lose sleep because of worries over deadlines, or fail to explore various points of view or approaches to problems. Students who prefer to stay open are quick to develop flexible thinking. When teachers overemphasize avoiding procrastination, they miss the gifts of openness and settle for the downside of sticking to plans.

But what does this have to do with differentiated instruction? Almost all the advice on study skills, strategies for preventing procrastination, and tips for avoiding Herculean last-minute efforts comes from experts who take the plan-your-work-and-work-your-plan approach. Myers and colleagues (2018), who popularized Jung's (1921/1923) personality type framework, describe those on the left of figure 6.1 as having a preference for *judging*—not being judgmental but rather loving to come to closure or judgments. They describe those who prefer staying more open as having a preference for *perceiving*—not being more perceptive, but rather staying open to more information and perceptions before acting (Myers et al., 2018). Of all the type tendencies, this pair causes the most conflict in schools, homes, and businesses (Murphy, 2013; Vîrgă et al., 2014). For doable differentiation, what really matters is the following.

- The strategies that work naturally for judging types to stay on task do not work for perceiving types.
- If perceiving types are forced to use judging strategies, the quality of their work often decreases.

So, how do teachers accommodate these pressure-prompted students in the schedule-bound world of school? They do so by reframing in their minds who their students are and what their students need. The following sections provide strategies you can use to accommodate the work style of your pressure-prompted students. You will also learn about two big essentials for success with pressure-prompted students and how to counter arguments against differentiation for these students. If you prefer to start with the research that supports the strategies, you can first check out the research base on page 99.

DOING DIFFERENTIATION

Consider the visible behavior of the following two students. How might you reframe their behavior in a positive way? In other words, what strengths might their work habits demonstrate? If you aren't sure now, revisit this question after you finish reading this chapter.

- **Elise:** Elise doesn't seem to use class time wisely. When she receives work time for writing assignments, she tends to doodle, chat with friends, and stare out the window. When teachers announce that work time is drawing to a close, she always seems startled but often buckles down to the task at hand. Much of her work is of good quality, but her teacher can't help but think Elise would do better if she used the entirety of the time for writing rather than daydreaming.

- **Kandhi:** Kandhi's father drove him to school this morning because he'd overslept after staying up past midnight to finish a project he had restarted multiple times. As Kandhi hands over a pass from the school office, his teacher tells him, "If you had stuck with the project you started, instead of changing your mind and changing your mind and changing your mind, you'd end up doing far less work, and you wouldn't be up late the night before it's due. You need to learn to focus before you get to college."

The Pressure-Prompted Accommodation Strategies

This section presents three strategies for helping pressure-prompted students experience success in the planful world in which they live: (1) Reframing, (2) Backward Planning, and (3) Pressure-Prompted Project Planning. Each of these strategies is designed to help pressure-prompted students use their strengths while helping them rethink when they need to start and what a project will encompass.

Reframing

Differentiation to meet the needs of the pressure-prompted requires teachers to reframe how they view students' behaviors to interpret them through an equity mindset rather than a deficit mindset. Look back at figure 6.1 (page 88). Most Western cultures value the left-hand side so strongly that they seldom see the value in those who operate best on the right. Yet entire cultures (India, the Anishinaabe nation, and others; Kise, 2017) and professions (emergency medicine and early childhood educators, to name just two) thrive through the strengths of the right side. Reframing changes deficit thinking around pressure-prompted students to language that honors their strengths, helping teachers recognize the value in their approach as well as varied cultural values. Scan through the following *If you're thinking* statements. Do you often find yourself having similar thoughts about your pressure-prompted students? Reflect on the reframing suggestions aligned with each statement, remembering the reality that perceivers do their best work under pressure.

- If you're thinking, "This student procrastinates" or "This student can't make up his or her mind about topics or projects or plans," reframe it as, "Some students love to generate and play with ideas."

  The opportunity to embrace possibilities attracts pressure-prompted students, who find it painful to let go of any avenues that still have merit. Starting an assignment too soon (or choosing anything too soon, from party costumes to colleges) often means they end up starting over later when they identify a topic they find more intriguing. Or, they suffer from buyer's remorse if they choose before they're ready, wishing they could travel the road not taken.

  To simplify choices for students, you might say, "If you're still stuck in five minutes [or tomorrow], we can do rock paper scissors to decide among your favorites." For bigger choices, such as project-based learning, see Backward Planning (page 91).

- If you're thinking, "This student doesn't plan ahead," reframe it as, "Some students have a valuable talent for scanning the current environment and noting what can be done."

  Once plans are set, pressure-prompted students worry they might miss something that no one is looking for. They do their best when plans include some flexibility, such as, "You can choose your water-quality experiments before we head outside. Or, you can bring the supplies for your top two choices and make up your mind once we get to the pond."

- If you're thinking, "This student has no focus," reframe it as, "Some students are attuned to the moment."

Remember that school schedules often interrupt students. They might be intensely interested in finishing a task or observing a spider or testing whether they can improve the angle of the ailerons on the paper airplanes you just had them make, and all of a sudden, a bell or the schedule randomly moves them on. (Even though the bell isn't random, it *feels* random to them.) If the next thing isn't as interesting to them, it's no wonder that their attention picks up the habit of wandering. Providing transition warnings, such as a five-minute reminder about the time remaining, can be very helpful to these students.

- If you're thinking, "This student doesn't finish anything," reframe it as, "Some students are distracted by their own creativity."

Students can lose interest if their project fails to meet the potential their imagination envisioned. Check in with these students before they start. Can you help them gauge whether their idea is realistic for the time they have? Alternatively, sometimes these students are further along than you think, but all the learning they must demonstrate remains in their heads. Graphic Organizers (page 162), particularly Freeform Organizers (page 165) might help them make their progress more visible.

- If you're thinking, "This student is sloppy and irresponsible," reframe it as, "Some students are caught up in the world of ideas, so sometimes, the details of reality, such as turning in homework or picking up after themselves, are just about invisible to them."

Have these students picture what will happen during the day in order to remember what they need to put in their backpacks. Set clear expectations for classroom responsibilities. Post pictures if necessary!

The goal of reframing is to move from thinking of pressure-prompted students as problems to solve and to start providing the differentiation strategies they need for time management in order to do their best work. These strategies lead to success and to more maturity through mastering strategies they can use for a lifetime, the *S* and *M* in STEAM[2].

Backward Planning

Almost all work-completion strategies assume that people should start early and finish quality work as soon as they can. Your pressure-prompted students instead need to learn to accurately answer, "How late can I start and still do quality work?" This is something many educators refer to as *backward planning*, and it's an increasingly common approach throughout the educational world (McTighe & Curtis, 2019). Yet, it has untapped potential as a student motivator.

To help students plan backward, your part of the conversation might go like this: "You're saying that you can start this paper Sunday night and turn it in on Monday. But don't you need to access information at the library, which is closed Sunday? Do you have a game Saturday? And don't forget the requirement to conference with a peer partner regarding your outline. With all of that in mind, Sunday will be too late, right? When do you think you need to start?" Note, as I explain in the next section, that these conversations also reveal steps students need to take sooner if they are to happen at all, like getting to the library.

You can turn this into a bit of a game for using class time well. Ask students to estimate how long they think it will take them to complete a task. Provide your estimate. Then, students can do the work and see how accurate they were. Should they have started earlier in class?

Pressure-Prompted Project Planning

The big, deep, essential application of accommodating the pressure-prompted is helping them learn how to finish multiweek projects. Using the three steps in this section— (1) shift students' mindset, (2) plan for completion, and (3) issue an alternative assignment— I've seen schools with failure rates on multiweek projects as high as 30 percent reduce the failure rate to zero (Kise, 2017). Assignments such as History Day projects, science projects, and other independent learning projects all come together for pressure-prompted students using this approach. This four-step approach takes teaming and persevering on the teachers' part, but here's how teachers and I have collaborated to reap such results.

Shift Students' Mindset

"You mean we're not broken?"

That was the reaction of a group of students at risk as they reconsidered their struggles through the lens of preferring perceiving and being pressure prompted. Students have to know that there isn't anything wrong with the way their brains operate. They just need to understand their brains and adjust their processes to align with their strengths. Here are three key mindset shifts teachers should present to students (and remember for themselves).

1. **Set high expectations:** High expectations can be tough with students who have stopped trying, but that behavior often covers up a fear of not being up to a task. When teachers convey high expectations to these students, that fear can change. Walk around and use encouraging pressure until every student has a pencil and paper and is writing. Usually, within a few class periods, students understand that they are expected to do the work. At the secondary level, setting high expectations works best when those expectations exist in every classroom.

2. **Do it right or do it twice:** The first time we announced that students who didn't meet the success criteria on an assignment had to redo it, cries of "That's bogus!" rang out. (Specifically, students needed to rework any

grade lower than a B-.) In this context, being unrelenting and repeating, "I have high expectations for you, and you should have them for yourselves" eventually ends complaints, and students redo their work. When you see students doing sloppy work, remind them of the success criteria while ensuring there are no roadblocks to success that require more direct support.

3. **Make them do something rather than allowing them to do nothing:** Big assignments almost always have some element of choice. For major assignments, let students know from the start that they will be completing an alternative teacher-chosen assignment should they not finish their original projects (see Issue an Alternative Assignment, page 95). To avoid that alternative assignment, students ask for lunchtime passes, leave messages on their phones as reminders of what they need to do, and work feverishly during class—anything to avoid the fallback assignment.

Plan for Completion

Completing a project requires understanding the steps involved, the amount of time each step will take, the time available, and the project requirements. This is not a natural ability for everyone. For major assignments, have students try the following: (1) identify project steps, (2) fill out a calendar, (3) set daily goals, and (4) reflect on progress. Let's review each step.

Identify Project Steps

The purpose of this step is to help students identify key intermediate milestones, especially those that are time-sensitive, such as getting feedback or accessing resources. Teaching students to complete step sheets to organize key project steps may take time, yet you'll quickly understand why so many students fail to finish what they start—they don't know how to get from start to finish! Many pressure-prompted students plan for two steps: (1) start project and (2) finish project. Coach them to think of the intervening steps rather than providing the steps for them. Such a conversation might go like this.

Teacher: You've chosen to create a board game to show what you know about French restaurant vocabulary. What's the goal of your game?

Student: To win.

Teacher: Well, think about board games and how you win them—reach the last square first? Collect the right game pieces?

Student: Um, collect the right game pieces.

Teacher: Do you need rules before you design the board?

Student: Oh, yeah . . .

Then, help them identify the *many* steps involved in the actions they identify. In this case, adopting board game rules involves choosing a format, writing out the rules, checking them for errors, drawing out what the game will look like, using the vocabulary to generate moves or questions that demonstrate a grasp of the vocabulary, and so on.

If all students are doing the same project, you might generate the completion steps as a class. Think of your efforts as helping the students build little synapses in that under-developed prefrontal cortex of their young brains (Fuller & Fuller, 2021).

Two things happen during the step-sheet creation process. First, on assignments where there are choices, students can evaluate whether their choice is realistic, given the time they have. Using a step sheet, like the one in figure 6.2, makes the scope of the project visible. Is it too complicated? Can they get the materials? Can they find enough information? For example, students might realize, just a week before a deadline, they won't have time to gather and organize information, develop a persuasive argument, and turn it into the high-quality hip-hip performance they had in mind. Second, the step sheet helps students plan out their real deadlines. For example, knowing that the papier-mâché features on their game board will need to dry for a day before they can paint them changes the deadline for starting to construct the game board.

Step	Action
1	Choose a topic.
2	Write out key information my speech needs to include.
3	Have someone review whether my information is complete.
4	List, then gather props I will need.
5	Practice my speech with a partner.
6	SHOWTIME!

Figure 6.2: *A sample step sheet for a demonstration speech.*

The step sheet in figure 6.2 is quite simple, but you or students can modify the design however you need. You might, for example, have students include key submission deadlines, such as for turning in rough drafts. Consider giving points for the step sheet and calendar (explained in the next section) with students self-assessing their planning efforts.

Fill Out a Calendar

The second part of planning is having students fill in a calendar that shows when they will complete each step. Have them work *backward* from the deadline (see Backward Planning, page 91). By when do they need to complete each step to make the final deadline?

To help facilitate this step, provide students with a blank calendar, including weekend days. As a class, fill in the mini-deadlines (see Keep Mini-Deadlines Ungraded, page 97) and final deadlines. Next, have students fill in other events in their personal lives: a school dance, babysitting gigs, soccer games, family events, and so on. Finally, have them fit their own project steps from the last section into their calendars, starting with the last step.

We asked students to take their calendars home and have a parent or guardian sign them. The adults told us, "The calendars help us know how far our child is truly behind!"

More importantly, students have a visual representation of whether they still have time to complete the project they have chosen to do.

Set Daily Goals

If you are providing in-class work time, have students use their step sheets to jot down goals for class time or homework. What are they going to accomplish *today*? We had students place these at the corner of their desks so we could see what they had chosen to focus on. Writing daily goals gives students a concrete reminder of what using their time wisely will look like.

Reflect on Progress

Periodically, based on the length of the calendar and the number of steps involved, ask students to reflect on their progress, rating on a scale of one to five stars how confident they are that they will make the final deadline. Then, have them journal on how well they're using their time, how they will adjust their work habits, and, in some cases, whether they need to switch projects if they chose something too complicated.

The team I worked with saw definite improvements in work behavior after implementing these reflection exercises. Students wasted less in-class time, identified how they needed help, and often showed us when they'd completed a step. The students who chose to change projects were the ones who had struggled to complete projects in the past. Here are two sample journal entries.

1. "I used the first half of my time wisely, and I wasn't going to start over after that. But then it was like, 'Oh, I'm almost done, and I still have a long time,' and I started watching TV. If I had used the time I spent watching TV to write my game directions, I would have finished on time."

2. "I did get to do the project I wanted, but it took a little more effort than I thought it would. I think I managed my time OK, but I could have done it better. I got it turned in at the last second, but we had to come in for lunch and type two pages the day it was due."

Obviously, not all students need this level of scaffolding. Making planning part of their grade often eases complaints. If students still complained, we asked them to consider whether other students in the class might benefit from the backward-planning strategies.

Issue an Alternative Assignment

If students have a history of not succeeding, even the planning structure may not keep them on track the first time they try to plan out a project. With a mindset of "make them do something rather than let them do nothing," structure an alternative assignment for them to complete. Let them know what the alternative will be as they're making their choice of projects. One teacher I worked with created a station-based assessment for students who failed to finish a lengthy report. She spread primary sources around the windowsills and bookshelves in the classroom, with a short-answer question to complete at each station. The students ended up completing a similar amount of research and writing as they would have done in completing their original reports.

There are two keys to making alternative assignments work.

1. **The alternative assignment needs to simulate as closely as possible the initial assignment:** For example, if students failed to write a report, then the alternative assignment might require taking notes from text excerpts, writing an opening paragraph based on those notes, completing bibliography entries for given resources, answering questions about where certain kinds of information might be found, and so on. Occasionally, teachers I've worked with used commercially available worksheets on science units or novels as the alternative assignments where we were assessing content knowledge. In one case, students who failed to turn in their work had to stay after school and complete a standardized science project, chosen by the teacher.

2. **Focus on student success but with a bit of regret:** Because administering the alternative assignment often requires class time, consider assigning the rest of the class a curriculum-based enrichment activity. Teachers often use figure 1.5 (page 28) to create a task menu to increase student interest and motivation. While students working on the alternative assignment may feel left out, focus their reactions to completing the alternative assignment on a sense of accomplishment, not on what they missed nor on the scaffolding they received.

Again, the goal is to help students experience academic success. Teaching them to plan *how* to complete a project and meet their goals helps them develop the skills they need to be responsible students in the future.

VIRTUAL CLASSROOMS

Ensuring that students complete an alternative assignment can be a bit more difficult in the virtual environment than when students are in the same physical space with you. Creating engagement, the *E* in the STEAM[2] framework, is perhaps most crucial to making this work. Consider grounding the alternative assignment in a curiosity creator such as Visual Entry Points (page 127). Think about whether the success criteria can be met if students work in pairs rather than in isolation. After they have planned their project, consider using a planned movement strategy (chapter 13) to enhance engagement. What if they, as did one of my graduate students, complete a concept map on their driveway with sidewalk chalk while a guardian or sibling films their explanation for submission? Enhancing engagement puts the emphasis on success in learning, helping to ensure these students don't feel they're being punished.

Two Big Success Essentials

Ensuring that pressure-prompted students learn how to use their strengths to meet expectations means getting the right balance of teacher responsibility for providing skills and scaffolding with students learning to take responsibility as they mature—the *M* in STEAM[2]. What follows are lessons learned and summaries of how to make these strategies work from teachers who have successfully used them.

Teach—and Embrace—the Both-Ands

Many cultures, such as many Native American nations, as well as multiple countries south of the equator, work on the premise that it's better to do what's right when the time comes than to spend tons of time planning (Kise, 2017). Those of us from scheduled, time-bound cultures have a hard time adjusting to this assumption, but we also know the merits of, for example, attending to a student's immediate needs or slowing down a lesson to ensure everyone grasps a foundational concept. In life and in learning, it's often necessary to hold two seemingly contrary ideas or concepts in your mind at the same time; that is, it's necessary to embrace both-and thinking.

There are a number of *interdependencies* (or *polarities*) at work in your classroom. These are paired ideas or concepts that exist on opposite ends of a spectrum or cycle but depend on each other (Kise, 2019). Differentiation involves several polarities, such as teaching to mastery *and* covering the curriculum, or meeting the needs of each student *and* meeting the needs of the class as a group. Teachers cannot solve these interdependencies once and for all. Rather, embracing the upside and downside of each, as featured in figure 6.1 (page 88), allows teachers to plan to get as much of the upside of both as possible.

In your classroom, talk about keeping the following interdependencies in balance.

- Finishing your work *and* finishing work that you are proud of
- Meeting deadlines *and* exploring options
- Being responsible *and* being flexible
- Doing high-quality work *and* doing good-enough work that avoids the perfectionist trap

Unleashing the Positive Power of Differences: Polarity Thinking in Our Schools (Kise, 2014) provides additional learning and tools for using these interdependencies in schools.

Keep Mini-Deadlines Ungraded

Pressure-prompted students are especially vulnerable to failure on big projects if there are no intermediate progress check-ins. Mini-deadlines, similar to what you read about in Set Daily Goals (page 95), can fill this void, but teachers often make the mistake of grading work done for mini-deadlines. Not everything you assign as a teacher has to be graded. Sometimes, a mini-deadline marks when students move to the next stage of a project after showing they've finished a prior stage. For example, once students turn in a drawing of their initial idea for a Rube Goldberg machine (an overly complex device that performs a simple task like ringing a doorbell), they can step into the science lab and start assembling. You may require the drawing by a mini-deadline and yet not grade it. Or, have them turn in a learning map with at least three essential questions before beginning to read a biography they've chosen. (See the Essential Question Priming approach, page 217.) Possibilities that provide students with ungraded mini-deadlines are endless.

You can even use ungraded mini-deadlines during class time. Let's say students are exploring a topic before beginning to produce their product. When you feel the moment has come, announce, "Class, based on my experience, if you want to finish your work by the end of class, you need to stop exploring now and move on to production."

Common Concerns About Pressure-Prompted Accommodations

The following statements represent common concerns I hear from educators as they consider using pressure-prompted accommodation strategies. Beside each statement, you'll find text on how you might address any resistance you encounter (by yourself or with colleagues) because of such concerns.

- **"Isn't completing work before play a lifelong skill?"** The proverb to stop and smell the roses is as important to students' health and creativity as it is to adults. Put another way, your students are human beings, not human doings. Like all people of any age, they need to play outside when the sun is shining, capitalize on spending time with those they love, and refresh their souls through life-giving practices. Ponder what other areas of life require the flexibility of being in the moment.

  Further, remember that always working before playing can result in negative habits, stress, anxiety, and struggles with unproductive perfectionism. Some judging types simply cannot sleep until their work is done. Some students don't need help meeting deadlines but instead need help understanding when it's OK, for example, to pause, get a good night's sleep, and get help with an assignment the next day.

- **"But the real world won't adjust for students."** This is why you must teach skills rather than take responsibility for student work. One of my colleagues, New Zealander Sue Blair, puts it this way: "Don't power over. Scaffold up" (personal communication, April 6, 2020).

  Even though we adults technically hold the power, we shouldn't use it to gain pressure-prompted students' compliance; instead, we can shift our thinking about the pressure-prompted from "Here's how you're going to meet this deadline" to "What do you need, and how can I help you?" Nagging or managing their time *for* them often makes the problem worse (perhaps not in the short run, but think of the students who struggle once they get to university because they weren't responsible for completing schoolwork; adults ensured that they complied with schedules). The strategies in this chapter scaffold up for success and maturity, part of STEAM[2].

Consider sharing the following strategies with parents and guardians to help them develop a better balance between adult responsibility and child responsibility as well.

‣ If a parent or guardian has to drive a forgotten item to school, the child gets an extra chore (mine had to cook dinner—macaroni and cheese from a box didn't count).

‣ If a deadline means a child is up too late, the parent or guardian sets the schedule for the next deadline in partnership with the child, helping them improve their time estimates.

‣ If a child struggles to estimate how long an assignment will take, the parent or guardian uses a timer and turns it into a game. The adult asks, "How long do you think it will take to do a quality job on this?" The adult also gives an estimate but sets the timer to the child's estimate to see who was closest. Make sure the child understands that this is about time *and* quality, so they don't cut corners. This helps the child become more aware of the time requirements of various efforts.

All of these ideas are designed to help pressure-prompted students develop needed skills.

• **"But I'm not that great at breaking out the steps in projects."** If you tend to plunge into big tasks and let the process emerge, great! You've figured out how to make it work for you, or else you wouldn't have the degrees and certifications that allow you to teach. However, in the interest of equity, understanding how to build high-level skills in students is essential, especially for those who respond best to pressure-prompted environments. Try out backward planning for yourself. Plan out the steps for creating a unit, completing a continuing education assignment, engaging in a volunteer effort, or navigating other areas where you tend to wing it. You'll have real experiences to relate to students who operate as you do. And, before trying out the planning with students, think through project steps, and ask a colleague whether you've identified what students will find helpful.

Why Pressure-Prompted Accommodations Work

Planning and prediction—students' determining how they will perform and planning what they need to do to do it well—has an effect size of 0.75 and ranks in the top 25 most effective influences on student learning (Corwin Visible Learning+, n.d.a). While full-blown implementation of this differentiation strategy is complex, the payoff is huge in both immediate results and the development of skills students will need for the rest of their lives.

Let's place this strategy in the context of neuroscience. Research shows that the very last part of the brain to fully develop is the prefrontal cortex, which manages executive functions like planning, setting priorities, organizing thoughts, suppressing impulses, and so on (Arain et al., 2013; Davidow et al., 2019). Referring to the prefrontal cortex, Wallis & Dell (2004) further assert that "the final part of the brain to grow up is the part capable of deciding, I'll finish my homework and take out the garbage, and then I'll [text] my friends about seeing a movie." This research suggests that having students practice those skills helps the brain develop.

While many students complete work without any prodding, the judging and perceiving functions described at the beginning of the chapter provide a potential explanation for why others struggle that doesn't assume such behavior is abnormal, immature, or even that it might require clinical evaluation. Instead, we can celebrate students who love options while helping them succeed.

Reflection Activity

Consider the following actions and questions as you reflect on this chapter's content.

1. As you read through the *If you're thinking* statements (page 90), did specific students you've taught come to mind? Be honest. How might you reframe those pressure-prompted students now?

2. About 70 percent of teachers have a natural tendency for the plan-your-work-and-work-your-plan approach to work and life (McPeek et al., 2013). Reflect on your own learning experiences.

   ‣ Do you naturally start projects early, or do you benefit from last-minute pressure?

   ‣ If you try to start early, what happens? Do you ever rush through? Do you find that you change your mind, so starting early ends up wasting time?

   ‣ How well do you estimate how long things will take? Is this a natural skill for you, or have you improved in estimation along the way?

   ‣ How do your experiences affect how you view your students and the scaffolding you tend to offer?

   Compare your answers with those of other educators. Do any of your or other educators' policies place pressure-prompted students at an unintended disadvantage? Do any policies accidentally create too much stress in students who tend toward perfectionism?

3. Consider how deadlines for the adults in your building are handled. What information in this chapter might lead to better outcomes?

CHAPTER 7

Student-Centered Discussions

Lucy West is a leader in mathematics coaching and a colleague. In 2012, as we prepared for a conference presentation, she shared with me an amazing video of student discourse. In the video, the following sequence plays out.

As a student finishes sharing her solution to an algebra problem, the teacher thanks her and asks, "Who came up with a different solution?"

Another student places his solution under the document camera, turns to the teacher, and says, "Now that I've heard her explanation, I know mine is wrong, but I can't find my mistake."

The teacher says, "Who can help him out?" What follows is a respectful discussion. Students listen to and build on each other's ideas, ask for justification, and finally agree on how their classmate's mistake arose.

As the students talk, the teacher is almost silent. She adds to the discussion by pointing to the student's work to ensure all the students clearly know which part they are discussing. She also acknowledges raised hands to lend a bit of order to responses, and she occasionally asks questions such as, "Who can rephrase what she just said?" "[Student name], how does that compare to your explanation?" and "Who can summarize what we've discovered so far?"

Teacher-facilitated discussions among students, such as the example detailed here, ensure students are listening to each other, building on ideas, using evidence, reasoning, and justifying, thereby engaging every student in higher-level thinking with complex content. Such discussions are student centered in that students take the major role in facilitating a good discussion, with the teacher adding, prompting, or redirecting toward a new topic or emphasizing an important conclusion as needed. These discussions ready students to produce more robust demonstrations of learning and mastery. Discourse is a top equity and inclusion strategy that provides ample

Student-Centered Discussion Strategies
(From quickest to deepest)

- ✓ Practice Prompts, page 103
- ✓ Mistake Modeling, page 105
- ✓ Anonymous Examples, page 107
- ✓ Volleyball Contest, page 108
- ✓ Discussion Protocols, page 108
- ✓ Group Work That Works, page 110

opportunity for differentiation. Consider how, when well-managed, these discussions meet the needs of each of the four cognitive processing styles.

- Structure-and-certainty students (let me know what to do) get to feel confident because of the structures and protocols they get to practice using.

- Experience-and-movement students (let me do something) get to verbally engage while testing out their ideas and receive immediate clarifications.

- Vision-and-interpretation students (let me follow my own lead) enjoy voicing different ideas and connections, especially when using protocols that include wait time (chapter 4, page 63).

- Question-and-connection students (let me lead as I learn) enjoy the collaborative building of knowledge and debate.

Think on the example of student-centered discussion that led off this chapter. Can you see the elements of student-centered discussion the teacher has put into place? These elements include:

- An atmosphere of safety and trust where mistakes are accepted as opportunities for learning

- A volleyball pattern of discussion, where the teacher "serves up" the topic and norms, and students then "volley" as they listen to, build on, and respond to each other's ideas

- An emphasis on explanation, reasoning, and justification

- The use of visuals to foster shared understanding and clarify the points being made

Note that every student in this urban classroom mastered the mathematical standards for that grade level that year, even though many were behind at the start of the year. Also, note that it took six weeks before students mastered the art of purposeful academic discourse. Ingrained habits had to be undone. The teacher had to master several ideas, including the following.

- Avoiding only seeking right answers and instead emphasizing reasoning and problem solving

- Using prompts that keep thinking in the hands of the students

- Sometimes assigning fewer problems and instead exploring a few problems in depth

- Ensuring her questions don't prompt a ping-pong teacher-student pattern of discourse but instead a teacher-student-student-student (and so on) pattern

Writing on the importance of equity, education authors Douglas Fisher, Nancy Frey, and John Almarode (2019) assert that adopting a strategy such as student-centered discussions has to be accompanied by essential and equitable activities and practices, such as those in this chapter. Using these strategies ensures these discussions fulfill their promise for creating successful, thriving, engaged, agile, and maturing students (STEAM[2]).

In this chapter, you'll also find four big essentials for success when using these strategies and answers to common concerns teachers have about using them. To review the research supporting these strategies and see how to turn your classroom into a student-centered discussion hub, see Why Student-Centered Discussions Work (page 115). Note that many of the wait time strategies in chapter 4 (page 63) will help all students prepare for discussions.

DOING DIFFERENTIATION

Chances are, you've seen colleagues struggle to listen to each other, build on each other's ideas, respectfully disagree, provide sound justification for their own positions, and elaborate on their thoughts to improve clarity. Remembering this can be helpful when watching students struggle to develop these essential skills.

If you introduce students to the discussion skills separate from class content, students usually develop the skills faster (Lespiau & Tricot, 2019). For example, if you're introducing a specific discussion tool, such as the sentence starters explained in the Practice Prompts section (this page), focus the discussion on materials the students are familiar with. If your lesson requires that you focus on new content, use a discussion strategy students have already practiced.

All the strategies in this chapter are designed to introduce trust-building and skill-building techniques that you can then quickly transfer over to content-rich lessons once students understand the basic norms and benefits.

The Student-Centered Discussion Strategies

This section presents six strategies for facilitating student-centered discussions, helping teachers act as facilitators while students take charge of learning from and with each other: (1) Practice Prompts, (2) Mistake Modeling, (3) Anonymous Examples, (4) Volleyball Contest, (5) Discussion Protocols, and (6) Group Work That Works. Each of these strategies is designed to build a safe atmosphere for discourse and introduce key tools you and your students will be using.

Practice Prompts

Prompts, as most teachers are familiar, are sentence- or thought-starters that signal students as to what they might add to a discussion. The sentence starters in figure 7.1 (page 104) and figure 7.2 (page 104) serve two key purposes: (1) they provide suggestions to students as to the contributions they might make to the discussion, and (2) they promote respectful phrasing of comments and questions, regardless of whether or not students agree with what others have said. Both are crucial to creating a safe space.

As you begin a discussion, display the prompts on a slide or poster, or provide students with cards that have the prompts printed on them. For primary students and English

Figure 7.1: Sample sentence-starters poster.
Visit **go.SolutionTree.com/instruction** for a free reproducible version of this figure.

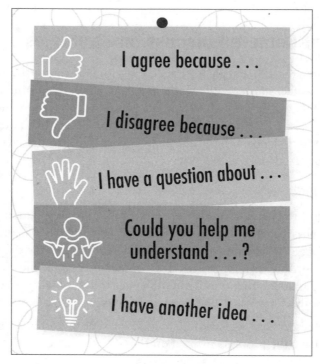

Figure 7.2: Sample-prompts poster for primary students and English learners.
Visit **go.SolutionTree.com/instruction** for a free reproducible version of this figure.

learners, consider starting with a shorter list of prompts and adding emojis, as shown in figure 7.2. Explain the prompts' purpose to students: "Perhaps you sometimes wonder what you might add to a discussion. These prompts can help you share the valuable thoughts you have. If we all use them well, everyone will feel respected."

The following are sample activities that allow students to practice using prompts for a discussion about content that is familiar or easily accessed through prior knowledge.

- **Grades K–2:** Set out three books you and your class have recently used as read-alouds. Inform the class that you all will be practicing sharing ideas and listening to each other. Explain the prompts, and give examples of how you might use them to respond to someone saying, "_____ is my favorite of the books we read." Emphasize showing respect and taking turns. Ask, "Who would like to share which of these books was their favorite and why?" You may need to prompt students to expand their reasoning.

- **Grades 3–12:** Select a picture book that creates a story around situations or objects with which students are familiar, such as *The Day the Crayons Quit* by Drew Daywalt (2013). Why picture books at all grade levels? With picture books, you can quickly convey the main ideas you will be discussing and get to the real point of the lesson—learning to use the prompts (Massey, 2015). Read aloud enough of the story for students to grasp the gist of the author's intent. For *The Day the Crayons Quit*, you might read the following:

  > Hey Duncan,
  >
  > It's me, Red Crayon. We need to talk. You make me work harder than any of your other crayons. All year long I wear myself out coloring fire engines, apples, strawberries and everything else that's red. I even work on *holidays*! I have to color all the Santas at Christmas and all the hearts on Valentine's Day! I need a rest!
  >
  > Your overworked friend,
  >
  > Red Crayon (Daywalt, 2013)

  Then, provide a discussion prompt. For this book, the prompt might be, "Choose another crayon color. What might that crayon say to Duncan? What might it be happy about? What other emotions might it express? Let's see how many ideas we can come up with for various colors."

Note that practice prompts provide some structure for what might otherwise seem like freewheeling discussions to structure-and-certainty students while still leaving plenty of freedom for question-and-connection students who love discussions.

Mistake Modeling

Students grow comfortable with sharing mistakes when they know classmates won't shame or tease them (Sullivan et al., 2020). Start off a discussion by sharing a mistake of your own or mistakes from other sources. At all grade levels, you can simply display a distractor answer for a complex problem. *Distractors* are answers that result from a common misstep, such as doing addition before multiplication in the equation $2 + 3 \times 2 = x$, not understanding the difference between the odds of something happening and the chances of something happening, or not listening closely to a question that includes words such as *before*, *after*, *including*, and so on.

With this strategy, students become comfortable with not being sure their answer is correct before sharing. You can also capitalize on the teachable moments involved in having students work backward from an answer to understand where the thinking went wrong, and it works across content areas, such as looking at mathematics problems or science experiments for which measurements don't make sense or a historical conclusion that doesn't seem to fit all the facts.

Here are some other suggestions.

- **Grades K–3:** Access www.setgame.com/set/puzzle, and select the option to play an online version of SET, a card game that engages players in finding patterns. Explain that in a set for this game, all cards have to be the same on an element (color, shading, shape), or they all have to be different on an element. Select two cards that might be part of a set, point to another card that doesn't work, and say, "I think this will work. Am I right? Why or why not? Who agrees? Does anyone disagree? Why?" Choose one more set, making one more mistake. Then let volunteers choose a potential set, asking their classmates, "Am I right? Why or why not?" The free version has one puzzle a day, providing practice for finding patterns, unpacking mistakes, and for practicing the prompts.

  Or, put up a simple riddle such as the following, and say, "I thought the answer was five, but I was wrong. Who can help me understand what I did wrong and what the answer is?" (It's six.)

  > I am between two and ten.
  > I am less than eight.
  > I am the number of sides on two triangles.
  > What number am I?

  For these puzzles, students might work with cards with the numbers 1–10 on them or use a laminated strip printed with those numbers.

- **Grades 4–12:** A good strategy for modeling mistakes is admitting you had no quick answer for a problem. For example, say, "This problem asks us to figure out how to make the biggest enclosure possible for my chickens if I have thirty-two feet of fencing. I know that the answer will form a square, but then someone asks, 'What if one side is a building, so the fencing is only needed for three sides? Is the answer still a square?' I don't have a quick answer. How can we figure that out?"

  Another quick idea is to share a flawed definition. For example, state, "Share why you agree or disagree with this definition: a triangle is a flat shape with three sides and three acute angles." An easy way to show this definition is flawed is to draw a triangle with a crooked line on one side. Or, you can state, "A polynomial is an expression consisting of variables and coefficients," and show $2x^{-3}$ to illustrate why this definition isn't complete.

If you don't teach mathematics, logic puzzles are still a handy way to generate discussions about mistakes. The Math Is Fun website (www.mathsisfun.com /puzzles) has puzzles of a wide variety of types and ranges of difficulty. I've seen ELA and foreign language teachers achieve success by asking students to find teacher-embedded grammatical mistakes. In physical education, as you referee a competition, let students know you will purposely make a few inaccurate calls. Challenge them to *politely* give the correct call based on the game's rules.

The fastest path to helping students share mistakes, uncertainties, and difficulties in understanding is to demonstrate the kinds of vulnerability illustrated in the preceding examples. This leads to assisting students to self-assess their own mistakes. For example, if you want students to reassess whether their first answer is the best answer, model taking time to think. This conveys that coming up with the fastest answer doesn't mean having the best or right answer. To support this modeling, try using one of these prompts.

- "Good question. Class, let's figure this out together."

- "I hadn't thought about that. Hmm, let's look at a diagram together while I think out loud."

- "I wonder if that's an exception to the rule we're discussing. Let me work with it during your individual work time, and I'll share my thinking at the end of class."

While this strategy specifically builds confidence for structure-and-certainty students who would rather not speak up until they know they have a right answer, everyone needs to understand that mistakes are normal and can be powerful sources of learning for ourselves and others.

Anonymous Examples

Having students assess the work of other, anonymous students is an excellent approach for first tries at high-level small-group or large-group discussions. Students usually enjoy assessing the work of other students, and they gain knowledge of high-quality work by doing so.

The easiest ways to acquire work samples are to save samples from a previous year or to partner with another teacher so that you each have samples from students who are not in your class. Rewrite them if you worry that any students may be identified. The assignment might be a short-answer response, the opening paragraph for an essay, a visual diagram comparing and contrasting two story characters or historical figures, or a mathematics problem. Make sure that reasoning, not right answers, is the point of the assignment. If students are working in small groups, roam the room, encouraging the students to use the discussion prompts (see Practice Prompts, page 103) to ensure they share ideas respectfully.

To set up discussion on the assignment, follow these steps.

1. Have all students first complete the assignment themselves. Otherwise, they may not understand the content well enough to assess the samples you will provide. As they work, answer their questions using the roaming strategies in chapter 9 (page 137).

2. Introduce the grading rubric, and ask students to assess their own work.

3. Provide the groups with a sample of another student's work, reproduced in a form big enough for all students to see it at once (you might project the image or use handouts).

4. Ask all students to use the rubric to independently assess the work.

5. Begin the discussion to agree on a rating. When first using this strategy, use an all-class discussion to model and guide this process. Once students understand how to come to an agreement on a rating, provide samples to small groups, have members assess the work independently, and then have each group discuss the sample and rubric, eventually coming to an agreement about the appropriate rating.

Note that this is a discussion protocol that honors all cognitive processes. There's a clear structure for the structure-and-certainty students, and both they and vision-and-interpretation students benefit from the chance to form their thoughts on the proper rating before the discussion begins. Experience-and-movement students simply enjoy the interaction and hands-on practice with rubrics for self-monitoring progress. Meanwhile, question-and-connection students enjoy engaging in persuasion and discussion.

Volleyball Contest

If students are used to giving either right or wrong answers to teachers' questions, using the analogy of a volleyball game, where a teacher "serves" the discussion topic and the students are to "volley" for as long as they can, responding to one another without having the metaphorical ball go back to the teacher, can be a fun way to change the norm. Ask an open question (for ideas, see chapter 9), and challenge your students to see how many volleys they can make, listening to each other and using the prompts, before you need to enter into the discussion again. You might keep score using the codes from the Spiderweb Discussions strategy (page 146) to improve discussion quality and participation. Remember, students with all cognitive processes benefit from student-centered discussions, and it is a key equity strategy because it improves discussion quality through greater student participation.

Discussion Protocols

The Discussion Protocols for Wait Time section of chapter 4 (page 63) covered how discussion protocols can provide students with wait time. With student-centered discussions, such protocols can also be key to ensuring equity. Zaretta Hammond (2020) points out that, while structured protocols may seem at odds with free-flowing discussions that welcome all students, without them, discourse often remains in the hands of those from the dominant culture. In U.S. classrooms, the dominant culture includes the students who are fluent in English and who are comfortable speaking up. Hammond (2020) recommends using structured protocols and allowing time for some informal small talk to pave the way for social and emotional safety in later academic discussions. Note how talking about favorite picture books or having fun with a picture book as illustrated with *The Day the Crayons Quit* (see Practice Prompts, page 103) can allow for safe small talk.

There are innumerable protocols to facilitate group discussion. Keeping in mind what you have learned in this chapter about high-level student discussions, search the internet or use your teaching resources to locate excellent instructions on the following protocol types.

- **Fishbowl discussions (Learning for Justice, n.d.b):** Using this protocol, students take turns sitting in several central chairs and actively discussing a topic, while other students sit in a surrounding circle and listen. Students rotate in and out of the central chairs so that everyone can participate, but only a few voices compete at any one moment. With everyone from kindergarten students to adult learners, teachers experience success with this strategy.

- **Last Word protocol (Averette, n.d.):** I introduced this protocol in chapter 4. A student reads a quote from a text. Other students then comment on it, following the regular norms for discussion. The student who chose the quote then gets to have the last word, explaining why he or she chose it. This protocol often leads to careful listening, building on ideas, and respectful commenting, as no one knows whether the first student likes or dislikes, or agrees or disagrees with, the quote.

- **Four As (Vilen & Berger, 2020):** This simple strategy prepares students for a discussion by focusing their thoughts as they read a text, watch a film, listen to a lecture, or otherwise acquire background knowledge. About this strategy and its benefits, educators Anne Vilen and Ron Berger (2020) write:

  > Students in EL Education schools often use the 4As protocol to prepare for a discussion on a controversial claim. They record one *assumption* the author makes, one thing they *agree* with, one thing they want to *argue* with, and one question they want to *ask*. Then students each begin the discussion by sharing one of their "A" statements. This gives every student a choice and a voice. (pp. 43–44)

- **Read and say something (Learning for Justice, n.d.a):** Use this protocol with an informational or narrative text for groups of four to six students. Designate who will go first in each group, perhaps alternating based on whose birthday is closest or who most recently ate an apple. That first person begins reading the text aloud until he or she reaches a spot where he or she would like to make a comment, a prediction, or a connection, or otherwise say something related to the text. Other students in the group then use the usual discussion prompts (see Practice Prompts) to discuss the first student's comment. Then, the next student begins reading, pausing to say something and engaging in discussion. Continue until students have finished the reading.

Note that the read-and-say-something protocol is safe for students with all the cognitive processes discussed in chapter 1 (page 15). Extraverted students know they'll have chances to talk, and introverted students know they'll get to talk about something of their own choosing and they won't be put on the spot. Sensing students relax because there is structure, and intuitive students know they can use their imaginations rather than only give right-answer responses. As you look for more ideas for changing up group discussions, consider using figure 1.1 (page 18) for reflection on whether the formats may favor some students or disadvantage others.

Group Work That Works

The difficulty with small-group discussions is that you can't monitor all of them at once. Entire books, such as the following, are dedicated to ensuring students work well together, using role assignments, and so on.

- *Designing Groupwork: Strategies for the Heterogeneous Classroom* (3rd edition) by Elizabeth G. Cohen and Rachel A. Lotan (2014)

- *Productive Group Work: How to Engage Students, Build Teamwork, and Promote Understanding* by Nancy Frey, Douglas Fisher, and Sandi Everlove (2009)

Nonetheless, helping students transfer the norms and practices they've learned about student-centered discussions in a large group to small-group work shines a slightly different light on small-group processes. The following key elements ensure productive small-group conversations.

- **Wait time:** Once you provide the discussion topic or task to the group, provide a minute or two of wait time to allow students to do a quick write (informally capturing ideas) to restate the problem, form a question they have about the assignment, or record a few thoughts or ideas on how to proceed. See chapter 4 (page 63).

- **Group notes:** Provide a way to capture student thinking that focuses every student's attention on the group's thoughts and processes. Chapter 11 (page 175) offers strategies for using big notes for group work. Alternatively, use manipulatives, card sorts, and other moveable organizers (see chapter 12, page 187). Have each group share one set of notes. Similarly, if students are to draw a diagram or capture their ideas in other ways, provide one whiteboard or tool for the group. The point is to avoid students' working on their own ideas on the side and instead have them share ideas, reason and justify out loud, summarize, and elaborate together as they collaboratively use these tools.

- **Discussion prompts:** Emphasize using Practice Prompts (page 103) for small groups as well as large groups.

- **Unanimous understanding:** Set the standard that even if the group chooses one person to explain the group's work, you might ask questions of any group member. Everyone is responsible for understanding and being able to explain the group's ideas or solutions.

No one likes working in ineffective groups, but students from among all the cognitive processes benefit from learning, reasoning, and creating with others in small groups. These elements add enough structure that both structure-and-certainty and vision-and-interpretation students have chances to be heard, yet there is plenty of interaction for the students who prefer work aligned to experience and movement, and question and connection. This frees teachers to monitor whether groups are on task and hold all students accountable for the learning targets.

Four Big Success Essentials

When teachers take the time to help students build SEL skills required for student-centered discussions, such as listening and respect and turn-taking, the equity and learning payoffs can be significant. What follows are lessons learned and summaries of how to make student-centered discussions work, from teachers who have successfully used them.

Use Teacher Moves

Teacher moves are the techniques you use to increase reasoning and justification, to redirect students, to encourage participation, and so on. They are key to student-centered discussions. If you struggle to know exactly what questions and strategies you might use to ensure students share ideas, listen to each other, justify their conclusions, and build on what has been said, you are not alone! The following are several tried-and-true teacher moves that foster equitable discourse, therefore differentiating by ensuring that everyone benefits. Choose a few, practice using them for a few days, and then come back for more. Start with the moves that fit best with your teaching style.

- **Revoice:** After a student speaks, repeat what he or she said such that the student must agree or disagree: "So you said . . . ?" This move helps you listen carefully to the student and keeps the student involved in justification or explanation. You might also revoice what the student said to demonstrate using better academic language and then check for understanding.

- **Restate:** Instead of revoicing something to a student, have another student restate what a peer said. Ask, "Who can restate what _____ said?" Or, call on someone to restate it. This keeps more students listening closely. Did they understand what a peer said? Do they have questions? If a student is unable to restate something, help him or her refocus. This reassures all students the class won't move on until everyone understands a concept. If you use the right language, you won't put students on the spot: "You aren't sure? That's fine—I'll come back to you after you've heard ideas from some of your classmates. Who has another way to say it?"

- **Check:** When a student restates what a peer said, ask the first student, "Is that what you said or meant?" This keeps the original speaker involved in the dialogue.

- **Require precision:** Every subject area uses a specific academic language, and it's important that students are precise when using it. Before the discussion, list terms students should use on the board and add to the list during the discussion. Be careful to avoid giving away themes, ideas, or solutions that could decrease student thinking.

- **Wait:** Pausing before students answer gives more students a chance to reflect. Pausing after a student answers lets the speaker rephrase or add to his or her answer if something occurs to the student, and it increases the chances for student-student interaction, rather than a student-teacher ping-pong pattern. See chapter 4 (page 63) for strategies to add wait time to discussions. For example, use the Ten Hands Up approach (page 66), customizing the number of raised student hands as you prefer. If only a few hands go up, or the same students are answering over and over, declare how many hands you want to see before you'll take an answer.

- **Use Think-Pair-Share:** This can jump-start or restart a stalled discussion. If you think students should be questioning what someone has said, or they aren't sure why they agree or disagree, have them turn to a partner or their table group to figure out what they should ask or say.

- **Embrace learning opportunities:** Ask the class to identify how a misunderstanding arose. Normalize mistakes as useful, and establish that students are responsible for politely identifying mistakes and for reasoning out how the misunderstanding arose.

- **Clarify drawings:** Help students learn to use visuals as effectively as possible to explain their reasoning. Add or ask students to add labels, shading, arrows, different colors, and so on.

- **Justify with sources:** Use this move when a student seems to be relying on a personal opinion or when the class seems divided on its conclusions or interpretations. Ask, "Who can support your idea with a quote? What page number?" or "Let's check notes you took in class. What support do you have for your reasoning?"

- **Require reasoning:** Ask students to explain answers. In this case, students don't have to source their answers, but they do have to show high-level thinking. They should not just say, "That's what we learned last year" or "I just know." Have students practice reasoning after discussions in journal entries, and emphasize precise definitions or references to texts and tools of the discipline, instead of opinions. As you question students, monitor your tone of voice to ensure it doesn't convey incorrectness, and avoid common habits like repeating incorrect responses as a question ("Twenty-two?").

- **Use prompts:** Use the same prompts that you ask students to use. Common prompts such as the following gently remind students of phrases they can use to enter the conversation.

  ‣ "Who agrees? Who disagrees? Why?"

  ‣ "Who can add to that?"

  ‣ "Who has a question?"

  ‣ "Who could help us understand that better?"

Facilitate All-Class Discussion First

Because listening, reasoning, justifying, and building on what has been said are all difficult for students (and for adults), start with all-class discussions so that you can prompt and guide high-level, respectful discussions. Once students demonstrate proficiency with the skills in all-class discussions, using the Anonymous Examples approach (page 107) is an excellent first small-group experience. See Group Work That Works (page 110) to determine whether tasks are groupworthy.

Rearrange Seating

Discussions flourish when students can see each other's faces. Traditional straight rows, facing the front of the room, discourage participation. Try arranging desks in a circle, horseshoe, or double horseshoe so students can see all or most of their classmates. If students generally sit at small tables or desk clusters, have them move or turn chairs so that as few classmates as possible see their backs. Another arrangement that works is creating two long rows of desks on each side of the room. While the desks need to be close together, creating aisles at the back of each row, as well as having a large center space, maintain a feeling of roominess.

Or, if you have a large enough classroom, have students pull chairs to a designated area or sit on the carpet in ways that allow them to see most of their classmates. If you're worried about the time it takes to move seating, try timing students on moving from "individual to group formation," challenging them to improve how fast they can do it.

Use Visuals

Although it's not always possible to use them, visual aids often make it much easier for teachers to help students understand ideas. For mathematics instruction, use document cameras, drawings, or diagrams on slides or whiteboards, or use large magnetized manipulatives so that you or the student who is talking can point to the shapes, numbers, or portions of a diagram he or she is explaining.

For other kinds of discussions, make use of the Thinking Maps strategy (page 160), spider maps, lists on the board, and other note-taking methods that will help students track what has been said. Chapter 11 (page 175) offers more ideas for using big notes with groups.

VIRTUAL CLASSROOMS

The essentials for good student-centered discussions hold true in virtual environments, like Zoom. You can use all the teacher moves (page 111) with virtual instruction. Also consider the following.

- Get creative with technology features such as the ability many tools provide to raise a virtual hand on the screen.

- Use fishbowl discussions (page 109) to model how breakout room discussions should function. To focus attention, have students outside the fishbowl turn off their cameras so that everyone can see the students who are participating. Have them record big ideas from the fishbowl using a note-taking strategy from chapter 10 (page 159) or chapter 11 (page 175).

- Use random breakout rooms for a Think-Pair-Share activity.

- Use both analog and digital visuals. I've had students in remote locations use shared digital whiteboards and documents but also position their computer cameras so they can share what they've recorded on their real whiteboard, on their window (with parental permission), or on their sidewalk with chalk.

As you facilitate group discussion, monitor students' comfort level with being on camera. Would allowing them to use a virtual background rather than share images of where they live make them more comfortable? Do their cultures frown on looking others right in the eye? Are you building community and safety with *home groups* where specific student groupings learn to work together well, even if you use random groups for other activities?

Discussions provide for the kinds of active learning experiences that enrich distance learning. With the right planning and tools, virtual discussions can be at least as effective as in-person discussions. Think about the opportunities technology creates for facilitation, and make the most of the tools available.

Common Concerns About Student-Centered Discussions

The following statements represent common concerns I hear from educators as they consider using student-centered discussion strategies. Beside each statement, you'll find text on how you might address any resistance you encounter (by yourself or with colleagues) because of such concerns.

- **"But only some of my students speak up."** Yes, and it might take six weeks before all students feel safe and feel that they have valuable contributions to make. Don't give up! Look back at the Use Teacher Moves section (page 111); the revoice, restate, and check moves are all useful in helping every student learn to speak up. If only a few students seem ready for the discussion, use a turn and talk to allow them to try out an idea.

For example, say, "OK, everyone, turn to someone and talk about this. Practice what you might add."

You can also try laminating a seating chart, marking who has spoken, and letting your students know that everyone needs to add to the class wisdom before those who have already spoken will have another chance. However, if you always do this, students may disengage after contributing, knowing they are off the hook for a while. To counteract this, randomly ask for a revoice, or use another move to ensure students pay attention.

Drawing names, perhaps having each student's name on a wooden craft stick, also works to ensure participation and helps the daydreamers stay more focused.

- **"But hearing incorrect responses and ideas may just confuse students or even upset them."** Although this is a common concern, when students jointly engage in sense making, *and* you remember to summarize what they have learned, the opposite happens. Refer to the opening example in this chapter (page 101).

- **"But discussions take time—and learning to do them well takes time."** Yes, most new approaches take time to learn and more time to master. But because student-centered discussions are a core equity strategy for ensuring that all students are engaged in higher-level tasks, this time investment pays off. Further, students, like all people, are social beings whose well-being depends on productive interactions with others, not solo performance, in the real world. Matthew D. Lieberman (2013), in *Social: Why Our Brains Are Wired to Connect*, points out:

  > The human brain didn't get larger in order to make more MacGyvers [referring to the inventive, save-the-day television hero]. Instead, it got larger so that after watching an episode of *MacGyver*, we would want to get together with other people and talk about it. Our social nature is not an accident of having a larger brain. Rather, the value of increasing our sociality is a major reason for why we evolved to have a larger brain. (p. 33)

Student-centered discussions take advantage of how our brains developed to interact socially—they learn and mature as their social skills improve.

Why Student-Centered Discussions Work

Student-centered discussion strategies are high-leverage strategies that engage all students in reasoning, justification, collaboration, synthesis, and evaluation, all of which are higher-level-thinking skills. As Dylan Wiliam (2018), an expert on formative assessment, points out:

> Engaging in classroom discussion really does make you smarter. So, when teachers allow students to choose whether to participate or not—for example,

by allowing them to raise their hands to show they have an answer—they are actually making the achievement gap worse, because those who are participating are getting smarter, while those avoiding engagement are forgoing the opportunities to increase their ability. (pp. 92–93)

Student-centered discourse is also perhaps the most powerful cross-disciplinary, K–12 differentiation strategy you can master. Why is it worth the effort?

- Student-centered discussions foster student success. Out of 277 influences on student achievement, John Hattie ranks classroom discussions as 16th, with an effect size of 0.82 (Corwin Visible Learning+, n.d.a). An effect size of 0.4 indicates that an influence provides about one year's academic growth, so classroom discussions, well implemented, provide a significant boost.

- Classroom discussions are a vital strategy for equity. In *Culturally Responsive Teaching and the Brain*, Zaretta Hammond (2015) provides two reasons why discourse is so important. First, the brains of students who come from traditionally oral cultures are primed to learn from story and dialogic talk. Second, rigorous classroom discussions ensure that all students engage in higher-level thinking, especially since oral skills develop more quickly than writing skills. Further, talking through ideas helps students prepare for the harder task of writing sound narratives, persuasive arguments, and other written forms of communication.

- Talking aloud draws on two basic facts: (1) people are social creatures who learn socially and are designed to enjoy conversing with others (Lieberman, 2013), and (2) students who are mastering English or academic concepts can orally communicate higher-level thoughts at complex levels much sooner than they can write about them (Hammond, 2020). This is also true for most students as they tackle more and more complex tasks.

However, student-centered discussions only have the desired effect when teachers pay careful attention to the crucial elements discussed in this chapter. For example, ensuring students refer to visual representations may not seem all that important, but researchers Robyn M. Gillies, Kim Nichols, and Asaduzzaman Khan (2015) show that when students can refer to nonverbal representations, their use of scientific language and their ability to engage in classroom discussions increase.

Further, keeping an atmosphere of safety and trust is crucial, especially when one considers many adolescents' fragile self-esteem. Lieberman (2013) finds that adults use different brain areas for self-assessing and for assessing what others think of them. Adolescents use the same areas for these two tasks; when asked to self-assess, they seem to ponder, *What do others think of me?* This means they may have difficulty building self-esteem separate from how they perceive how others have judged them! If carefully facilitated, classroom discussions have the potential to foster self-esteem and other components of social-emotional learning as students experience being listened to, feeling valued for their input, and taking risks in a safe environment.

Improving the quality of student-centered discussions is well worth the time it takes.

Reflection Activity

Consider the following actions and questions as you reflect on this chapter's content.

1. Creating space for great student discussions involves several teacher competencies. Where might you concentrate first? Use this list as you review the chapter and decide which strategy you might try first with your students.

   ‣ Create an atmosphere of trust.

   ‣ Use teacher moves that create verbal volleyball rather than simple ping-pong discussions.

   ‣ Avoid rewarding or acknowledging right answers; instead, allow students to explore multiple ideas and solutions.

   ‣ Ensure all students engage in discussion.

   ‣ Add your own areas for skill building: _____.

2. Volunteer to be filmed while facilitating a student discussion. Or, find a partner, and observe each other during a discussion. Then, use the video to meet with colleagues you trust to review it or meet with the colleague you shared observations with. You get to choose what to focus on as they watch you during the filmed student discussion or reflect on your live instruction. Here are some ideas.

   ‣ What teacher moves did I make that engaged more students?

   ‣ What worked for scaffolding struggling students?

   ‣ When did I indicate or not indicate whether an answer was right or wrong?

   ‣ What worked in encouraging students to use the sentence starters?

   ‣ What indicators did you see of student trust, student anxiety, or other student emotions during the discussion?

   ‣ What prompted good student reasoning and justification?

3. Practice using the sentence starters (see Practice Prompts, page 103) in collaborative discussions with colleagues. In fact, try any of the strategies with colleagues. What learning surfaces from engaging in the activity?

CHAPTER 8

Curiosity Creators

At a middle school where I provided ongoing professional development, a new teacher asked me to observe one of her classes, seeking help to engage students with informational texts. The students were restless as they read. Only a few students spoke up during the ensuing question-and-answer discussion of the text. "I just don't know what else to do. We simply need to get through this content," the teacher said and sighed. She gave me the next day's reading and pleaded, "How would you teach this? I'm out of ideas."

I took the reading home and failed to make it through the first paragraph because, on a scale of one to ten (where ten is *boring*), it was a ten. Can I confess that I used the research-based strategy of sipping a small glass of red wine to increase my creativity (Jarosz, Colflesh, & Wiley, 2012) as I pondered what differentiation strategies might work best? It occurred to me that, in any classroom, some students read just fine whether or not they are interested in a text, but the best course to differentiate for those who have other interests is often to make them curious (Hammond, 2015). Curiosity creators take advantage of the brain's penchant for novelty. Think of a time when you felt slightly drowsy, and a sound or sight pulled you to full wakefulness. Curiosity activates the same reactions in your brain. Thus, curiosity creators capture student attention, motivating them to engage in more complex texts, increase knowledge retention, activate prior knowledge, and develop thinking skills such as inferring and synthesizing (Dejarnette, 2018; Tan, 2017). Note, too, that most of them work with all age groups, including adults.

The next day, the teacher and I discussed some curiosity creators she'd seen during professional development. We then selected and worked together to develop an anticipation guide (page 123). The result? Not only did the guide help facilitate good student discussions, but 100 percent of students went on to read the incredibly boring article from start to finish. The article involved the same students and the same complexity as previous readings did, yet it had a totally different engagement level.

Curiosity Creator Strategies
(From quickest to deepest)

- ✓ Mystery Draws, page 120
- ✓ Key-Word Prediction, page 122
- ✓ Anticipation Guides, page 123
- ✓ Stop the Story, page 125
- ✓ Visual Entry Points, page 127
- ✓ Tea Party, page 129
- ✓ Bug Lists, page 131

In this chapter, you will engage with a variety of strategies designed to stimulate students' curiosity. Note that these are designed to foster curiosity in students with any of the cognitive processing styles for which a lesson's content doesn't intrinsically motivate them. You will also learn two big essentials for using these strategies effectively and answers to common concerns teachers have about using these strategies. As always, it's your choice to either read the research first (see Why Curiosity Creators Work, page 135) or proceed right into the strategies.

DOING DIFFERENTIATION

Consider the following terms: *rugby, boredom, 70 percent, ice fishing, school, anting*. How might each be related to the topic of crows? Compare your ideas with those of a friend or colleague.

Now, are you a bit curious about the actual connections among these terms? If you are, do a web search for the article "Has Success Spoiled the Crow?" (Quammen, 1985/2008). Think about how quickly you could create a similar list of terms for a reading you might ask students to engage with.

The Curiosity Creator Strategies

This section presents seven strategies for sparking student curiosity: (1) Mystery Draws, (2) Key-Word Prediction, (3) Anticipation Guides, (4) Stop the Story, (5) Visual Entry Points, (6) Tea Party, and (7) Bug Lists. Each of these strategies is designed to intrinsically motivate students to engage with content and learning strategies via their own curiosity. You can easily add most of these to existing lessons.

Mystery Draws

When conducting a mystery draw, instead of receiving questions or tasks in list form, either teachers or students draw them from a container. This simple strategy takes advantage of the natural question, "What's inside?"

Place questions or problems on strips of paper, and put them in an interesting container. For example, purchase a sturdy gift bag from a party store, decorate a box, or use a fishing net with a handle that makes it easy for you to extend the net toward a student—whatever suits your personality and your students' age. You're adding a bit of novelty, chance, and fun to assignments that might otherwise be rather rote.

One middle school teacher asked me to observe her classroom after attending a weeklong differentiation workshop I facilitated for her district. She used a decorated coffee can, filling it with tasks on pieces of paper. It gave off a satisfactory rattle when she occasionally shook it while providing instructions. The students couldn't wait to find out what was inside the can and enjoyed getting to draw a task for their group when the time came.

Here are two additional uses for mystery bags.

1. **Task draws:** Assign students to groups of four to six, and give each group a mystery bag filled with tasks. A group can then draw one task from the bag, complete the work, draw another, and so on. Foreign language dialogue prompts, mathematics problems, vocabulary word exercises, creative writing tasks, internet searches—the relatively quick and straightforward tasks for which this approach might add novelty are endless.

2. **Task sets:** Determine an even number of student groups, and create task bags with each task on a separate sheet of paper or card. If you have four groups, you'll need two pairs of bags, each pair having identical tasks; if you have six groups, you'll need three pairs of bags; and so on. All groups might have the same tasks. Or, you might have different sets, but color-code the task sets and number the tasks for easy sorting. Figure 8.1 shows task card sets for use with six groups.

   Groups then work independently, drawing each task and completing it. When they finish, they compare their answers and approaches with the group that has the same set of tasks. Note that students, not the teacher, are in charge of determining which answer is right or complete or meets whatever criteria are established for the task. The intergroup discussions will tend toward reasoning and justification rather than right-answer thinking. Using this approach, you'll also successfully apply a planned movement strategy (chapter 13, page 201).

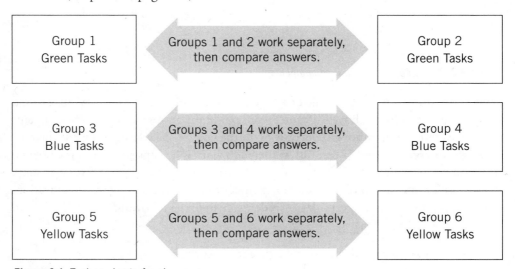

Figure 8.1: Task card sets for six groups.

Again, Mystery Draws activate the human brain's preference for novelty, helping students engage whether or not they are inherently interested in content. They can be especially useful with tasks that embed the kinds of practice that vision-and-interpretation and question-and-connection students find boring.

Key-Word Prediction

Key-Word Prediction is an approach from the National Urban Alliance (2005) that offers a simple way to activate prior knowledge, provide practice in making connections and justifying them, and stimulate curiosity in a topic; you experienced it in connecting crows with rugby and other terms in this chapter's Doing Differentiation (page 120). If you didn't track down the related essay, the correct answer is that crows seem to play a game with stones on the fly that is rather like rugby. To begin, choose a word that is central to the theme of a text, fictional or informational, that students will be reading. Then, choose seven to ten other words or phrases found in the text. Figure 8.2 illustrates how to display the word cluster for an article on the history of Play-Doh (http://bit.ly /Play-Doh50; Goulis, 2019). Using a fun article makes teaching the strategy easy, but the opening story in this chapter illustrates how you can dive right into important text as well.

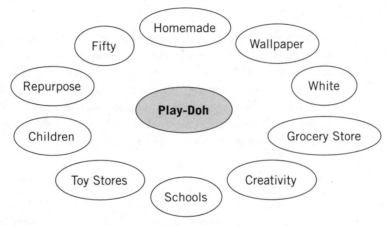

Figure 8.2: *An example Key-Word Prediction cluster.*

Place the key word in the middle of a slide or whiteboard and the other words around the outside. Alternatively, leave the center word out of the array, and see whether students can make connections among the words, with the goal of speculating on what the article might be about. In either case, ask students to work in groups (two to four students) to predict how each word might relate to the article's theme. Have the groups share their ideas for one or two of the words; remember to ask for reasoning and justification. Potential prompts you might use with students include the following.

- "Tell us more about your idea."

- "What prompted you to make that connection?"

- "What have you read or heard that gave you that idea?"

Do your best to comment on the quality of their responses rather than their correctness. For example, the correct connection between *wallpaper* and *Play-Doh* is that the creator of Play-Doh stumbled onto the formula while trying to make wallpaper paste. Responses that are high quality but inaccurate and plausible might include "Play-Doh might harm wallpaper if you stick it on a wall" or perhaps, "You can hang a picture by making a hook out of Play-Doh, sticking it on a papered wall, and letting it dry there." Both are plausible. Support the students in providing good reasoning and justification; often, they come up with amazing ideas that further their creative problem-solving and inference skills and their confidence.

After discussing all the words, have students read the source text independently. Students pay attention as they check whether their guesses were right. You'll often hear exclamations of "I was right!" or "Cool—I was way off, but that makes sense." Teachers may worry that this strategy could result in students' remembering incorrect hunches instead of the text, but this doesn't happen. The aha moments seem to embed the correct answers in the students' minds.

Note that, while making the kinds of connections this activity requires is natural for vision-and-interpretation and question-and-connection students, it also provides safe practice for structure-and-certainty and experience-and-movement students if you let them try out ideas in small groups before voicing them to the class. However, the latter two groups may need some direct instruction to understand that their predictions may require guessing or using their own knowledge rather than what they've learned in class. Demonstrate with one of the words you've chosen, saying, for example, "Let's look at the local grocery and Play-Doh. Hmmm, maybe they sell it. Or, maybe they use it to make displays."

VIRTUAL CLASSROOMS

Use online breakout rooms to form groups of three to four students. Have the groups make their predictions for each word and designate one group member who will share answers. Then, use the chat feature for the all-class discussion. Tell the group which word they're to share their connection for and have the sharer type his or her group's answer in the chat box. Then, debrief using the same kinds of prompts as for a live classroom, asking others from the sharer's group to respond. Alternatively, use the whiteboard; type the word or phrase being discussed in the center and have the sharers type their group responses around it.

Anticipation Guides

Anticipation guides activate prior knowledge and build curiosity. They consist of statements that students are asked to agree or disagree with, based on what they already know or might conclude through hunches or making connections. Readers can find the correct answer within a text. Figure 8.3 (page 124) shows a short anticipation guide for the first few pages of the introduction to this book.

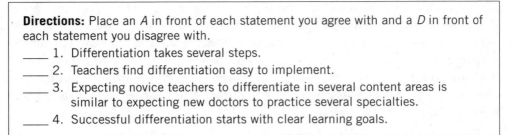

Directions: Place an *A* in front of each statement you agree with and a *D* in front of each statement you disagree with.
____ 1. Differentiation takes several steps.
____ 2. Teachers find differentiation easy to implement.
____ 3. Expecting novice teachers to differentiate in several content areas is similar to expecting new doctors to practice several specialties.
____ 4. Successful differentiation starts with clear learning goals.

Figure 8.3: An anticipation guide example.

For a given text excerpt, article, or short story, generate six to ten declarative statements that students can answer with *agree* or *disagree*. Some of your statements should be true, and some not true. Create two to four that correspond with the opening paragraphs of the text to immediately capture students' attention and allow students to experience early success with determining whether they correctly anticipated an answer once they begin the reading.

Before assigning the reading, hand out the anticipation guide and ask students to read through the statements individually, marking whether they agree or disagree with them. This can work even if students have little prior knowledge about the topic. I once saw a teacher use an anticipation guide for an article on salt mines; simply knowing what salt is was enough for students to engage with the anticipation guide. Encourage students to make a note or two on why they gave each answer. In fact, when you first try this strategy, combine it with a slight variation on the Retrieve-Pair-Share strategy (page 66) so the students can discuss their notes with one other person before the discussion begins.

Begin an all-class discussion involving one or two of the statements to model how small-group discussions should proceed. Ask, for example, "Who agreed with statement 1?" Probe for students' reasoning. Then ask, "Who disagreed with statement 1 and why?" Make sure that you stay neutral, not indicating whose answer is correct. Then state, "We've heard two viewpoints. Our goal is to come to an agreement. I'd like a show of hands. How many agree? Disagree? Let's hear some more reasoning and evidence from each side."

After this round, ask for another show of hands to see whether students are coming to a consensus. Depending on how engaged students seem, you might move on to the next statement or continue to work for agreement. Once students understand the discussion protocol, you can continue with the whole class or have students follow the protocol in small groups. Then, ask students to read the text. When they have finished, direct them to review the anticipation guide and discuss with a partner or in a small group how their thinking has changed.

Recall in the story that opens this chapter how using an anticipation guide sparked student engagement so that students dug in on reading a low-interest but content-rich text. Intrinsic motivation is the main role of anticipation guides, but they also provide practice with the critical thinking skills of making connections and hypothesizing that sensing students need, a structured process to make it easy for introverted students to participate, and easier access to texts for students whose reading skills aren't as robust as others.

Stop the Story

"What happens next?" is a natural human reaction as we listen to stories. Stop the Story takes advantage of this by using the first part of a story to build curiosity and thus engage students for an upcoming task. The reward of hearing the rest of the story increases motivation for the task. Note that stories in and of themselves are powerful learning tools. From the time we're as young as six months old, our brains work to make sense of what we're seeing and experiencing through stories. For example, if you add a button resembling an eye to a triangle shape, babies interpret the shape as a character. If you use various shapes in a simple puppet show, such as one shape helping another climb a hill and another shape giving the climber a shove, babies will reach for the shapes that helped other shapes (Tasimi & Wynn, 2016). The simple words *once upon a time* capture people's attention at an early age. All these things tell us making creative use of stories is an effective way to motivate students for rigorous tasks.

Using this simple strategy, curiosity springs from students' wondering what happens next. Here are some ideas for reading aloud just the beginning of a short story or picture book or the first chapter of a longer book.

- **Decision matrix:** In *Creativity in the Classroom*, Alane Jordan Starko (2018) suggests using Dr. Seuss's (1997) *Horton Hears a Who!* to introduce students to decision matrices. A social studies teacher and I tried this with eighth graders the afternoon before winter break began, often a time when students aren't particularly interested in academics. The teacher read aloud about Horton's dilemma, and asked, "Horton has picked up a clover blossom and discovered that on it rests a whole world populated by the little Whos. If he puts it down, their world will fall to pieces. What is he to do?" Every student group worked diligently to decide criteria (feasibility, cost, time involved, and so on) by which to evaluate different decisions Horton might make; all the students were eager to hear the rest of the story as a treat.

  Figure 8.4 (page 126) highlights a sample decision matrix for another popular book, *Nya's Long Walk* (Park, 2019). This book poses a dilemma: *Nya is a refugee in South Sudan. She and her little sister walk to a distant well to get water for the family, but as they start back, her sister becomes ill. Nya isn't big enough to carry her sister and the water, but they desperately need the water.* Stop reading to students after the sentence, "Nya felt worry swelling inside her. They were at least half a morning's walk away from home" (Park, 2019). Ask the class to work in small groups to come up with different actions Nya might take and write them in the first column of the matrix. Then, have groups brainstorm criteria by which to rank these suggestions, placing them in the first row of the matrix, and have groups debrief by sharing the alternatives they chose and the criteria they used. Note that the example in figure 8.4 reflects a tie. If a tie happens, ask the group to come up with a tiebreaker, such as, "Which decision seems wisest to you?" If you use this strategy with students in grades 1–3, brainstorm one or two columns and rows as a class to model the higher-level thinking you're asking students to demonstrate. After the debriefing, finish reading the story.

Possible Solutions	Decision Criteria					
	Time it will take	Nya's strength	Is realistic	Sister's safety	Total	Rank
Wait for help.	5	1	3	4	13	3
Leave the water.	2	2	2	3	9	1
Leave her sister.	1	3	5	5	14	4
Carry the water and her sister.	4	5	4	2	15	5
Empty out some of the water.	3	4	1	1	9	1

Figure 8.4: *Decision matrix for* Nya's Long Walk *by Linda Sue Park (2019).*

DOING DIFFERENTIATION

Why picture books? Picture books are short, leaving plenty of class time for the lesson content. Some create interest in the story itself, while others launch teaching of higher-level thinking strategies, unit themes, STEAM projects, and more.

- **Predictions:** Having students predict what comes next in a text is a time-tested strategy. However, this strategy suggests including an interesting twist that builds curiosity. Instead of asking, "What do you think will happen next?" ask, "What would you do next if you were this character?"

  For example, introduce elementary students to *The Wall in the Middle of the Book* by Jon Agee (2018). Then, read what the knight has to say as he climbs a ladder to put a brick back in the wall that keeps him safe from the ogre and other horrors on the other side of the wall. He fails to notice the floodwaters rising, a crocodile swimming toward him, and other dangers on his side—until the waves reach his feet. Say to students, "You can see the ogre on the other side. What would you do next? What do you think will happen next?"

  Note that this simple book could also launch secondary student discussions about the dangers of unexamined mindsets. Ask students to propose situations when people adopt a mindset of making fast, default decisions. Suggest possible answers like *choosing socks in the morning, avoiding dangers*, and so on. Ask students, "Is this mindset dangerous? If it is, when and why is it dangerous?"

- **Empathy inroads:** Use fiction to spark interest in a science, social studies, foreign language, or engineering unit by helping students see how it is relevant to their own lives, how those involved felt, or why the topic is or was so important to many people. For example, an eighth-grade social studies teacher and I worked together to introduce a unit on the Middle East. We used the fiction title *The Breadwinner* by Deborah Ellis (2000). The students knew very little about the events surrounding the Gulf Wars; as the teacher started reading from the first chapter, where young Parvana's father is taken by the Taliban, her students thought the events had happened at least a hundred years ago.

  To help students relate the story to the unit themes, we asked them to journal on the question, "What three things would you find hardest to deal with if you were Parvana?" after the first chapter. Sample answers from students included "living in a small room with your whole family," "not being able to go outside without your father," and "being in a long robe all the time." The teacher prepared a different journal prompt for each chapter, with the goal of helping the students understand how much they had in common with Parvana even as they learned about cultural differences and the impact of war.

All of the Stop the Story techniques in this section harness the power of story to more quickly engage students. More engagement with content leads to more learning success. After all, how much learning takes place when students remain disengaged? In this case, instead of differentiating for student interests, you're using stories to create interest in all students.

Visual Entry Points

When it comes to building curiosity, a picture really can be worth a thousand words. Instead of thinking of pictures, films, and other images only as information sources, consider using them to spark interest in a lesson, a problem, or an entire unit of study. Here are some examples. Note that these strategies work across K–12; only the content changes.

- **Photographs:** To get students to think about the themes or content you'll be introducing, display one or more photographs and ask questions or other prompts. For example, find photographs of the opera house in Guangzhou, China; the Signature Towers in Dubai, United Arab Emirates; and other buildings designed by architect Zaha Hadid. Several are shown at the end of the picture book biography *The World Is Not a Rectangle* by Jeanette Winter (2017). Ask, "What do these buildings have in common?" Note that one key commonality is how Hadid used nature as inspiration for her buildings. Then, read aloud the simply told but fascinating story of her career.

  For older students, expand the theme by finding more pictorial examples of women in architecture and engineering. Go beyond Marie Curie using a resource such as *Headstrong: 52 Women Who Changed Science—and the World* by Rachel Swaby (2015).

- **Three acts:** Mathematics educator Dan Meyer (n.d.a, 2011) coined the term *three-act mathematics problem*. He points out that stories can provide a curiosity-provoking framework that is both usefully prescriptive (how to construct such a lesson) and usably flexible. As a teacher, identify a real-world mathematics problem and set it up with the following three-act structure.

  › *Act 1*—Introduce the problem through a photograph or diagram, a video from the real world, a movie, or a scenario. State the mathematical question you have. This can be as simple as displaying a picture of students waiting in line at an amusement park ride and wondering how long the wait will be. Ask students to predict an answer; predicting engages them in a way that motivates problem solving.

  › *Act 2*—Meyer (2010) emphasizes how teachers strip the thinking— and the fun—out of mathematics by giving students everything they need to solve problems. This is a far cry from how they'll encounter mathematics in the real world. Encourage students to determine the information they need to solve the problem; then have them work to solve the problem.

  › *Act 3*—Demonstrate the answer through a video, demonstration, diagram, or picture.

  Meyer has archived an ample supply of these problems, targeting standards for third-grade mathematics and up (visit http://bit.ly/Meyers3Act). Peruse a few examples, and you'll quickly understand how to create ones for your curriculum. I promise that you'll enjoy his "Bucky the Badger" problem (Meyer, n.d.b) whether or not you teach mathematics.

- **Information removal:** Meyer (2010) also suggests using illustrations already in your mathematics textbooks but removing the information so the students need to decide what is important. For example, a typical textbook problem might have a diagram labeled to match the text, such as, "If a gallon of paint covers 350 square feet of wall, and a room is 16 by 16 feet with eight-foot ceilings and only one door, how many gallons of paint would you need to buy?" Instead, ask, "Let's say we could repaint the walls of this classroom. What would we need to know to estimate how much paint to buy?"

- **Visuals to spark inquiry:** In content areas other than mathematics, use visuals to spark inquiry in students. For example, to introduce the picture book *Her Right Foot* (Eggers, 2017), you might either seek a used copy of a book about the history of the Statue of Liberty or search the web for "Statue of Liberty history." Display a variety of pictures showing the statue in pieces, in Paris, and with scaffolding, as well as close-ups of various parts of Lady Liberty. Make sure to have a close-up of the way her right heel is lifted off the ground. Have students examine the pictures and organize their thoughts either as good inquiry questions or in a K-W-H-L chart (What do we know? What do we want to learn? How might we learn it? and What did we learn?).

Hold a student-centered discussion on why her right heel is lifted. Use the Retrieve-Pair-Share approach (page 66) on the message the sculptor was conveying. The book *Her Right Foot* (Eggers, 2017) contains interesting facts about the statue and one theory about the foot.

- **Pictorial history:** Pictures can effectively ground students in how their own lives differ from those of people who lived in a different period of history or different culture. Or, they can quickly convey the prior knowledge students need for an upcoming lesson. For example, for a unit on the struggle for civil rights in the United States, consider locating a used pictorial history book and cutting out (for display) several key images with which students may not be familiar. Those images might feature racist signs over drinking fountains, protest signs, or police and demonstrators. The pictures can tie to your learning targets for the upcoming unit. Select the intensity of the pictures depending on the age and maturity of the students.

  You might ask students to generate inquiry questions or to step into the shoes of one of the people depicted and write a first-person fictional journal entry on the depicted event. Or, have students draft a potential newspaper story—capturing the who, what, when, and where of the event and why the event was important.

  Consider applications for this approach in *any* content area, such as the following.

  ‣ In a physical education class, what might students learn from looking at pictures from throughout the decades that show the evolution of sports equipment and protective gear, the changes in who plays certain sports, or the changes in where or how people play?

  ‣ In an art class, how might you use a display of oil paintings, watercolor paintings, or artworks in other media to prompt students to develop a signature style of their own?

  ‣ In a science class, display a set of vehicles, and have students hypothesize about which vehicle is the fastest or about which design flaw its manufacturers targeted in a subsequent iteration. Have them use wind dynamics, laws of motion, or other concepts to support their hypothesis.

As with other curiosity creators, pictures spark intrinsic motivation to engage students more quickly with content. In many instances, pictures also do a better job of conveying information about events, places, and those involved than text can. They also allow students who struggle with text to grasp essential information tied to learning targets.

Tea Party

A tea party is a structured way to have students engage in multiple, quick conversations that will spark their curiosity and provide information for an upcoming lesson or unit. Kylene Beers (2003), author of the seminal *When Kids Can't Read: What Teachers*

Can Do, named this activity to reflect how it plays out rather like the many short conversations one has at a social event. Use it to begin a discussion about a poem, a novel, a nonfiction text, or a new unit topic. You can pull quotes directly from a text or create statements based on a story or a nonfiction text.

For example, you might ask students what the following facts have in common.

- In the United States, Scandinavia, and western Europe, trees virtually stopped growing for an entire year. Growth did not return to normal for twenty-three years.
- The greatest government on the continent of North America collapsed.
- Workers under age twenty-five began to die at a rate almost twice that of the previous year—68 percent versus 38 percent—mainly due to starvation.
- Levels of pollution in the troposphere (lower atmosphere) increased dramatically at different times during the year because of massive forest fires and dust storms.

Allow students a few minutes to consider and discuss the facts. They likely won't determine the common thread (all the facts have to do with a volcanic eruption in 535 AD that precipitated the historical period known as the Dark Ages), but you will have successfully engaged them in a discussion about these facts as a preamble to introducing a new text, *Catastrophe: An Investigation Into the Origins of the Modern World* by David Keys (2000). This text tells of the scientific journey to identify the volcano eruption as the cause of the phenomenon listed here.

You can adapt this approach to any content area. For example, physical education teachers have used tea party discussions to introduce new units with rules, equipment, and player position names and were pleased with the positive spin it gave to different sports. For nonfiction, you might select quotes from various parts of a text or unit information, thinking about your students' prior knowledge and their ability to make connections. Or, you might select quotes from people involved if, for example, the reading will be about a historical event or a scientific discovery.

Because hearing things more than once is helpful in identifying commonalities and connections, Beers (2003) recommends having about half as many sentences or phrases as you have students and making two identical sets of cards with the quotes or information.

Instruct students that they will have ten to fifteen minutes to accomplish the following directives.

- Compare cards with as many classmates as possible.
- Listen carefully as you read cards to each other.
- Consider what the cards have in common.
- Speculate about what the overall theme or topic might be, or how all the cards you've reviewed might be related.

After the sharing period, form student groups of four to five. Ask group members to work together to make a prediction, using the following prompt: "We think this is about _____ because . . ." Reinforce that their justification is as important as their prediction. What did they see in the texts that supports their prediction? Note the higher-level skills involved, such as comparing and contrasting, drawing on prior knowledge to speculate and infer, looking for patterns and themes, and identifying key ideas.

Adapt the Tea Party approach for grades K–3 students by using fewer cards on topics with which they are somewhat familiar. Here, your purpose is to provide practice in making inferences and connections even as you spark curiosity. Follow these steps.

1. Decide how many small groups you will form. Choose an equal number of topics, and prepare that many sets of cards, six to eight cards per set, with tea party–style facts or quotes. Consider printing each set on a different color of card stock.

2. Provide each small group with a document to record its answer to the question, "What is the common topic for these cards?"

3. Use a practice set with the whole class. For example, if you were starting a unit on different ecosystems with first graders, a set about swamps might consist of *toad*, *cattails*, *algae*, and *mosquitoes*.

4. Have the groups work with one set of cards at a time, returning the sets to you and taking another as they finish. When all groups are finished, the class can compare answers and discuss what the students think they'll be studying.

Besides sparking curiosity in students, tea parties engage experience-and-movement students as they move around the room for new conversations. Structure-and-certainty students have a specific protocol to follow even as the protocol stretches them to make connections. Question-and-connection and vision-and-interpretation students will feel at home as they strive to synthesize what they are reading and hearing. This is another strategy that has something for everyone.

VIRTUAL CLASSROOMS

For online learning, consider sending students their tea party facts in advance via email or classroom message board. Then, assign them to a series of random breakout rooms, with two or three participants, to compare strips. In the last round, form groups of five or six to determine a theme. You might also adapt the Key-Word Prediction approach (page 122), eliminating the topic circled in the middle, and have groups of four to six work together in breakout rooms to engage in conjecture about the theme.

Bug Lists

Great ideas often come from people motivated to solve problems they've identified. In *Conceptual Blockbusting: A Guide to Better Ideas*, James L. Adams (2019) develops the idea of creating a *bug list* to spot problems you might be motivated to solve. Bug lists help students engage in this kind of solution-oriented thinking.

Have students start a notebook or a document to record things that bug them that they'd love to see fixed. Provide some examples of things that bug you to prime the pump. Pick a category such as the physical school environment, cleaning, sports equipment, or libraries—an area over which you have at least some influence—and show some of your bug list examples. For example, your list might include the following.

- The difficulty of dusting ceiling fans or metal window blinds

- How pencil lead smears on your hand as you write

- The difficulty of getting the last mayonnaise out of a squeeze bottle

Then, have students record their bug list ideas for about a week. Give them a few minutes in class each day to record their list items; you'll also find some students add to their list in between designated writing times as their curiosity grows. At the end of the week, have students pick one item for which they think they can devise a viable solution, either as individuals or as a group.

Use the resulting discussion to generate a topic for a variety of coursework. Consider the following.

- **An invention science fair:** Students as young as six years of age, as my own children can attest from their school experiences at that age, can succeed if they're focused on things they've noticed. As they choose the bug they want to fix, make the resulting project simple, like having them make a model of their idea. The solutions become more sophisticated with secondary-level students. (See http://inventionconvention.org if you believe your students would benefit from this blend of science, curiosity, problem solving, and real-world learning.)

- **Essays:** These essays should cover the problem students want to fix, their proposed solution, and information on why they think the solution will work. For example:

  ‣ *What is the current normal you are trying to fix?* "At school, I have to use a pencil to write essays, and pencils are messy. As a left-hander, I get lead all over my hands."

  ‣ *What moment prompted your motivation to fix it?* "Last week, a friend started laughing at me in the hall, and I realized I'd smeared lead all over my nose. I thought, *This has to stop!*"

  ‣ *What is the new normal your solution produced?* "At home, I tried using one of my dad's gloves—he's a nurse. And it worked! The lead stayed off my hands. He gave me a box of gloves for our class so that I'm not the only one using them. No more smeared noses!"

- **Service projects:** Assign a bug list topic, such as things on the playground (for younger students) or in the community (for older students) that the students believe they might be able to improve. Form small groups in which members compare top choices from their individual bug lists, decide on criteria, and then choose one project to work on as a group.

Besides tapping into students' own curiosity as to how they might fix something that bugs them, bug lists have something for all learners. Structure-and-certainty students build on the real, known world around them. Experience-and-movement students can touch, manipulate, and observe their worlds to discover what bugs them. Vision-and-interpretation students can use their imaginations, and question-and-connection students will enjoy discovering problems and communicating how they solved one.

Two Big Success Essentials

Curiosity creators can help students thrive via accomplishing a real-life solution to a problem; think with more agility via learning to infer, make connections, and more; and increase engagement, the *T*, *E*, and *A* in STEAM[2]. What follows are lessons learned and summaries of how to make curiosity creators work from teachers who have successfully used them.

Master a Strategy, Then Change It Up

Just as with many other strategies in this book, you and your students may need to experience the strategic approaches in this chapter five or six times before everyone understands how they work and reaps the benefits. Repeating the Key-Word Prediction approach (page 122) twice a week for three weeks, for example, will cement how to use the strategy. Then, take a break from it for at least a week, try something else, and start rotating the strategies you use. Yes, even curiosity creators can become boring if overused!

Teach Students to Infer and Trust Their Ideas

If you have students who are used to right-answer thinking or have been taught that the answers are all in the text, it will take time to build their skills and comfort with making inferences, connecting new information to what they've learned in the past, and drawing on prior knowledge that may not seem directly related to the topic they're reading about. For example, as a group of students explored several curiosity creators in preparation for reading a story about the destruction of Pompeii, they asked, "We can't find any information in the article about why people still live on the sides of Mount Vesuvius. What are we doing wrong?" I asked them to think about why people still live in California in spite of earthquakes or why people live along the local river that floods frequently. I encouraged them to use that inherent knowledge to speculate (infer) on why the people of Pompeii might behave similarly.

Another time, a group of students who were discussing an anticipation guide asked, "How are we supposed to know whether the state forests have always been the way they are?" I asked them to think about forests they visited, including the one adjacent to the school. "You mean we can make up answers?" they said. I helped them frame this in a different light, saying, "You'd be basing your answers on something you can verify or have learned before."

Some students, especially those who prefer structure and certainty (figure 1.1, page 18), need permission to infer. They might consider it making things up. One of my colleagues said that only in high school did it dawn on her that inference was a skill to master as opposed to some kind of cheat. As an example, she mentioned a test question on *Pride and Prejudice* (Austen, 1813/2003), which asked about Mr. Darcy's feelings as he finally proposed to Elizabeth. While taking that test, she realized that the answer wasn't in the text and that she was supposed to use clues to "make stuff up," as she put it. She now, of course, knows that inferring based on text isn't making up answers; but as a teen, the skill violated her conviction that there can only be one right answer.

Common Concerns About Curiosity Creators

The following statements represent common concerns I hear from educators as they consider using curiosity creator strategies. Beside each statement, you'll find text on how you might address any resistance you encounter (by yourself or with colleagues) because of such concerns.

- **"But we have so much to cover."** Yes, and you'll have more class time for instruction if students are engaged than if, as with the opening story about the uninteresting reading, students aren't interested in the topic.

- **"Don't students need to learn things that don't interest them?"** We know that intrinsic motivation—when students want to do something—leads to more learning (Froiland & Worrell, 2016). If the content isn't motivating to some students, think of curiosity creators as a way to provide motivation via the learning process you're providing rather than via the content.

- **"But my high schoolers need to read boring, technical stuff!"** A teacher challenged me, "Google 'Python code documentation.' How would you create curiosity and open questions for these kinds of documents?" Good one.

  After looking up Python code documentation, I knew that I could still make use of both curiosity and another crucial human motivator: purpose (Pink, 2009). I'd make clear before introducing a single line of code, "As dry as this documentation is, imagine having to reread and reread to catch your errors. I'm going to help you invest the time *now* to learn to do it right." Then, I'd work through the same differentiation process as for any other lesson.

  ‣ Start with the foundation of good differentiation: clear goals. Create your learning progression (page 37). To understand Python documentation, what might students do first? This is something that an amazing number of tutorials and games on the web can support.

  ‣ Determine which cognitive process naturally fits mastering the basics. In this case, students should master definitions, conventions, commands, shells, and so on, which requires memorization. This is the domain of learners who prefer structure and certainty. Creativity comes later!

› Differentiate so that those least comfortable with this kind of learning—in this case, students who prefer question and connection—stay interested long enough to master the knowledge they'll need before they can create and innovate with Python. This is where curiosity creators would come in; check the web for ready-to-go-introductions that have students program games such as Mad Libs or rock paper scissors that might even impress their friends. You'll find strategies throughout this book that can support this step.

Remember, not every moment needs to be differentiated. Direct instruction, online tutorials, practice, memorization, and other strategies that fit the content are fine. Sprinkling in these other approaches helps keep all students motivated as they move toward the real goals of coding.

Why Curiosity Creators Work

Students who exhibit curiosity achieve at higher levels (Michigan Medicine, 2018; Pluck & Johnson, 2011). They are more persistent, goal driven, and intrinsically motivated to learn (Kashdan & Steger, 2007; Sendova & Boytchev, 2019). Thus, don't teachers owe it to all students to help them develop curiosity, regardless of their preferred learning style? Note that the strategies in this chapter move from simple (but effective) parlor tricks to methods that truly engage students' intellectual curiosity. Employing them serves the simple purpose of getting students engaged, but curiosity does much more than that.

You've probably heard of the *lizard brain*, the oldest part of our brain in terms of evolution. Our brain stem and cerebellum control our body temperature, breathing, heartbeat, digestion, and involuntary reactions to stimuli (Fuller & Fuller, 2021). Within this lizard brain is the *reticular activating system* (RAS), which constantly scans for new or novel happenings, events, information, and so on that might affect our physical safety, emotions, social status, or potential reward. Curiosity creators put the RAS to work. Approaches like Key-Word Prediction (page 122) and Tea Party (page 129) signal the brain that what is coming deserves attention. Activating the RAS prepares us to learn new information.

Reflection Activity

Consider the following actions and questions as you reflect on this chapter's content.

1. Try using a Tea Party strategy, such as the one provided for *Catastrophe* (Keys, 2000), with your collaborative team. Or, use the following excerpted example, geared for grades 7 and up. (Visit **go.SolutionTree.com/instruction** for a free reproducible version containing all fifteen statements.) Volunteer

to create a fresh set of cards and put them to use. Discuss what happens to curiosity about the topic as you work together to find the theme.

‣ Egyptian pharaohs and Roman emperors included these animals in victory parades.

‣ They are a keystone species in their ecosystem, meaning that other animals will be negatively affected in a drastic way if they become extinct.

‣ Because of hunting, their numbers had been drastically reduced in South Africa by 1906.

‣ In 1956, a woman became the first zoologist to come to Africa to do field research on a large mammal, predating male scientists. All of her letters to government officials were ignored. She finally used her initials to disguise her gender and gained permission from a farmer to study these animals as they roamed his land.

‣ These animals naturally range over hundreds of miles of savanna habitat. However, increased farming, resulting in deforestation, livestock grazing, and the building of roads and other infrastructure has fragmented their habitat, reducing their food and water resources and causing inbreeding.

‣ Only about 50 percent of this animal survives its first year of life. The youngest in the herd are easy prey for lions, hyenas, cheetahs, and crocodiles.

2. You can find an anticipation guide and related article on student motivation on the Solution Tree website (www.SolutionTree.com/free-resources /plcatwork/cacc). Try it with your collaborative team.

3. Try the Key-Word Prediction strategy (page 122) with your students, using the Play-Doh article referenced in that section. Consider recording your teaching so that you can watch and review your teacher moves. Did you do the following?

‣ Provide sufficient wait time.

‣ Prompt students with an example of good thinking if they were stuck.

‣ Stay neutral regarding whether their responses were right or wrong.

‣ Encourage them to share their reasoning or the thought behind the connection they made.

‣ Use a strategy such as Ten Hands Up (page 66) or Retrieve-Pair-Share (page 66) if students seemed reluctant to share their ideas.

CHAPTER 9

Open Questions

Most teachers can think of times when students were set loose to discover information or concepts and, as a result, didn't discover what they needed to discover. Because of this, teachers often resort to asking explicit, right-or-wrong questions to ensure that students focus on the content linked to learning targets. However, this strategy can backfire if, for example, a student can simply access key points of a reading or other text instead of engaging with the information at a high level. Put simply, a student should *never* be able to do just as well or *better* on an assessment of a novel or other reading by simply reading the SparkNotes (www.sparknotes.com) version of that text (Tovani, 2015). Using *open questions*, questions that have multiple correct answers or can be approached in various ways or require critical thinking, is a guaranteed strategy for ensuring that students benefit from accessing and engaging with the original work, not summaries.

Open questions quickly engage the vision-and-interpretation and question-and-connection cognitive processing styles because the natural tendency of the intuitive information gathering embedded in these styles automatically seeks connections and creates hunches and analogies. (Refer to table 1.3, page 26.) For structure-and-certainty and experience-and-movement learners, open questions support the development of essential higher-level-thinking skills such as exploring multiple points of view, investigating different approaches to problems, working with paradoxical questions, and making inferences.

The following lists several pairs of questions or tasks; think about what might happen in your classroom if you asked the first or the second question in each set.

Open Question Strategies
(From quickest to deepest)

Open Question Strategies for Interdisciplinary Literacy

- ✓ Question Taxonomies, page 139
- ✓ Student-Generated Open Questions, page 140
- ✓ Open Questions for Applying and Critiquing Text, page 140
- ✓ Catalysts, page 141
- ✓ Posthole Questions, page 143

Open Question Strategies for Mathematics

- ✓ The World in Numbers, page 144
- ✓ Multiple Right Answers, page 145

Open Question Discussion Protocols

- ✓ Spiderweb Discussions, page 146
- ✓ Student-Centered Discussion Roles, page 150

- What does 2 + 3 (for older students, 467 + 293) equal? *or* How many number sentences can you write, using addition and subtraction (for older students, using any combination of operations), where the answer is five?

- Read this text about kangaroos and provide answers to these questions based on the text *or* What questions do you have about kangaroos? How might you find the answers?

- How does someone register to vote in our city? *or* Read the information on the card you've been given about a citizen who wants to register to vote in our city. What barriers might this person face in the registration process?

- Look up the definition of *density*. How would you use density to measure exactly one solid cubic centimeter of salt? *or* How can you measure exactly one solid cubic centimeter of table salt, accounting for all the space in between the crystals?

The second suggestion in each pairing is an open question—a variety of answers or processes would be acceptable. However, without some planning, including structuring, scaffolding, or setting parameters for what good answers look like, open questions alone may not result in solid learning tasks.

Let's look at some strategies for open questions and how to ensure they work well. This chapter offers three strategy sets: (1) a set for literacy across all content areas, (2) a set for mathematics, and (3) two discussion protocols for open questions. Note that by increasing content rigor or question complexity, you can implement these strategies at all grade levels. This chapter also provides three big essentials for success with these strategies and answers to common concerns teachers have about using them. If you wish to explore the research supporting these strategies, first read Why Open Questions Work (page 155).

DOING DIFFERENTIATION

How might you turn the following yes-or-no questions into open questions?

- Did you like this book?
- Who was Grace Hopper?
- How many gallons of water will it take to fill a koi pond that is six feet by eight feet by four feet deep?
- What is the chemical formula for water?

Open Question Strategies for Interdisciplinary Literacy

While checking for student understanding often requires simple questions that have one right answer, we also want all students to develop agility with both answering and asking more complex questions as part of the STEAM[2] framework. This section presents five strategies for open questions: (1) Question Taxonomies, (2) Student-Generated Open Questions, (3) Open Questions for Applying and Critiquing Text, (4) Catalysts, and (5) Posthole Questions. Each of these strategies is designed to help all students go beyond right-answer thinking, both in generating their own questions and in developing skills in reasoning, inferring, comparing and contrasting, and other higher-level-thinking skills.

Question Taxonomies

Question taxonomies describe various kinds of questions by category of complexity. Planning for discussions using Bloom's taxonomy revised (Anderson & Krathwohl, 2001), Webb's (2002) Depth of Knowledge (DOK) model, or another favorite system helps you avoid natural biases. Try drafting the questions you might normally ask during a lesson, and compare them to a taxonomy for levels of questions. Then, rebalance your list to match your goals for the lesson. Do you tend to focus on questions that require recall (representative of lower thinking levels) or those that require application, synthesis, and other high-level-thinking skills?

Arthur L. Costa and Bena Kallick (2015), who cofounded and direct the Institute for Habits of Mind, provide a succinct questioning taxonomy with just three levels: (1) inputting data, (2) processing information, and (3) applying or evaluating information. Let's look at how these three levels might work with the familiar story of "Snow White and the Seven Dwarfs."

1. **Inputting data:** Questions and tasks at this level include describing, listing, reciting, naming, counting, defining, and recognizing.

    ‣ Describe what Snow White looks like.

    ‣ Name the seven dwarfs.

2. **Processing information:** Questions and tasks at this level involve comparing, organizing, summarizing, sequencing, analyzing, and estimating. Facts are terribly important, but these questions give them context and purpose.

    ‣ Make a timeline of important events in the story, listing the key events and a reason that each event is important to the storyline.

    ‣ Be ready to give a one-minute summary of the story.

3. **Applying or evaluating information:** Questions at this level involve predicting, applying, creating, and evaluating.

    ‣ Pose a what-if question regarding Snow White, such as, "What if Snow White hadn't wanted to marry the prince who awakened her? Write an alternate ending to the story."

    ‣ What stereotypes are depicted in this story? What might you change in this story to decrease stereotypes?

Remember that questions with one right answer aren't bad. In fact, they are ideal for checking for student understanding of specific facts, for example. Using a question taxonomy ensures you don't stop with these simple questions and instead engage all students in higher-level questions. These questions often motivate students who prefer the vision-and-interpretation and question-and-connection styles, and students with the other cognitive process benefit from the metaphorical stretch.

Student-Generated Open Questions

Research continues to reinforce that having students generate their own questions increases intrinsic motivation as well as provides practice in the higher-level-thinking skill of questioning (Sendova & Boytchev, 2019). I've included this strategy partly as a reminder to think through the tools you've already found effective. Which might you use more often?

To help students brainstorm their open questions, engage them in using the K-W-H-L structure (What do we know? What do we want to learn? How might we learn it? and What did we learn?), which facilitates building to questions that reflect high-level thinking. As an example, for the book *Ruby Bridges Goes to School: My True Story* (Bridges, 2009), first ask students what they *know* about Ruby. Then, prompt questions with the two-and-a-half-minute video "Civil Rights—Ruby Bridges" (McGrath, 2013) as a curiosity creator (chapter 8, page 119). Ask students what they *want* to learn about Ruby. Ask *how* they might learn those things. Gather their ideas, and then have students read the book. After the reading, have the students discuss what they've *learned* and which questions they've answered. At the conclusion, encourage them to think about how to learn more. Thus you've used the full scope of the K-W-H-L structure and circled back to *H* for questions they raised that the book didn't cover.

What other protocols have you used in the past besides this one to help students generate their own questions? Remember that while asking questions is natural for your question-and-connection students, their opposites, structure-and-certainty students, need to stretch to do this well. If some of your students seem stuck, start the *W* step with a bit of structure, such as, "Let's first think about things you might want to know about Ruby's school." Then provide a few such categories before asking the wide-open, "What else?"

Open Questions for Applying and Critiquing Text

Often, more class time goes to answering lower-level questions about texts than to applying the information or learning from a story. Teachers want students to go beyond the who, what, and where of a story to ask and answer, "What does this have to do with me? How might it relate to other things I've learned about? How might I apply what I've learned from this text?" Open questions facilitate thinking about story themes and relevance that go beyond the facts. Here are a couple of ideas for open questions.

- **Help students find big ideas:** A key element of helping students make meaning of texts is guiding them in finding the big ideas an author is trying to convey. Open questions assist in this exploration. For example, before reading the book *Layla's Happiness* (Tallie, 2019), ask students to think about what makes them happy. Consider having them write down an idea or two (kindergartners might draw a picture) or using a wait time strategy (chapter 4, page 63) to facilitate a discussion. Then, read about Layla. What do students notice about what makes her happy? What do the things she mentions have in common? There are several themes, and using open questions to explore them helps students go beyond simple text-based lists. For example, nothing Layla mentions can be purchased. She gives examples involving each of the five senses. She mentions the happiness that flows from watching those she cares about do things that make them happy.

These sorts of questions will feel quite natural in a secondary classroom, but they might seem like complex conclusions for the elementary-level students in this example. Even very young students *can* reach such conclusions. Consider providing copies of the book to groups of three or four students so they can review the content. Some scaffolding prompts you might use include, "Did you list any of the things Layla lists?" "Does something on her list remind you of something on your list? What do those things have in common?" and "What similar thing might you add? For example, you said you love watching your sister play with your puppy. Layla loves watching her parents dance salsa. What third thing might fit with those two? How might you label a list of such things?"

- **Question the moral or the stereotypes:** Questions that target a text's moral or a stereotype help students move from understanding to evaluating what an author is conveying. It's been a long time since I facilitated Junior Great Books discussions at my children's elementary school, but I still remember one suggested question from these discussions: "How might the story be different if Cinderella were beautiful and cruel or plain and kind?"

  Use these open questions for a prereading or postreading discussion. You could teach a whole unit on princess movies or fairy tales and what they're teaching, including modern-day retellings that tackle the stereotypes, such as *Cinderella Liberator* by Rebecca Solnit (2019). I'd love to see seven-year-olds wrap their brains around the open question, "Why might Disney make a film that makes fun of all the Disney princess films?" (This happens in a key scene in *Ralph Breaks the Internet* [Spencer, Johnston, & Moore, 2018].)

As you use this strategy, you'll find that many of your vision-and-interpretation and question-and-connection students are already asking these kinds of questions themselves as they read. The more you provide practice with these explorational questions for other students, the more you'll find that they, too, will begin to go beyond the mere facts to the real purpose of literary texts, both fiction and nonfiction.

Catalysts

Catalysts are objects students can investigate to stimulate their thinking for an open task. You might bring in a box of things related to a specific topic, historical items, or a collection of bizarre throwaways from your local thrift store. Author Katie White (2019) suggests having students engage with catalysts to help them explore ideas and to spark creativity. Before reading a historical novel, a biography, or another nonfiction title, bring in related pictures or postcards for students to peruse. What questions do these raise?

Catalysts can launch many tasks, such as the following.

- If students are about to write a story or fairy tale, set a few dozen curious objects around the room to spark ideas—old 45-rpm records, interesting seashells or rocks, bits of odd jewelry, trading cards, empty food boxes, some sports equipment, widgets from a hardware store for which the purpose isn't obvious, or souvenirs from faraway places. The possibilities are endless.

- Use catalysts to expand foreign language vocabulary. What objects from another culture might spark curiosity? Have students form questions and answer them, looking up new words they'll need.

- Use catalysts to form the basis for bug lists (page 141).

- Apply this approach to mathematics by setting out objects that could act as visual entry points (page 127), or use The World in Numbers approach (page 144).

Some students might struggle with moving from the objects to the assignment, while for others, the ideas will flow easily. White (2019) suggests supporting students by providing these questions:

- What materials [or objects] am I most curious about?
- What am I wondering?
- Were there any materials, images, questions, or problems that got me thinking right away? What does this tell me?
- Which topics are most interesting to me? Why? Do I have other questions about that topic?
- Can I imagine a different possibility?
- Which question, statement, video, image, or problem seems most interesting to me? Why?
- How do I know when something captures my attention?
- How do I imagine I might use these materials?
- Are there any other materials I wish to have?
- How might I change what is already here (materials, audience, setting, genre, function, perspective, values, variables) to get something new?
- How could looking at things from another perspective change what I might do and how I might respond? (p. 71)

While your vision-and-interpretation and question-and-connection students will most likely embrace catalysts and perhaps come up with more ideas than they need, your structure-and-certainty and experience-and-movement students will appreciate starting with reality-based objects and using the prompts as starting places for finding a good approach to these kinds of open-ended tasks.

Posthole Questions

Posthole questions are what-if scenarios that allow students to reason and support their ideas. They are useful in helping students synthesize, evaluate, or otherwise work with and apply the knowledge they have learned. In *Creativity in the Classroom*, Starko (2018) defines *posthole questions* as questions that:

- Clearly relate to the real world

- Build intrigue for your specific students

- Are without known solutions or methodologies

- Reflect ways in which students might see themselves as stakeholders

- Require that students access substantive content connected with curriculum and standards

Here are a few examples.

- You are the director of an art gallery in Germany in 1938. You receive a letter from the Nazi Ministry of Propaganda directing you to review your collection and discard any work that is degenerate. Failure to comply will result in severe penalties. What criteria will you use to review your collection?

- Schools in the United States waste over $5 million every day on food that goes uneaten. How can you calculate the food waste at your school? What practical steps could your school take to reduce the amount of food that is wasted by students eating school lunches?

- Some books really have changed the world. *Uncle Tom's Cabin* by Harriet Beecher Stowe (1852/2005) opened the eyes of millions of people to the evils of slavery. *The Jungle* by Upton Sinclair (1906/2001) exposed the unhealthy and dangerous practices of the meatpacking industry in the 1900s. *The Overstory* by Richard Powers (2018) is a more recent attempt to heighten awareness of our crucial interdependence with old-growth forests. As we've studied our democratic system of government, you've identified several themes regarding the conditions necessary for a democracy to flourish for all people. In your groups, create a thorough storyboard for a novel that might increase the population's knowledge of a crucial factor for democracy and motivate them to participate in making it a reality.

Posthole questions are a great example of excellent layer A tasks for Assignment Menus (page 55). Beginning in layer C, students build the foundational knowledge for the task, such as basic facts about books that changed the world. In layer B, they apply that information to understanding how these books addressed issues of their time and what made them popular. And in layer A, they synthesize the information to create a potentially world-changing storyline. While teachers might provide layers A and B through direct instruction, readings, or Knowledge Stations (page 206), note that the open question nature of posthole questions will engage your vision-and-interpretation and question-and-connection students. And, the foundational knowledge from layer A provides the structure the other students need to feel they can confidently undertake the open-ended task.

Open Question Strategies for Mathematics

This section presents two strategies for working with open questions in mathematics at all grade levels: (1) The World in Numbers and (2) Multiple Right Answers. Each of these strategies is designed to help students think like mathematicians who aren't merely using worksheets but using mathematics to describe the real world in ways that solve problems.

The World in Numbers

I cringe every time I see a T-shirt or internet meme that says something like, "There. Another day where I didn't use algebra." Even if you only asked, "How many episodes are left in the series I'm binge-watching?" today, you used algebra. Algebra is simply the art of finding the unknown, a way of describing the real world in numbers. Even simple word problems like, "How many blocks do you and I have?" use algebra. And calculus can include intriguing questions like, "How might we measure a rainbow?" Open questions are an easy and essential way to help students begin to think of mathematics as simply a language for describing and working with what they see in the world, useful for solving dilemmas and informing decisions.

Challenge students to come up with a mathematics question as they watch a movie, visit a new place, or read a story. Model this. Perhaps once or twice a week, share a mathematics problem you encountered at the grocery store, at a football game, or while making dinner that you were genuinely curious about. Use Catalysts (page 141) to prompt a question. Other ideas might include saying, "Look at this picture of a building made out of Legos." (Search *Lego Eiffel Tower* or *Lego Empire State Building* to see examples.) You could also ask, "I was thinking I'd love to make a model for _____, but how would you go about deciding how many bricks and what bricks you'd need?" or "I found this video of someone running *up* a *down* escalator. And I started to wonder how many steps that person would climb before reaching the top. What would we need to know to figure that out?" Encourage students to bring similar open questions.

Because educators often teach mathematics as algorithms applied to problem sets, students don't necessarily make connections between mathematics in the classroom and how they might actually put that learning to use in their lives. If you think about the four cognitive processing styles, question-and-connection students will flourish with this strategy. Vision-and-interpretation students will enjoy finding the quirkiest examples they can explain. Experience-and-movement students will come up with great problems if you ask them to think about what they are doing: "What does mathematics have to do with shooting a soccer goal? What about making a snack or playing a video game?" Finally, structure-and-certainty students will chime in as they gain experience with these kinds of problems with open questions.

Multiple Right Answers

Yes, asking mathematics questions that have only one right answer is often a great teaching strategy. The problem comes when students look to the teacher as the authority on what is true and not true at all times, when they wait for classmates to give the right answer rather than thinking for themselves, or when learning is limited to memorization or call-and-response rather than involving thinking skills. Use the following methods to offer students open mathematical questions with more than one right answer.

- **Add thinking to drills:** Open questions are a great way to get students to actually use mathematical concepts rather than practice using them without thinking about what they really mean. For example, "How many number sentences can you make where the answer is five?" requires students to think about concepts such as the commutative property of addition, order of operations, and more. Change the structure of the question depending on the age of your students. I once watched a seventh-grade class where small groups received wet-erase markers, assigned windowpanes (see chapter 13, page 201), and the instruction, "Come up with an equation that equals twelve that uses at least four operations. You'll be checking the work of the other groups."

- **Use supplements:** Parrish (2010) points out that when people rely on memorized rules and mathematics facts, they often fail to understand how to apply mathematics in real life. Carefully crafted open questions help students apply concepts in ways that make those concepts stick with them, and you can provide these questions by supplementing your curriculum with problems from other proven resources. Here are some simple resources for adding supplements to your curriculum that spark open questions. Not only are all of them organized by topic and grade level, but they also include valuable teacher resources.

  ‣ Use the menu on the NRICH mathematics resources website (https://nrich.maths.org), maintained by the University of Cambridge in England, to find your grade level, preK to grade 12. Then, search by topic. Many of the tasks include teacher instructions, samples of student work, handouts, and more. The teacher resources are extensive, and the site provides answers. To experience how the site works, search for the problem "How Do You Do It?" This group task is perfect for student-centered discussions; it encourages students to compare how they solved problems and determine who has the most efficient solution. While this problem is suggested for ages 7–11, I've had older students—and teachers—engage in the task for long periods.

  ‣ Use *Good Questions for Math Teaching* (a grades 5–8 resource) by Lainie Schuster and Nancy Canavan Anderson (2005, 2020) and *Good Questions for Math Teaching* (a grades K–6 resource) by Peter Sullivan and Pat Lilburn (2002). These are both filled with pull-off-the-shelf-and-teach questions, arranged by topic and grade level.

    ‣ For grades 6–12, review the Visual Entry Points strategy (page 127) for information on teaching mathematics problems using three acts. Come up with your own three-act problems, and encourage students to do the same. An example problem might be "How might you prove that the length of a traffic-signal yellow light didn't give enough warning to avoid running a red light?" Note that my twelfth-grade physics teacher created curiosity in us by showing how he beat a traffic ticket by answering this question.

- **Add open questions to fact worksheets:** Start with any set of practice problems, and add a related open question or two. You can use this technique as a supplement for drilling students on basic mathematics facts. Think back to choice strategies in chapter 3 (page 47), and picture a worksheet with some traditional problems as well as some open questions.

  Perhaps you have several basic fraction problems, such as ½ + ¼ = _____, so that students gain practice. The last questions could be "The answer is ⅗. What might the question be?" and "What three fractions might be added together to get an answer of ½?" (Schuster & Anderson, 2005).

- **Crack open a problem:** Instead of assigning problems that give students all the information they need, have them "crack open" a problem in their textbook by turning it into an open question. Use the Visual Entry Points strategy of information removal, such as the paint problem example in that section.

All of these are easy strategies to move students from right-answer thinking in mathematics to giving them experiences with the real kinds of tasks mathematicians play and work with. Note that if you add the multiple-answer questions after right-answer questions, as these strategies facilitate, you'll help your structure-and-certainty and experience-and-movement students move from what they know to more open-ended tasks.

Open Question Discussion Protocols

While some of the strategies from earlier in the book, such as Practice Prompts (page 103) or any of the wait time strategies in chapter 4 (page 63) will improve student discussions that involve open questions, the two approaches in this section—(1) Spiderweb Discussions and (2) Student-Centered Discussion Roles—place even more of the responsibility for facilitation, high-level discussions, and learning in students' hands.

Spiderweb Discussions

Spiderweb discussions are so named because a diagram that is part of the strategy looks like a spiderweb, owing to the way it depicts which students spoke and the kinds of comments they made. Educator Alexis Wiggins (2017) maps out in detail how to turn control of an all-class discussion—and responsibility for the discussion's success—over to students. In these discussions, the teacher sets a topic and the duration for the discussion (perhaps ten minutes for elementary schoolers, thirty minutes for middle schoolers, and forty-five minutes for high schoolers). The students do the rest, thus generating their own structure rather than responding to teacher questions. Wiggins (2017) lists four crucial elements for these discussions to work.

1. Students sit in a circle, which allows them to see every other student's face.

2. The teacher sits outside the discussion circle and takes notes by creating the spiderweb discussion map, staying silent unless the discussion deteriorates in ways that might cause emotional harm to any student. Figure 9.1 (page 148) shows a sample spiderweb discussion map. What is unique about this map is that it ensures students have a visual to reflect on when discussing their collaborative efforts. Note how you can code for various norms you are encouraging. In this example, *B* is for building on another student's idea, *C* is for making a connection, *I* is for interrupting, *S* is for making a superficial comment, *D* is for being distracted or off task, *Q* is for asking a question, *P* is for probing, *RJS* is for reasoning or justifying or synthesizing, and *Tx* is for making references to text. Not all of these appear in figure 9.1, but you can use these codes or make up your own codes that match the data you wish to share with students.

3. At the end of the discussion, display your notes, and ask students to self-assess how well they did on the discussion criteria you laid out in a rubric. Have them set a couple of goals for improving discussion dynamics the next time. Criteria might include the following.

   ‣ Whether students participate equally rather than some talking significantly more or less frequently

   ‣ Whether students listen, build on each other's ideas, and ask follow-up questions

   ‣ Whether students interrupt each other

   ‣ How deeply students probe the topic and stay on point

   ‣ The quality of students' reasoning, synthesis of ideas, summarization, and conclusions

   ‣ Whether students are able to stay on task during the full time allotted for the discussion

   ‣ Whether students' volume and tone of voice are appropriate and respectful

   ‣ Whether students use academic vocabulary pertinent to the discussion (which the teacher may provide in advance)

4. Using the clear criteria in the rubric, the students assign themselves an all-class grade that does *not* count toward their actual grades. The teacher then either agrees or disagrees with their grade, pointing back to the criteria. Figure 9.2 (page 149) shows a sample rubric you can use with students to add clarity to the evaluation process.

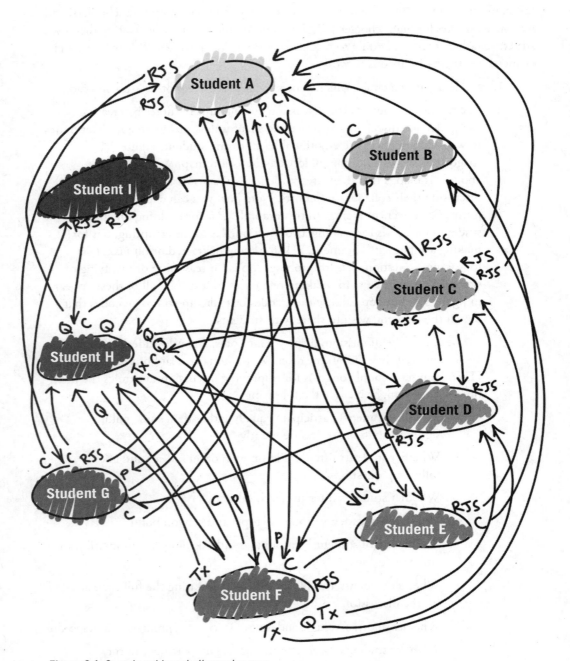

Figure 9.1: Sample spiderweb discussion map.

	Great! (3)	Good (2)	We Can Do Better (1)
Participation	We contributed equally.	Contributions from students were a little uneven, but everyone participated.	Some of us spoke significantly more than others while we missed the contributions of others.
Focus	Our discussion stuck to the topic at hand even as we made connections and synthesized ideas.	Our discussion had a few tangents, but we returned to our focus.	We wandered off topic and didn't draw conclusions or synthesize ideas.
Discourse	We listened to each other, probed thinking, built on ideas, and asked for clarifications.	We generally built on what others said, but sometimes, we rushed to put forth new ideas without connecting them to what we were discussing.	We made our own points with little connection to the ideas of others.
Reasoning	We gave reasons and justifications for our ideas, synthesizing and summarizing thoughts while checking for understanding.	We shared ideas, sometimes providing reasoning and justification, but we sometimes shared opinions without explaining how we arrived at them.	We gave opinions and didn't support them enough.
Use of texts and experiences	We used texts and specific examples from real life to illustrate our points, justify ideas, or foster discussion.	We used some texts and examples, but we also made generalizations from narrow experiences or failed to ground our thoughts in good evidence.	We relied on opinions rather than on good evidence.

Figure 9.2: *Sample rubric for class evaluation of a discussion.*

*Visit **go.SolutionTree.com/instruction** for a free reproducible version of this figure.*

Spiderweb discussions differentiate by ensuring that everyone is aware of making space for equitable turn taking. This fosters more participation from both introverted students and those who need more time to form thoughts. While students who prefer the question-and-connect style often favor these kinds of open discussions, the emphases on listening, building on, using text, and other specific criteria help the opposite style, structure and certainty, engage. As you will learn more about in chapter 15 (page 233), in the two-step differentiation model, if you begin with the style a strategy favors and adjust for the opposite, you have something for students with all of the styles.

VIRTUAL CLASSROOMS

Spiderweb mapping works for online discussions. Note that the iPad app Equity Maps (https://equitymaps.com) automates the process and lets students look at data by gender or other groupings, analyze how long they spoke, and more. It assists students in assessing their progress toward equitable and inclusive discussions.

Student-Centered Discussion Roles

Assigning students to specific discussion roles can also add reassuring structure to open question discussions, helping structure-and-certainty and experience-and-movement students be more aware of how they might contribute. When students facilitate their own discussions, Wiggins (2017) suggests assigning the following roles.

- **Three-questions asker:** This student prepares three thoughtful questions to spark discussion.

- **Key passage leader:** This student identifies two to four good passages for discussion.

- **Textual evidence leader:** This student is in charge of keeping the discussion based in the text.

- **Rubric leader:** This student speaks up to reference the criteria for successful discussions, including who participates and the rigor of the discussion.

- **Host:** This student invites all to join in with questions that build on what students discuss. The host might also summarize or ask questions of someone who has lost the thread of a discussion or perhaps isn't paying attention.

- **Vocabulary leader:** This student might highlight important new words and guide the group in articulating good definitions.

- **Feedback giver:** This student takes notes based on the scoring rubric for the discussion and reports out at the conclusion of the discussion on how it went.

Note that students at all grade levels can rotate in and out of these roles if they see high-level modeling. Consider conferencing with students as they first form discussion questions, or have them show you one key passage and explain how they chose it before they identify the others. In other words, scaffold by ensuring they are on the right paths. Alexis Wiggins (2020) sees this shift from assessing quantity to assessing quality in student discussion as part of social-emotional learning:

> After all, if we aim to produce graduates that have strong "people management," "coordinating with others," and "emotional intelligence" skills, then we have to assess those skills. A formative group grade for student-led collaborative inquiry is an excellent way to do just that. (p. 38)

Student-led collaborative inquiry, such as is fostered through these protocols, is a great way to measure whether the discussion you are holding is living up to the potential of discussing open questions. Are students discussing themes and ideas that apply, critique, evaluate, and extend what they have learned? Are they coming up with new questions? Are they learning from each other as well as learning to listen, reason, and justify rather than only express opinions (for which there is also a place in discussions)?

While structure-and-certainty students might appreciate the structure of roles for the clear paths to participation they provide, question-and-connection students may find them useful in developing better listening and reasoning skills. Vision-and-interpretation students will enjoy choosing texts and questions even as the discussion criteria help them clarify their comments and connect them with other students. Finally, experience-and-movement students will appreciate having roles that guarantee a chance to speak.

Three Big Success Essentials

Think how open questions increase student success and maturity as students learn to think at higher levels, how they become more agile as they realize many tasks have more than one correct approach or answer, and how they stay engaged when they're answering questions they themselves derived. Yes, open questions support the S, E, A, and M in the STEAM[2] framework, ultimately helping students thrive as well, which is the T. What follows are lessons learned and summaries of how to make open questions work, from teachers who have successfully used these strategies.

Find High-Level Tasks

Often, teachers mistake complex content for complex tasks. For example, they might assume any task involving a picture book or a game is low level. Or, they might take a high-level task and overstructure it so it is no longer rigorous. Students often know the difference. For example, for a survey that a seventh-grade team of teachers and I developed while I was consulting at their school, students reported an attitude that they could get good grades without working very hard. They were successfully memorizing significant content, but they knew they weren't being asked to think at high levels.

Work with your team to develop your own understanding of what high-level tasks look like. You'll find a sample set of tasks at the resources page for *Creating a Coaching Culture for Professional Learning Communities* (Kise & Russell, 2010; visit www.SolutionTree .com/free-resources/plcatwork/cacc). Rank the tasks individually as high or low, and then compare answers. Sometimes, ratings differ because of how colleagues envision implementing a task. Will they implement it as a worksheet? Through guided inquiry? At the start or end of a unit?

Then, bring your own tasks, and help each other decide whether their rigor is appropriate for your purposes. What might make the tasks more rigorous? How might you implement the tasks at a high level?

Maintain the Cognitive Demands of Tasks

Most learning standards have a goal for students to reach a certain thinking level. However, if the tasks students complete don't reach that level, they can't meet the standards' requirements. In *Implementing Standards-Based Mathematics Instruction*, authors Mary Kay Stein, Margaret Schwan Smith, Marjorie Henningsen, and Edward A. Silver (2009) find that teachers implement only 20 percent of high-level tasks at a high level. The following list highlights seven factors they identify as crucial to sound task implementation, along with the criteria I look for when observing mathematics lessons. The criteria are easily adaptable for other subject areas.

1. The teacher scaffolds student thinking and reasoning, as evidenced by the following.

   ‣ Emphasizing thinking tools

   ‣ Preparing roaming strategies (see the next section)

   ‣ Modeling good reasoning and justification

2. Students receive the means to monitor their own progress, as evidenced by the teacher doing the following.

   ‣ Providing learning progressions, rubrics, and worked examples

   ‣ Encouraging students to find flaws in their reasoning (use the roaming strategies in the next section)

3. The teacher draws frequent conceptual connections, as evidenced by the following.

   ‣ Establishing clear goals that are supported by lesson strategies

   ‣ Using summarizing techniques

   ‣ Emphasizing reasoning and justification

4. Students receive sufficient time to explore (not too little that there is insufficient time for students to reach a good solution, and not too much that they become frustrated or go off-task), as evidenced by the teacher doing the following.

   ‣ Using preplanned scaffolding techniques and extensions to keep all students engaged

   ‣ Monitoring students' use of class time

   ‣ Assessing students' engagement with a task

5. Tasks build on students' prior knowledge, as evidenced by the following.

   ‣ Choosing appropriate launch activities

   ‣ Focusing on clarifying or restating problems or the questions being asked

6. The teacher or capable students model high-level performance, as evidenced by the following.

  ‣ Maintaining the quality of class discussions

  ‣ Emphasizing reasoning, accepting correct answers only with justification

7. Students sustain their press for justifications, explanations, and meaning, as evidenced by the following.

  ‣ Responding to teacher questions, comments, and feedback

  ‣ Asking for clarifications until they can re-voice other students' thinking

Think about your lesson plan and these factors. What do you need to keep in mind to keep from decreasing rigor?

Use Roaming Strategies

As you plan a task, consider what you might see, hear, say, and do as you roam the classroom to answer questions, observe student work, and press for justification and reasoning. The following questions prompt students to think rather than tell students how to proceed.

- "Is there a strategy you can use?"
- "Is there another way to diagram it?"
- "Is there another way to organize your data or ideas?"
- "Tell me again: What is the question you're trying to answer?"
- "What do you know for sure?"

Prepare questions to help students revisit false reasoning, such as the following.

- "What if the people involved were . . . ?"
- "Explain your reasoning."
- "Did you think about whether this would apply to another situation? Does it work?"
- "Explain it to me as if I were a small child."
- "Does your answer make sense? Is it reasonable?"

In science or mathematics, if two groups are close to being on track, but their reasoning is off, pair them up and have them justify their reasoning to each other to correct their own thinking. In ELA, two groups might compare the themes they've identified and the text they are citing as evidence. Look for models of high-level reasoning. Ask those students to prepare to present their solutions or ideas to the class.

Consider what prompts might be effective to encourage justification for a given problem or open task.

- "How do you know . . . ?"
- "Where does that concept come from?"

- "Where did you get that number?"
- "Why do you think the character was motivated by _____?"

To adapt these questions for multiple content areas, consider in advance when you might point students back to texts, provide counterexamples to their conclusions, or otherwise help them re-evaluate potentially misguided reasoning, whether they are looking at character motivations, historical events and their modern implications, or science experiment hypotheses and data analysis.

Common Concerns About Open Questions

The following statements represent common concerns I hear from educators as they consider using open question strategies. Beside each statement, you'll find text on how you might address any resistance you encounter (by yourself or with colleagues) because of such concerns.

- **"My students just ask for the best way to approach tasks."** Remember that telling students doesn't prepare them for the real world, where questions are messy and the answers aren't in the back of a book. Here's the reward for helping students embrace these more complex tasks: if you properly scaffold open questions—and include them consistently over six weeks, even as you also include other kinds of tasks—you'll find that students' curiosity, motivation, and perseverance increase as they learn to trust their own reasoning.

- **"Some content involves right and wrong answers."** Use open questions when appropriate alongside direct instruction. Revisit your question taxonomy (page 139) and decide on the best strategy for your content. Remember that for some information required for standardized tests, students might need to create flash cards to memorize specific definitions, historical dates, plot details for a novel, or other content, but they can do so as they work with ideas in the ways that open questions allow.

- **"Some students aren't ready to tackle such tasks."** The best open questions reflect knowledge students can access using multiple thinking-skill levels and prior knowledge. For example, the roaming strategies I provide in this chapter (page 153) allow students engaged in mathematics to draw pictures, use manipulatives, try strategies ranging from arithmetic to geometry or algebra, and so on. In other content areas, the sophistication of student answers may vary, or you might need to develop different roaming questions to scaffold thinking. Think about this, though: If you asked students higher-level questions about their favorite movies, could they answer them? If so, then with the right scaffolding, they can answer them in academic content areas.

Why Open Questions Work

Questions with one right answer are necessary as students master facts, algorithms, and the plot of a story. However, they do not help students learn to think, reason, synthesize, evaluate, justify, and question—in short, right-answer questions can't teach higher-level thinking any more than learning how to turn on a stove teaches you how to create a dinner.

Further, open questions, properly introduced, help students move from being dependent on teachers and texts as their sources of knowledge and toward becoming the independent learners they need to be. They have to think for themselves—the engaged, agile, and maturing components of STEAM[2]. Doing so may create a bit of fear in some students who just want to know what they have to do, especially if they think being a good student means readying perfect work every time, but school should be a safe place to practice thinking.

Hammond (2015) points out that dependent learners are used to teachers carrying the cognitive load. They wait for instructions on how to tackle tasks, often saying they "don't get it" before making any attempts at new tasks. In contrast, independent learners are used to carrying more of the cognitive load, can use strategies to tackle new tasks, and know ways to get unstuck. Hammond (2015) adds:

> Dependent learners cannot become independent learners by sheer willpower. It is not just a matter of grit or *mindset*. Grit and mindset are necessary but not sufficient by themselves. We have to help dependent students develop new cognitive skills and habits of mind that will actually increase their brainpower. Students with increased brainpower can accelerate their own learning, meaning they know how to learn new content and improve their weak skills on their own. (p. 15)

Instead of thinking of dependent students as somehow deficient, reframe them as being in need of strategies—the strategies that work to help students on the left-hand side of figure 1.1 (page 18) feel comfortable when tasks require them to operate on the right side of that chart.

Many studies show that student learning increases when teachers employ higher-level questions, yet as low as 20 percent of questions used in classrooms are higher level (Peterson & Taylor, 2012; Tienken, Goldberg, & DiRocco, 2010). Jo Boaler and Pablo Zoido (2016) report that brain scans reveal how students who memorize mathematics facts don't store the information as securely as those who use strategies to solve problems. They detail three specific learning styles—(1) students who memorize, (2) students who relate (connect) new information to prior knowledge, and (3) students who routinely self-monitor and self-evaluate. They conclude:

> In every country, the memorizers turned out to be the lowest achievers, and countries with high numbers of them—the U.S. was in the top third—also had the highest proportion of teens doing poorly on the PISA math assessment.

Further analysis showed that memorizers were approximately half a year behind students who used relational and self-monitoring strategies. (Boaler & Zoido, 2016)

Open questions are essential to providing students with opportunities to apply knowledge, concepts, and strategies in ways that move them from working memory to long-term memory.

Further, open questions are essential to delivering the benefits of both all-class discussions and small-group work. Elizabeth G. Cohen and Rachel A. Lotan (2014) differentiate between routine tasks (where there are right answers and procedures to follow) and "groupworthy tasks that are open-ended, productively uncertain, and require complex problem solving" (p. 85). They state that groupworthy tasks:

- Provide opportunities for students to use multiple intellectual abilities to access the task and to demonstrate intellectual competence
- Address discipline-based, intellectually important content
- Require positive interdependence and individual accountability
- Include clear criteria for the evaluation of the group's product and of the individual report (Cohen & Lotan, 2014, p. 85)

Reflection Activity

Consider the following actions and questions as you reflect on this chapter's content.

1. Revisit figure 1.1 (page 18) and the list of seven criteria from the section Maintain the Cognitive Demands of Tasks (page 152), noting that teachers who prefer structure and certainty (let me know what to do) or experience and movement (let me do something) tend to overstructure tasks and may emphasize right-answer thinking. Teachers who prefer the other two styles (vision and interpretation, and question and connection) tend to understructure tasks and may not adequately press students to provide clear reasoning and justification (Kise & Russell, 2010). What traps do you fall into as you try to create high-level tasks in the classroom?

2. Work together with other teachers to assess the cognitive level of various tasks. To build trust and ensure that no one is worried about being judged, start by analyzing questions and tasks from your curriculum. Or, use the "Academic Rigor Task Cards" reproducibles from *Creating a Coaching Culture for Professional Learning Communities* (Kise & Russell, 2010; visit www .SolutionTree.com/free-resources/plcatwork/cacc).

Agree on criteria for rigor (see Question Taxonomies, page 139), but be careful to not simply see a word such as *evaluate* and assume it points to a high-level task. Instead, consider the following criteria.

- *Low-level cognitive demands*—These tasks require students to memorize information, or they do not make connections to enduring understandings and concepts. These are appropriate for mastering core content.

- *Medium-level cognitive demands*—These tasks require students to use procedures they receive. The goal is to produce a correct answer without any explanation required because the only explanation is showing correct use of the procedure. Examples of good use of these tasks include mastering science lab procedures, mastering standard algorithms in mathematics, and correctly applying rules of grammar.

- *High-level cognitive demands*—These are tasks students can approach in multiple ways. They promote a deeper understanding of concepts or foster connections across the curriculum, require self-monitoring, and engage students in productive struggle—where students experience uncertainty but still feel motivated to persevere. The open questions in this chapter model higher-level cognitive demands.

3. Select a task from your curriculum. Use the procedure in Maintain the Cognitive Demands of Tasks to plan how you will implement it. What do you need to keep in mind?

CHAPTER 10

Concept Maps

As a prelude to a group of sixth-grade ELA students beginning a personal narrative writing assignment, a teacher I was coaching quickly introduced and demonstrated a tool to help students brainstorm how they might add rich details to their stories. With the word *Details* in the middle, she drew spokes out to category headings such as *Characters*, *Place*, and *Feelings* and encouraged them to make their own map, jotting down their ideas for each of these categories. This approach helped the students preplan their writing without the restrictive feel that traditional outlines sometimes produce, and the teacher commented that, as a result, students' rough drafts included richer details than she'd seen from similar past assignments.

As you've probably guessed, the students were creating *concept maps*, which are visible, flexible ways, concrete or virtual, to display knowledge. They differentiate by helping students organize information and ideas so they can more easily activate prior knowledge, compare and contrast information, justify their thinking, find a logical way to organize ideas, monitor their own learning progress, and more.

Think of concept maps as *heuristics*, which are tools that let students learn something by themselves. Once students master how to use a heuristic, they can apply it in multiple content areas and use it in life outside school. For example, once you've been introduced to categorizing facts rather than simply listing them as you learn them, you might apply this heuristic to making a grocery list by store aisle, organizing your closet by color or articles of clothing, or using limitless other applications.

In this chapter, you'll explore several strategies for using concept maps to differentiate instruction in your classroom. Note that these strategies aren't specifically suited to any particular grade level. Their complexity increases as students' ability to perform complex thinking increases. Thus, these maps are just as useful in the world of work as they are in school. After the concept map strategies, you'll learn four big essentials for success using them and answers to

Concept Map Strategies
(From quickest to deepest)

common concerns teachers have about using them. To see the research that underpins success with this chapter's strategies, see Why Concept Maps Work (page 172).

DOING DIFFERENTIATION

To build experience using concept maps, try taking notes for a short informational video using a simple concept map; flip through this chapter and choose one that appeals to you. Then, choose a video of interest, perhaps from the list of the most popular TED talks (https://bit.ly/3kpimtb). How is this form of note-taking similar or different from your usual method and engagement with note-taking?

The Concept Map Strategies

This section presents six strategies for concept mapping: (1) Thinking Maps, (2) Graphic Organizers, (3) Freeform Organizers, (4) Advance Organizers and Learning Maps, (5) Learning Progression Study Guides, and (6) Graphic Recording. Each of these strategies is designed to help students organize information in ways that make it easier to learn, work with, and apply it.

Thinking Maps

Author and researcher David Hyerle's gift to educators is having developed and popularized a set of eight basic but powerful thought organizers that he has dubbed *Thinking Maps*® (Hyerle & Alper, 2011, 2014). You can learn much more about using them from the resources cited here as well as at the Thinking Maps website (www.thinkingmaps .com). Teachers can quickly and easily teach any of the map styles to students, but there is nothing simplistic about the power these maps have to help students at all levels organize information. Here are three of my favorite map styles.

1. **Bubble maps:** Have students place a word, concept, or character's name in the middle of a writing space. Then, instruct them to draw spokes out from the middle term, adding something they know about the term or an adjective that describes it to each spoke. This is a perfect way to have students summarize what they learned from a lesson. You might prompt students to add to their bubble maps by asking, for example, "Class, what have we learned about denominators?" "What do we know about gravity?" or "What did we learn about writing a good narrative poem?"

   Students quickly master using a bubble map to brainstorm ideas, capture knowledge, summarize takeaways, and more. See figure 10.1 for a sample bubble map on the contents of this chapter.

2. **Tree maps:** These are the classic organizational charts people use for family trees, classifications, detail organization, and more. For example, students

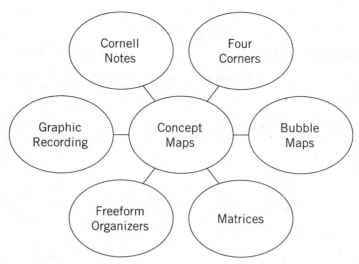

Figure 10.1: *Sample bubble map.*

might put the main topic of "Books I read this year" at the middle top of a page. In the next line would go subtopics such as science fiction, biography, graphic novels, poetry, and so on. Underneath, students have space to add books they've read over the course of the year. Figure 10.2 (page 162) shows a sample tree map for two uses of concept mapping. Note how you can form tree maps with manipulatives for big notes (chapter 11, page 175), which your experience-and-movement students will greatly appreciate.

3. **Flow maps:** These maps organize information by showing how steps or events or information build or flow from one element to the next, from left to right on a page. Thus, the first box on the left might describe the first scene in a story, with the next one showing the second scene, and so on. Uses for flow maps include making timelines, organizing steps in a science experiment, planning a project or computer program, or outlining a fictional or true story. Figure 10.3 (page 162) shows a double flow map for a history unit on the U.S. space program, with each item in the second row explaining the significance of the event directly above it. See Moveable Concept Maps (page 179) for an in-depth application of using a flow map as a mobile outline for writing.

Sometimes, schools get the idea that Thinking Maps are the only or best tools for concept mapping. And they are very good and versatile, but keep exploring other formats. You'll find some, including those described in the following sections, that work better for more complex learning tasks and some that work better for certain students, especially the vision and interpretation (let me follow my own lead) mavericks. In general, structure-and-certainty and experience-and-movement students like the most structured maps, including Thinking Maps. Vision-and-interpretation and question-and-connection students often gravitate toward the Freeform Organizers (page 165) and Graphic Recording (page 167). To consider whether a Thinking Map is the best choice, compare some of the options in the Graphic Organizers (page 162) and Advance Organizers and

Concept Mapping

Comparing and Contrasting		Organizing Notes	
Matrix	**Four Corners**	**Graphic Recording**	**Cornell Notes**
Is easy to label and makes it easy to read through comparisons	Can make a hexagon for six comparisons, a triangle for three, and so on	Lets you be creative in taking notes	Have a structure that leads to asking questions and summarizing
Is easy to expand	Require remembering to label the same topics in each corner	Uses your whole brain	Include questions that let you fill in what you missed or didn't understand
		Requires remembering to summarize and check for completeness	

Figure 10.2: *Sample tree map.*

Early Space Program Events and Significance

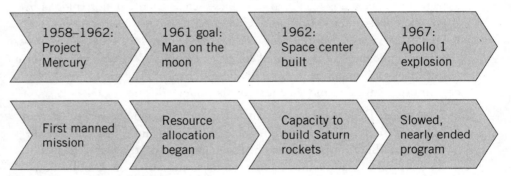

Figure 10.3: *Sample double flow map.*

Learning Maps (page 165) sections to any of the eight Thinking Maps for the same purposes related to your curriculum. If someone insists that you only use the eight maps, try responding, "I'm not saying I won't use Thinking Maps. I'm saying that in this case, it will be a better thinking tool for my students. Here's why."

Graphic Organizers

Graphic organizer is a catchall term for methods that capture information in ways that make clear the connections among the various pieces or that help organize how one thinks about the information. Graphic organizers range from tools that help students take better notes to diagrams that set loose creativity. The following are particularly useful for fostering higher-level thinking.

- **Four corners notes:** Students divide a workspace, such as a sheet of paper, into four quadrants. At the top of each, they list the topic for that quadrant. Here are some example topics.

> ‣ The four characters students will compare and contrast
>
> ‣ The four great civilizations (Mesopotamia, Egypt, China, and the Indus Valley) about which students will capture information
>
> ‣ The four microscopic organisms students are examining under a microscope
>
> ‣ The four mathematics problem-solving strategies for a daily lesson

Then, students can list similar information in each quadrant, using the same labels in each, such as *character background, strengths, motives, main goal, weaknesses*, and *dark secrets*. Despite the name, note that the organizer does not have to take the form of four quadrants; it can become three or five pie wedges, or a divided hexagon, for example. The format just depends on the number of categories students are comparing.

Demonstrate this organizer's power by filling in an example during an all-class discussion. Then, use different-colored markers to circle similar ideas, draw lines between connections students find, add generalizations or conclusions, and so on. Graphic organizers are not meant to be static information holders but active tools for prompting thinking.

- **Conversation roundtable:** This is a variation on four corners notes from author Jim Burke (2002) that emphasizes organizing the information for comparing and contrasting. First, draw a circle in the middle of your workspace (about two inches in diameter if working on copy paper), and then make lines for the four quadrants around the circle. Put the topic— such as a decision a character faces, a public-policy topic, or a proposed school or classroom policy—in the middle. Or, delve deeply into points of view by having students compare four real people connected with the Little Rock Nine, the Triangle Shirtwaist fire investigation, the 1968 Chicago Democratic National Convention riots, or NASA Mission Control during a mission catastrophe. How did their various backgrounds and roles influence their perspectives on the same event?

- **Matrices or spreadsheet notes:** Whether students make a grid or use spreadsheet software, this format works for comparing and contrasting, organizing information, planning a report, and more. Placing data into a matrix or spreadsheet is particularly useful for helping students who like to lay out logical arguments, if-then scenarios, cause-and-effect analyses, and more. This also works well for students just learning to write all the way through to students learning to structure a dissertation. Figure 8.4 (page 126) includes an example for decision making.

- **Cornell Notes:** Using this format from Cornell University (n.d.), students quickly master how to use notebook paper to record information, form questions and categories, and summarize. While Cornell Notes are part of Cornell University's recommendations for college study skills, students of any age can successfully use this format. The topic, lecture date, or resource for which students are taking notes goes at the top. Students draw a line down the page to form about a two-inch column on the left and a six-inch column on the right. (See figure 10.4 for an example.) The note-taking process includes the following six steps that promote questioning, synthesis, memorization, and reflection.

a. *Record*—Students use the wide column to take notes. These do not need to be complete sentences. Students might take notes on digital devices as well, given research that taking notes by hand has no significant advantage in information retention (Morehead, Dunlosky, & Rawson, 2019).

b. *Question*—Students record questions they have about the material in the left column either as they take notes or shortly afterward. What words or ideas do they wish to clarify? Help them develop the habit of finding the answers before studying further. What relationships or connections might they make?

Or, demonstrate a *Jeopardy!*-style use of the questions, anticipating assessments. (If this is the information, what might be the question?) This sets them up to study their notes.

c. *Recite*—Students then study by covering their notes, reading the questions they've written, and recalling the information.

d. *Reflect*—As they recite, encourage students to ask questions that allow them to go deeper. They should ask themselves, "Why are these facts significant? How do they relate to each other or to other things I've learned? How can I use them? What do I want to know more about?"

e. *Review*—Students should review their notes at least once a week rather than only at test-taking time. This kind of periodic review connects with long-term retention of information. Spacing out study time, rather than cramming at the last minute, has an effect size of 0.65 (Corwin Visible Learning+, n.d.a).

f. *Summarize*—Students use the bottom of their notes to summarize the big ideas, the most important things they learned, or the gist of the information they gathered.

The beauty of Cornell Notes is that they provide a method for structure-and-certainty and experience-and-movement students to go from the information they've written down to forming questions or defining topics and other application and synthesis tasks. Although vision-and-interpretation and question-and-connection students may not be fond of the linear, right-hand column, they enjoy adding items to the left-hand column, increasing their engagement. To learn more about using Cornell Notes, visit Cornell University's (n.d.) website.

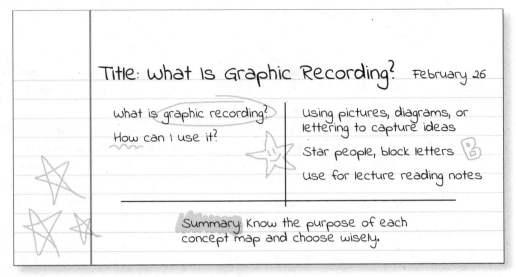

Figure 10.4: Cornell Notes example.

Freeform Organizers

Freeform organizers let students develop their own unique ways of organizing information and ideas. Instead of showing them a template, as in the previous chapter strategies, let students come up with their own format. If they wish to be creative, let them be creative even as you remind them of a particular purpose their organizer should fulfill. Perhaps they place character notes all over a simplified map of London for *Oliver Twist* (Dickens, 1838/2014) or on a floor plan of 4 Privet Drive for *Harry Potter and the Sorcerer's Stone* (Rowling, 1997). They might stack notes on culture in an Egyptian pyramid or keep track of important astronomical information in a drawing of the solar system. Suggest to students that they limit the time they spend getting creative so they have time to actually organize the information. Some students will need help with knowing when creativity needs to stop for productivity to start. Others need encouragement to ask the question, "What would be a unique and clever way to depict what I'm learning?"

Getting creative frequently leads to more time spent working with the information—especially for your vision-and-interpretation students who love showing their individual creativity but need some motivation to master factual information.

Advance Organizers and Learning Maps

I first introduced learning maps in chapter 2 (page 33) as a way for teachers to set clear goals and expectations. This variation for students expands their use as an actual study tool. Knight (2013) further clarifies the benefits of students' using learning maps:

> [A learning map] highlights the knowledge, skills, and big ideas that students should get from a lesson, unit, or course. The map depicts the most important information to be learned and how the different pieces of learning are connected. A learning map is a visual cue for the advance organizer (the introduction of

learning at the start of a lesson) and post organizer (the summary discussion at the end of a lesson), and a living study guide that students and teachers complete after each new learning. (p. 89)

Students can realize the benefits Knight (2013) details by using a tree map, which you learned about in the Thinking Maps section (page 160). Here is how you might accomplish this.

1. To introduce the unit, provide students with a tree map advance organizer, with the unit title at the top. In the next row of the tree map, have students place the main topics to be covered in the unit. For lengthy units, you might add a third level of detail. For example, for a unit on mountains, the second row might list the three main types of mountain formations: (1) fold, (2) fault-block, and (3) volcanic. Under each of these categories, an example might appear to anchor students in the knowledge the unit will cover.

2. Use the advance organizer to explain to students what the unit will cover and how they can use the organizer for organizing their notes.

3. Direct students to add to the organizer each day so they connect what they are learning with the overall unit goals. Daily lesson summaries can include fitting information into the advance organizer. Even if notes are detailed and kept in a separate place, completing the advance organizer will help students see the interrelatedness of the various topics.

4. Have students periodically examine the organizer to identify connections among the various topics.

As much as possible, remember to have students bear the cognitive load for creating the learning map. You might hand out a map with the main topics and then have students fill in the details during silent reflection at the end of a lesson. Then, hold a discussion so all students have all the main points down. Or, they might transfer their learnings from Cornell Notes (page 163) to a learning map for the unit so that they can see the flow of the unit in one place. This strategy helps all students review information, but it is especially useful for students who favor structure and certainty, and experience and movement so that they go from segmented information to seeing the themes and connections throughout the unit.

Learning Progression Study Guides

As I wrote in the Learning Progressions section (page 37), *learning progressions* are lists of learning objectives, also called *knowledge packages* (Ma, 1999, 2020; Popham, 2011). They help teachers recognize the piece-by-piece construction of knowledge, which may or may not be reflected in standards or in the curriculum. You can turn these into a study guide for students to help them take responsibility for their own learning. Figure 10.5 shows an example for part of a learning progression for adding fractions.

Learning Target	Student-Generated Notes That Show Mastery of Concepts
1. I understand how to divide shapes, groups of objects, number lines, and other things into equal parts.	I now know there are three models for fractions: set, area, and distance.
2. If you give me a fractional part of something, I can figure out what the whole is.	The bar-model drawing makes this easy. If you tell me that I have 2 red shirts and that's ¼ of all my shirts, I can draw this and know the whole is 8. [2	2	2	2]
3. I know that the actual size of a fractional piece depends on the size of the whole.	If I give you half of a fun-size candy bar and I get half of a regular one, we didn't get the same amount!
4. I understand that fractions also represent dividing things into fair, equal shares.	This doesn't show ⅓. But this does.

Figure 10.5: *Learning progression with student notes.*

When students fill in the right-hand column with examples that demonstrate they understand the learning target, they also show understanding of the success criteria (see Clear Success Criteria, page 33) and the ability to satisfy them. This makes Learning Progression Study Guides a high-impact strategy for all students.

Graphic Recording

Graphic recording, also known as *visual note-taking* asks students to think differently about what they are hearing. Purposeful inclusion of sketches and symbols, as well as words, makes graphic recordings a bit different from other concept maps. Remember that working with pictures and working with words use different parts of the brain, so this strategy can strengthen the retention of ideas (Einstein & May, 2019). And even as people write, they're often creating images in their brains that the words bring to mind. Encouraging students to add pictures to their notes engages them in synthesizing and summarizing. For example, how might you depict the following?

- Crows mate for life.

- The Battle of the Somme lasted almost five months.

- *I* comes before *E* except after *C*.

Wrestling with how to draw these concepts can serve to synthesize and solidify the ideas. Further, it turns out that doodling is an effective thinking tool, even improving test scores when students engage in drawing while thinking (Shellenbarger, 2014).

To use this strategy, find a resource that explains simple visual note-taking strategies, such as *The Sketchnote Handbook* (Rohde, 2013), which shows simple techniques like how to turn cubes into a city or organize ideas along a sketch of a pathway. Demonstrate one or two of the most useful and simple techniques to students, such as the following, which are illustrated in figure 10.6.

- **Star people:** Adding human features to a basic star shape posed in different ways

- **Paths:** A straight or curved line or series of steps or stepping stones, with ideas written along the way

- **Cubes:** Can be turned into cities or box people or used to box in main topics

- **Triple lettering:** Quickly emphasizes key ideas

Figure 10.6: Simple sketchnote techniques.

While graphic recording will, again, help all students remember information, vision-and-interpretation students often thrive when given permission to take notes this way. Remember that their inner world is rich; graphic recording can help them pay attention to what is being said in the outer world by putting their creative bent to good use.

Four Big Success Essentials

Concept maps lead to more student success (the *S* in STEAM[2]) as students visually capture and manipulate the information they're working with in ways that help them make connections, see patterns, remember facts, and more. Yet the maps that teachers introduce or students choose to use need to fit the purpose and, in some cases, be used in certain ways. What follows are lessons learned and summaries of how to make concept maps work, from teachers who have successfully used them.

Let Students Arrange the Information

If you hand a completed concept map to students, you've undone its purpose. It's through organizing the information that students compare, contrast, hypothesize, make connections, and more. Learning increases when students create concept maps for themselves (Schroeder, Nesbit, Anguiano, & Adesope, 2018).

Explore Virtual and Handwritten Maps

Have students experiment with whether taking notes on their tablets, laptops, or other devices works well for them. Perhaps everyone takes notes by hand one day and on their devices the next day. With which medium do they make more connections, find it easier to categorize information, or engage in other higher-level tasks?

Fortunately, many tablet apps allow for excellent concept mapping. Do an online search for "best concept-mapping apps for students," and choose one that you can use intuitively. Microsoft's OneNote app (www.onenote.com), which works on multiple platforms, has a Cornell Notes form, for example.

Bolster Note-Taking Skills

Students may need scaffolding in how to take *any* form of notes. The Advancement Via Individual Determination (AVID) Center (2017) has excellent suggestions for making note-taking more accessible for all students. Here are some of those recommendations, which you can pair with this chapter's strategies (AVID Center, 2017).

- **10-2-2:** Lecture, or let a discussion run, for ten minutes. Let students talk with a partner for two minutes about each other's notes. Then, provide another two minutes for students to reflect on the information, revise their notes, and write down questions they have. Save time at the end of class to answer their questions.

- **"Wait, wait, hold on!":** Teach students to leave blanks in their notes rather than ask you to slow down if they didn't quite catch something that you said. This technique builds in time for them to make sure they have all the information while allowing you to keep class flowing. Monitor, perhaps by walking around, whether students are leaving too many blanks, indicating you really are setting too fast a pace!

- **Think-aloud note-taking:** Display a text page or have students read text aloud as you take notes. Explain your choices.

- **Pay-attention-to (PAT) list:** Post at the front of the room a PAT list before students read or watch a film. Such a list might include statements such as, "Pay attention to the attitudes of the four adults," "Pay attention to the explanations given by the three climatologists," or "Make sure you note the information on sterilizing lab tools."

- **Word bank:** Post at the front of the room a list of key words a lesson will involve. You might preview a few meanings without going into a full vocabulary study. Students can then refer to this list as they are taking notes, or raising questions, so that they use correct terms.

Teach Digital Note-Taking Skills

To further students' note-taking skills in a digital age, it's also vital to understand the differences in how the human brain processes print and digital text. In *Reader, Come Home: The Reading Brain in a Digital World*, researcher Maryanne Wolf (2018) chronicles research on the importance of understanding this difference in order to guard the crucial ability to engage in deep reading and critical thinking. Of particular note for educators is the fact that everyone tends to process digital texts—online information and ebooks—in the same way they watch films. Humans are used to not being able to turn back the pages when watching movies; our brains seem to think the same is true when reading digital texts. Thus we read on screens in the moment, just like we watch movies. This means people don't sequence the events as well as when reading a printed text, they absorb fewer details, and they don't tend to take notes. With digital texts, we seem to use a Z pattern of reading, skimming rather than reading every line. This *doesn't* mean that students shouldn't read digital texts; it means that everyone needs different strategies for electronic texts. Here are some suggestions.

- **Carefully explore app features:** Most ebook apps and platforms include various tools for note-taking, such as highlight text; make notes with a stylus, finger, or keyboard; and use a feature that collapses the document into just those highlighted and annotated lines for future, quick reference. But students need to know *how* to use these tools effectively. Research already shows that simply highlighting content doesn't accelerate learning (Corwin Visible Learning+, n.d.a). Students often need guidance in understanding what they should highlight and how they can effectively review highlighted texts. Popular e-readers include features for taking notes on why something is important, why you agree or disagree, the questions you have, and so on. Model using these features as well as exporting your notes and using them for study sessions.

- **Emphasize sequencing:** Students often struggle with sequencing events even when reading print materials. Introduce using concept maps for sequencing when students are reading digital texts.

- **Slow down details:** In literature, point out rich, detailed descriptions. Have students close their eyes and imagine the scene or the person or the events unfolding. This is also a differentiation strategy to increase reading comprehension; experienced readers do this naturally while struggling readers, focused on decoding, aren't aware of this enriching skill and need scaffolding and practice.

- **Emphasize empathy:** Wolf (2018) calls attention to startling evidence of a 40 percent decline in teen empathy in the early 21st century, highlighting the need for social-emotional learning. Reading fiction about the lives and experiences of people from different backgrounds has been shown to increase empathy and understanding. Wolf (2018) summarizes research on how the brain regions connected with empathy activate during reading about dramatic events.

  As students read ebooks, interrupt the skimming pattern with exercises in deep reflection on how texts make them *feel*. Have students step into the shoes of characters and keep a journal as they read, write fictional letters to and from someone in the culture they are learning about, or otherwise go beyond the text in order to vicariously experience another's experience.

Standardize Concept Maps *and* Give Choices

Explicitly teach students how to use several concept maps. Use your favorites for all-class discussions. When students work in small groups, require the use of the same map if it will simplify the debriefing process. However, once students understand the uses of different concept maps, offer one or two as *suggestions*, but allow the groups to use any note-taking approach that works. A small percentage of your students—especially vision-and-interpretation students—*hate* being told what to do, even if you truly know what is best. Let them learn through creativity and through trial and error what works for different tasks.

Common Concerns About Concept Maps

The following statements represent common concerns I hear from educators as they consider using concept maps. Beside each statement, you'll find text on how you might address any resistance you encounter (by yourself or with colleagues) because of such concerns.

- **"Filling in the blank is efficient, and many of my students want it."**
  When teachers allow this approach, it may be easier for everyone involved, but teachers aren't teaching students to think. Concept mapping is actually an equity strategy, addressing many problems. By using concept mapping and fostering high-level thinking, you're helping students of all cognitive processing styles.

  - Concept mapping helps students most comfortable with structure and certainty or experience and movement do the following: work comfortably with higher-level thinking skills where the answers can't be easily found in the book or their notes, work with processes and applications rather than focus only on getting the right answer, *and* engage with materials beyond the goal of getting a good grade or checking off a standard.

- ‣ Concept mapping helps students most comfortable with vision and interpretation or question and connection learn to do the following: focus on classwork that requires memorizing, work with specific information, or follow specific structures (for example, persuasive writing assignments or science projects) *and* use heuristics to improve their mapping skills, no matter their initial skill level. (Allowing choices provides the autonomy and uniqueness these students crave.)

- ‣ Concept mapping also helps students with learning disabilities. Explicitly teach these students how to do the following: color-code their maps to highlight key ideas or make connections *and* arrange information to more easily show connections and other insights.

An excellent resource for exploring how to use concept maps is the article "Color-Coded Graphic Organizers for Teaching Writing to Students With Learning Disabilities" by Kathy B. Ewoldt and Joseph John Morgan (2017).

- **"Students just want study guides."** If students just need to memorize information for a test, this is fine. If you want them to forge connections, synthesize information across the curriculum, understand real-world implications, and transfer the knowledge to long-term memory, teaching concept mapping equips them with a lifetime tool for deep thinking.

- **"Some students hate conforming."** As established in the Four Big Success Essentials section (page 168), if you tell most students, "Engage with creating this kind of map this once. I'd like you to experience the way in which it supports thinking. Know, though, that you'll be able to choose how to map in the future for most assignments," the certainty that they won't always have to do as they're told with these often creates buy-in for trying each map.

- **"My students are so disorganized they'll lose their maps."** Keep it simple. You might provide student folders and keep them in the classroom. Or, have students keep just one spiral notebook into which they staple loose handouts and freeform maps. I used to keep my notes in a two-pocket folder, with both lined and copy paper on the right, and completed papers on the left, numbered and in order.

Why Concept Maps Work

You'll note I've already cited much of the research supporting this chapter's strategies along the way, including how human brains are hardwired to process visual images. Hattie finds that using concept mapping in all content areas has an effect size of 0.64 (Corwin Visible Learning+, n.d.a). David Hyerle's Thinking Maps support students as they develop specific cognitive skills, such as comparing and contrasting, organizing information, arguing logically, forming analogies, and so on (Hyerle & Alper, 2011).

Concept mapping allows intuitive students (vision and interpretation, and question and connection) to play with connections and a task's big ideas. And they provide sensing students (structure and certainty, and experience and movement) with the strategies they need to use the intuitive preference. Further, this approach avoids teaching exclusively right-answer thinking, which Hammond (2015) explains can stunt brain development:

> The brain's main purpose is to get smarter at surviving and thriving in life. Brain growth is stimulated when we have to figure out something new, engage in a complex task, or complete a puzzle. The brain's response is to literally grow more capacity in the form of neurons, dendrites, and synapses, topping it all off with a thick coat of myelin to increase speed. When we look at the educational experiences of many groups marginalized by race, language, or socioeconomics, we see that they often get a "watered down" curriculum that doesn't require higher order thinking. Consequently, they don't build the capacity to do higher order thinking on their own. (p. 49)

The effectiveness of concept maps is solidly grounded in research. And, you can use different maps to better engage students in capturing information and ideas, making connections, reviewing information, and more—all crucial tasks for learning. In short, concept maps are worth the effort of helping students learn to use them.

Reflection Activity

Consider the following actions and questions as you reflect on this chapter's content.

1. Try taking notes during professional development or as you read books or articles, using some of the concept maps in this chapter. Which concept maps do you find useful? Which will help your students organize their thoughts or capture classroom learning?

2. Which of the concept maps in this chapter is least appealing to you? Most appealing? Compare your choices with those of your colleagues. Probe whether your preferences reflect your own styles, or concerns about how students will use them, or uncertainties about whether they will fit your purpose, and so on. Are there any ways in which your own biases, or unfamiliarity with a strategy, might be keeping you from trying a concept map strategy that might just help some of your students thrive?

3. Search the web for other graphic organizers that might work well with the content you teach—the possibilities are just about endless. Before using them with students, make sure you consider the following.

    ‣ Identify the thinking skill that the graphic organizer fosters (comparing and contrasting, sequencing, and so on).

    ‣ Explore whether students can both hand-draw with the graphic organizer and work with it digitally so that you know the options.

‣ Think hard before handing out templates. A graphic organizer template's spacing might limit students' thinking and might also plant the idea that they can't use this particular kind of map unless they have the form. Note that your "let me know what to do" and "let me do something" students often crave templates. Explain with an example how templates don't fit all circumstances. For example, show a tree map without enough branches for the topic. How else can you gain buy-in to help these students create their own maps from scratch while at the same time helping the "let me follow my own lead" and "let me lead as I learn" students learn that using some standard maps can be really helpful?

CHAPTER 11

Big Notes

A team of sixth-grade teachers I worked with decided to help their students understand their cognitive processing styles so they'd have a common language around learning strengths and stretches. To close the unit on the cognitive processes, all 130 students joined the five teachers and me in the school library for a Forced Choice planned movement exercise (page 203). The teachers and I organized students into sixteen groups. Each group then answered, "What would make your style the final survivor? What might get you voted off the island?" At this point, you might wonder how we managed to keep groups on task with this sort of assignment. We did it using big notes. Each group gathered around a piece of chart paper so all could easily see and contribute to what was being written, and teachers could see with a glance whether each group was providing quality responses.

Big notes are literally big notes; students record notes or ideas in a large, easy-to-read format. They help students work in groups by facilitating collaboration (everyone can see what the group decides or tries) and keeping the group members focused on reasoning together rather than trying strategies on their own or forming their own opinions on individual papers or devices. Note that they accommodate the needs of students with the various cognitive processes in the following ways.

- Structure-and-certainty students appreciate how big notes provide a clear path for group work. This helps them stretch when engaged with question-and-connection processes—the style opposite their own—such as small-group discussions involving open questions.

- Experience-and-movement students benefit when a big notes strategy lets them stand and write at a whiteboard or when manipulatives are involved.

- Vision-and-interpretation students benefit because this format often keeps them from getting lost in their own thoughts about the assignment. They can see what the group is seeing, more easily make connections, and then contribute ideas.

> ### Big Notes Strategies
> *(From quickest to deepest)*
>
> ✓ Chart Paper, page 176
> ✓ Group Whiteboards, page 177
> ✓ Laminated Tools, page 178
> ✓ Big Manipulatives, page 178
> ✓ Moveable Concept Maps, page 179
> ✓ Hint Cards, page 179
> ✓ Visual Representations for Group Summaries, page 180

- Question-and-connection students generally enjoy the collaborative discussions involved in big notes. Sometimes, these "let me lead as I learn" students find that big notes help them listen better as they debate or drive toward group consensus.

Big notes also help teachers by making it easier for them to monitor group progress, facilitate in-the-moment scaffolds based on group progress, and provide immediate feedback, which is time-consuming as well as potentially disruptive without using big notes.

Big notes allow for simultaneous implementation of several strategies that accelerate student learning, such as open questions (chapter 9, page 137) and Group Work That Works (page 110). If you ever attend one of my workshops, you'll find me employing big notes with adults for many of the student and teacher benefits I outline in this chapter introduction.

In this chapter, you'll find several strategies for using big notes in your classroom, essentials so that the strategies foster good collaboration and listening, and responses to common concerns about using them. Note that almost all the big notes strategies work at all grade levels. If you prefer to review the research first, skip to Why Big Notes Work (page 183) to gain an understanding of the research underpinning these strategies.

DOING DIFFERENTIATION

Use big notes at your next team meeting. You might select a concept map (chapter 10, page 159) and have one person use it to record notes on a whiteboard that everyone can see. Or, if just two or three people are present, put markers in everyone's hands; each person adds to the group notes as they add ideas to the conversation. Alternatively, take notes in an electronic document but project them on a screen for all to see. Afterward, discuss whether sharing the same big notes helps with engagement, collaboration, listening, building on each other's ideas, making connections among thoughts, or other areas that improve group processes.

The Big Notes Strategies

This section presents seven strategies for using big notes for small-group or all-class tasks: (1) Chart Paper, (2) Group Whiteboards, (3) Laminated Tools, (4) Big Manipulatives, (5) Moveable Concept Maps, (6) Hint Cards, and (7) Visual Representations for Group Summaries. Each of these strategies is designed to foster better collaboration, ensure that each student understands group thought processes or approaches to a task, or facilitate student-centered discussion.

Chart Paper

Providing groups with a large piece of chart paper lets them literally take big notes. Every group member can see the group output—and so can the teacher—whether they are recording how they solved a mathematics problem, brainstorming ideas for a research project, comparing and contrasting two fictional characters with a graphic organizer (page 162), and more. Some educators are surprised when I pass out chart paper while facilitating a workshop, even suggesting this is a Luddite strategy. Then, they realize how focused it keeps their group, especially during the afternoon doldrums, and they understand why they might use it with students.

To use this strategy, purchase the cheapest newsprint pads you can find. For many purposes, a half sheet is enough. Often, students can use both sides. For example, the scented markers I use don't bleed through, and they come in a washable formula. During instruction, provide criteria (questions you want students to answer, suggested concept map format, worked example, and so on) that clarify the information you expect to see groups record. Often, thinking through how you'll summarize or debrief the activity helps in deciding what should be on the charts. Emphasize that the sheet of chart paper is a shared workspace; work is recorded when group members agree to it.

Students who prefer the structure-and-certainty cognitive process will appreciate the clarity and focus chart paper can bring to group tasks, and experience-and-movement students enjoy the bigger writing surface (and may even prefer to write with the paper posted to a wall so they can stand). Vision-and-interpretation students will experience a bit of stretch in explaining their ideas to be included in the group process, and question-and-connection students will enjoy the collaboration.

Group Whiteboards

Are your classroom whiteboards serving as bulletin boards or only as projector screens for static information? While whiteboards are useful for these purposes, they're also great big notes surfaces. Whiteboards, which help you save on paper costs, lend themselves to easy revision via dry-erase markers. Students can code information with different marker colors and draw connections or easily squeeze in new thoughts.

To use whiteboards as big notes, allocate whiteboard space to each student group. If there isn't enough space for all student groups, look into whether your collaborative team members or other colleagues might be able to share whiteboard easels or a two-sided rolling whiteboard. These can be as valuable as any other technology purchase—and they may be more durable and less likely to become obsolete. Also, consider whether there's a way you can use chalkboard paint or wallpaper and chalk markers. Can you cover the side of a file cabinet, a closet door, or some other surface? Include possibilities for horizontal surfaces too. For many tasks, a fourteen- by seventeen-inch whiteboard is big enough for a small group.

Whiteboards usually allow students to stand, to the delight of experience-and-movement and question-and-connection students. When coupled with teacher direction or group consensus on a concept map (chapter 10, page 159) or note-taking format, they lend structure for structure-and-certainty students and a focal point for vision-and-interpretation students.

Laminated Tools

If your initial reaction to using chart paper is, "I don't want to waste paper," lamination may be your first answer. Laminating the tools students will use makes them reusable and also allows students to revise their work. You can use laminated tools, including chart paper and graph paper, again and again. Also, note that lamination products are increasingly eco-friendly (visit https://lam-on.com for an example). Consider laminating a standard outline for literature circle reporting, the scientific method, or the five Ws and H (who, what, when, where, why, and how) of news reporting, all big enough for groups to use.

Groups can use sets of blank laminated copy paper or large strips of paper (chart paper cut into four or five pieces) in infinite ways. They might individually brainstorm ideas on the strips and then compare and synthesize their ideas. See Moveable Concept Maps (page 179) for more ideas. You might also laminate templates of a few graphic organizers, such as four corners (page 162), so that groups can quickly engage in a comparison task. Note that you can also use document sleeves and plastic folders for this purpose, which are more durable. Consider placing several graphic organizer templates inside a document sleeve, one sleeve per group. Then, students can pull the relevant map for a given activity to the top.

The big draws for lamination are reuse and flexibility with student thinking. Students are more likely to revise their thoughts if erasing is easy, and reading what they've written will be easier for you without cross-outs and erasure smears.

Big Manipulatives

Big manipulatives take familiar tools students use to work with concepts and make them big enough for a group to use together. Some standard manipulatives meant for individuals are fine for groups; fraction tiles, counters, chips, and card sets are usually easy for everyone in a group of four or five to see. However, consider fraction circles (circle-shaped manipulatives that break into multiple pie wedges to illustrate fractions). With a set intended for individual use, the size difference between the pieces showing $\frac{1}{8}$ and $\frac{1}{12}$ may not be distinct enough for all group members to grasp concepts. You may need to make a bigger cardstock or laminated set with larger diameters and laminate the pieces.

Think of big manipulatives as an easy way to increase student engagement in group work, our E in STEAM². If you wish to have students collaborate as they think about higher-level-thinking tasks, they all have to be able to see the thinking revealed in the manipulatives the group is using. All students benefit from this approach, but experience-and-movement students probably experience the biggest engagement boost while modeling their thinking by manipulating objects that help make abstract ideas concrete. For an additional boost for these students, glue magnets on the back so students can use the manipulatives at a standing whiteboard, and watch their engagement rise.

Moveable Concept Maps

Many concept maps (chapter 10, page 159) work well as big notes to facilitate high-level conversations. For this strategy, turn the maps into moveable big notes. For example, students might each write information, ideas, or questions on large strips of paper, on individual whiteboards, or even on their tablet devices. Student groups can then organize the ideas by theme or category into a tree map (see Thinking Maps, page 160). They might also collaborate on the design of a science experiment, writing each step on a separate card and constructing an easily adjustable flow map. Not only does this allow student groups to improve the categories they are working with or rethink the most important ideas, but it reinforces revision as a key part of the thinking process.

By implementing concept maps as moveable big notes, the notes also help facilitate all-class discussions that allow for reflection and interaction. See All-Class Brainstorming (page 196) for an example of how to involve students in setting success criteria using big notes. Or, think about how students might reflect on ideas to add to a group concept map. Provide every student with a laminated, magnetized oval paper—perhaps twelve inches long. Write a term, a concept to review, or another topic in the middle of your main whiteboard. Have students write down their own idea on their paper. Appoint a couple of students as map organizers. As students bring up their individual ideas, the organizers help with grouping similar ideas.

Moveable concept maps reinforce agility, the A in STEAM^2, by making it easy for students to revise their thinking through adding, subtracting, connecting, or rearranging ideas. If you recall from chapter 6 (page 87), pressure-prompted students often want to stay open and resist locking down on an idea or structure. Moveable organizers facilitate their style. Also, structure-and-certainty and vision-and-interpretation students, who may be more likely to want to move toward completing their first idea, can more easily stretch by changing their minds when a moveable map makes doing so painless.

Hint Cards

Remember from Why Open Questions Work (page 155) that only about 20 percent of cognitively demanding tasks are implemented at a high level? Stein and colleagues (2009) identify one of the major errors teachers make is focusing on whether student work is right or wrong. Tap into the content in Use Roaming Strategies (page 153) as a way to ensure the prompts you give let students determine for themselves whether they are on a good path. One of the advantages of big notes is that you can quickly see student thinking and then apply the right roaming strategy. One way to do this is to prepare cards with the hints you've preplanned.

Carol Ann Tomlinson and Marcia B. Imbeau (2010) suggest preparing hint cards in advance by thinking through common student thinking errors, how you might enrich a task, ways to help students think more deeply, or how you will ensure everyone is engaged. This strategy deepens big notes for teachers as well as for students. Picture being able to walk up to a group, review its big notes, and simply hand over a card with one or two questions or hints that will help the group members redirect their thinking without discussing what is correct or incorrect. The Hint Cards strategy allows you to give immediate feedback without allowing students to default to right-answer thinking. You might also have cards that enrich the task. For example, if one group quickly finishes comparing and contrasting two historical events, add a twist. Perhaps a card asks them to each discuss one of the events from the viewpoint of a different person involved. What would be their main concerns? What would you want to ask them? Preplanning lets you extend their thinking, keeping them engaged while other students finish.

Note that besides the benefit of leaving thinking in the hands of students, structure-and-certainty students will appreciate the clear direction hint cards provide while their opposites, question-and-connection students, will benefit from the autonomy of not being told exactly what to do.

Visual Representations for Group Summaries

Instead of limiting summaries to words, visual representations add pictures. When students have engaged in deep reading of complex texts, this strategy is perfect for ensuring they understand the big ideas and remember the important facts (Gillies et al., 2015). To demonstrate this technique with teachers, I often use the essay I mentioned in chapter 8's Doing Differentiation (page 120), "Has Success Spoiled the Crow?" (Quammen, 1985/2008), which you can find online by searching for the article's title and author. The article combines humor with intriguing information, and there are plenty of ideas to illustrate.

In the classroom, students mark the passages they believe to be important. Then, in groups of four to six, they use only pictures to capture the most important concepts on a poster. The teacher then does a poster walk. Figure 11.1 shows an example of a teacher-created poster.

Figure 11.1: Sample visual representation for group summary.

Thinking about the implications for the classroom, the teachers made the following observations.

- Students can easily see, via consistency among the posters, the big ideas they need to remember.

- If one group's members miss something important, they'll see it on another poster.

- The teacher can ask students to point out similarities and differences as a way to summarize the material.

Having to think visually keeps students from skimming over ideas. They have to work awhile to come up with some of the facts in the article. In the example from figure 11.1, students had to consider how to illustrate the mortality rate of fledglings, the fact that crows mate for life, and activities they engage in. One group concluded, "What about a recognizable drawing of crows playing a game with rocks that they drop on the fly to each other—think quidditch!"

Set norms, such as stick figures being artistic enough for this purpose, how students can use color to add meaning, and that an occasional use of words is OK. You'll find that there is enough structure for students who need it, while those who need room to roam, such as vision-and-interpretation students, will come up with some amazing representations that engage everyone.

Five Big Success Essentials

Big notes facilitate better student collaboration and allow teachers to monitor group progress and work quality. However, there are five organizing principles that ensure big notes work as you intended. What follows are lessons learned and summaries of how to make big notes work, from teachers who have successfully used them.

Ensure Everyone Can See

This includes you. Model, and then insist, that students print large enough so that their work is visible from at least six feet away. This allows you to conduct poster walks as well as quickly assess a group's progress and process.

VIRTUAL CLASSROOMS

Visibility becomes even more important for small groups working together online, as some may be accessing the internet on small mobile devices. Think creatively; for example, if one student's feed can focus on a whiteboard or window where he or she is taking group notes, the print may be large enough for all to see. A virtual whiteboard, using larger fonts, may work as well. When students share documents, set a norm of using a bigger font size and checking whether everyone can read the common big note.

Everyone Must Be Able to Explain

Set the expectation that when you walk up to a group (or visit a virtual breakout room), any member of the group needs to be able to explain the group's work. If someone is unable to answer a question, you'll be back in a couple of minutes to ask again. This ensures that even if one person is doing more of the thinking, everyone in the group grasps the strategies and conclusions.

Know What You're Looking For

As you observe big notes, it's important to know what you're looking for (see Use Roaming Strategies, page 153). For example, know how you'll redirect a literature circle that isn't delving deeply enough into character motivation or how you'll prompt science lab partners to reconsider whether their measurement method is accurate enough without telling them how to fix it. Know the text page you might refer a group to if it's stuck or the generic prompts that might apply, such as, "Have you tried using the textbook index to find information that might get you unstuck?" Planning in advance lets you redirect students without giving away the answers.

Make Big Notes Meaningful

Big notes are for high-level group tasks where students benefit from considering multiple approaches, organizing their reasoning and justification, and employing skills such as problem solving, logical analysis, evaluation, or creation. If students are working together to create study notes, though, using a shared Google Document or sharing thoughts via a reciprocal teaching activity might be better.

Know How You Will Summarize

Know your plan to summarize students' group work when the exercise is complete. Will every group share its work? Will you post all the big notes so students can view them via a poster walk before you lead a debriefing discussion, asking what they note? Will they look for similarities and differences, strategies their own group didn't think of, key takeaways, and so on? Having a plan for summarizing students' learning allows you to organize for the lesson summary as you monitor the groups.

Common Concerns About Big Notes

The following statements represent common concerns I hear from educators as they consider using big notes strategies. Beside each statement, you'll find text on how you might address any resistance you encounter (by yourself or with colleagues) because of such concerns.

- **"My students will mess with the supplies rather than work."** You'll be able to catch if students are off task much more quickly when they're using big notes than when they're sharing a tablet device. More important, you can use the gradual release of responsibility model (Fisher & Frey, 2014;

Mooney, 1988) to initiate a hands-on, directed experience with big notes and gradually provide student groups with increasing autonomy as they learn to complete big notes themselves. To use this model, follow these steps.

    a. *I do*—Model use of the big notes process, demonstrating how you listen to students for agreement before recording work or rearranging concept map pieces.

    b. *We do*—Take student groups through a big notes process step by step. Perhaps they don't get into their groups until they've done the individual portions. Perhaps the first time, you group them so that the students who might go off task are closest to you. Perhaps you gather students' markers as soon as the students have written the individual portion. The goal is to help them experience the delight of being able to stand, wiggle, or talk while they work on a task together, with the support they need to succeed.

    c. *You do*—Set the groups free as they show they can handle the responsibility.

- **"But we have no budget for materials."** Ask to use part of a professional development meeting to explore how you might get supplies. Who might make a scouting run to a used office supply store? What business might donate old plastic folders to make moveable concept map pieces? Does the local hardware store or builder have anything that might be turned into whiteboards? One teacher I worked with found a lumberyard willing to slice up an acrylic-coated shower stall a builder had removed during a home remodeling project. This resulted in whiteboards and an illustration for students about the idea of reduce, reuse, and recycle.

  Also, discuss what materials teacher teams and colleagues can share among classrooms. Take time to search through school storage closets; it's amazing how often forgotten supplies can be repurposed.

- **"Our rooms are set up for students to share technology."** If a group can use technology in a way that satisfies the five big success essentials from this chapter, great—use it! Otherwise, carefully determine when students' digital devices will or won't be as effective as big notes in promoting high-level discussions, allowing you to monitor progress and provide feedback, and facilitating summary discussions.

Why Big Notes Work

Big notes let you walk up to a group of students and accomplish the following.

- Know exactly where the students are in a task, allowing you to extend or shorten the time you've allocated for the task. Allocating appropriate time is crucial for maintaining rigor in high-level tasks (Stein et al., 2009).

- See how the students are thinking about a task and quickly provide the right amount of support. You can then provide targeted feedback and improve task clarity—teaching moves with effect sizes of 0.64 and 0.76, respectively (Corwin Visible Learning+, n.d.a).

- Provide an extension or ask a question that deepens how the students are thinking about the project. Ensuring that students have appropriately challenging goals has an effect size of 0.59 (Corwin Visible Learning+, n.d.a).

- Decide whether having a group immediately share its approach might foster better thinking in the other groups. The group may have an exemplary approach or a crucial element for maintaining rigor (Stein et al., 2009). Or, its work may reflect a common misunderstanding. If you've established that mistakes are learning opportunities for everyone, you might have the class work together to locate the misunderstanding (see Mistake Modeling, page 105).

Big notes strategies also increase participation, as all students can see what the group is deciding, ensuring all understand the content the big notes contain. They also increase focus, especially since you can easily redirect a group by reviewing its workspace at a glance. Table 11.1 captures how big notes strategies help students of each cognitive processing style.

Table 11.1: How Big Notes Differentiate for Cognitive Processing Styles

Structure and Certainty	Vision and Interpretation
<ul><li>Directions for group workspaces are clear.</li><li>Students receive quick feedback as they work, meeting their need to not waste time on dead ends.</li><li>Students gain practice in tasks that do not involve a specific process or a clear right answer, increasing their ability to be comfortable with ambiguous tasks.</li></ul>	<ul><li>Group processes allow for individual thinking before the group commits to recording work in the shared workspace.</li><li>Students gain experience with effective processes through standardized big notes, yet for many applications, students can receive some flexibility in how they organize the big notes.</li><li>Groups can tackle higher-level tasks with multiple approaches, which these students enjoy.</li></ul>
Experience and Movement	**Question and Connection**
<ul><li>Big notes easily lend themselves to movement and interaction, keeping these students energized for learning.</li><li>Many of these students learn best when something is happening in the real world, including physically moving things to show connections, sequences, and more.</li><li>Students can shift more easily between concrete representations—their natural environment for problem solving—and abstract ideas.</li></ul>	<ul><li>Students get to learn through the kinds of high-level discussions that big notes facilitate.</li><li>Big notes make it easier for a teacher to guide these students in collaborating rather than leading the group.</li><li>Big notes allow students to move and interact while engaging in higher-level tasks with multiple approaches that they enjoy.</li></ul>

Reflection Activity

Consider the following actions and questions as you reflect on this chapter's content.

1. Facilitate a collaborative team activity with big notes. Sit in a semicircle around a whiteboard or a flip chart stand. Or, try this: Individually, read the essay "Has Success Spoiled the Crow?" (Quammen, 1985/2008). Use the Last Word protocol (page 69) for team discussion. Then, use Visual Representations for Group Summaries (page 180). Discuss how your team might use the strategies with students.

2. Here are potential results from using big notes in your classroom. Reflect on which might be most significant to the success of your students. Which big notes strategy might be easiest for you to implement to work toward these results?

   ‣ Knowing exactly where students are in a task, allowing you to extend or shorten the time you've allocated for the task

   ‣ Seeing how students are thinking about a task, and quickly providing the right kind of and amount of support

   ‣ Deciding whether having a group immediately share its approach might foster better thinking in the other groups

   ‣ Providing planned movement and interaction to decrease off-task behaviors during tasks that require sitting still

3. With your collaborative team, create a four corners chart (see Graphic Organizers, page 162) on large-format chart paper to discuss possibilities for using big notes with students. Figure 11.2 shows an example.

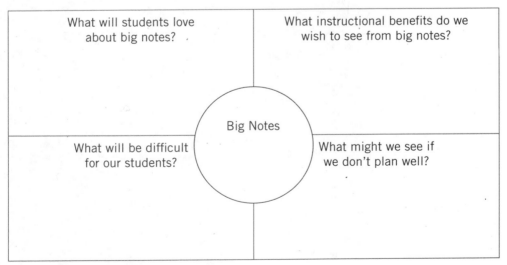

Figure 11.2: A four corners chart on big notes.
*Visit **go.SolutionTree.com/instruction** for a free reproducible version of this figure.*

CHAPTER 12

Moveable Organizers

In 2008, a team at a middle school where I provided ongoing professional development asked for strategies to help students complete and improve the quality of major assignments—science fair projects, reports, presentations, and so on. Notice that each of these requires background research. I demonstrated to the team an organizing system that used note cards placed inside envelopes with numbers labeled on them. The envelopes were then stapled inside a folder (see figure 12.1), and students crossed off a number each time they placed a completed card in an envelope, marking the progress they were making.

Figure 12.1: Envelopes for organizing segmented notes.

During this demonstration, a teacher who prefers the question-and-connection cognitive process mumbled, "Who would want to do this? And worse, I'll get 120 identical reports. I'll fall asleep grading them."

One of his teammates, who prefers the experience-and-movement cognitive process, actually leaped to her feet and jumped up and down with each phrase as she said: "I. Would want. To make. Those check marks. Wonderful!"

"Really?" said the first teacher. "I guess I'll try it, then, but I don't see how it'll keep students more organized. They'll just lose the cards."

A week later, he reported, "So many of my students are hugging those folders as if they're life preservers. They know if they check off each number, they'll be done. Better yet, they're on track to finish the reports." He also commented on how his own preferred ways of learning had almost kept him from trying the strategy. "I would have resisted as a student, but you know? Several of my question-and-connection students are the happiest with the folders. They see the path to success, and they're willing to give up a bit of the autonomy they usually fight for." We chatted about how the folders provide a roadmap for structure-and-certainty students and perhaps serve as guardrails for the students more like him. Moveable organizers meet the needs of different learners in different ways.

> **Moveable Organizer Strategies**
> *(From quickest to deepest)*
> - ✓ Segmented Notes, page 189
> - ✓ Personal Manipulatives, page 191
> - ✓ Story Aids, page 191
> - ✓ Card Sorts, page 192
> - ✓ Concept Map Manipulatives, page 193
> - ✓ Moveable Outlines, page 193
> - ✓ All-Class Brainstorming, page 196

Moveable organizers are simply ways of organizing thoughts, information, or work in progress that involve moveable pieces. Cards, pieces of paper, manipulatives—all kinds of tools can be made moveable. The reason this strategy is popular with students is that human brains can only handle so much information at a time. Strategies that use moveable organizers differentiate learning by expanding the working memory of all students, and greater working memory capacity is tied to better academic outcomes (Audusseau & Juhel, 2015; Schulze, Lüke, & Kuhl, 2020). Using cards, manipulatives, and other moveable organizers spread out on a flat surface, such as a table or board, decreases a task's cognitive load by letting students process information externally, freeing up working memory. The table or board becomes a brain extension, a canvas for students to express their thinking in an external and physical form, so students can devote more internal working memory to applying concepts. In this way, moveable organizers are concrete, real-time aids that expand working memory.

I've grouped together this chapter's strategies because they let students physically manipulate ideas in ways that reflect the nonlinear nature of creativity and higher-level thinking. These strategies often strike some adults as being more time-consuming than they're worth or even as fostering lower-level thinking. If you happen to prefer the vision-and-interpretation style, you might even be thinking, *I do this kind of thinking in my head.* Although *you* may not need any of these, some students do. After learning about the strategies, you'll also find two big essentials for using them successfully and answers to some common concerns teachers have about using them. If you want to start by reading about the research that underpins these strategies, see Why Moveable Organizers Work (page 199).

DOING DIFFERENTIATION

Many schools still have blank overhead sheets, plastic folders, or page protectors stashed in closets. Cut one or two into notecard-size pieces. Try writing items for your to-do list, one to a card. Or, use them to brainstorm potential enduring understandings for a unit, essential questions for that unit, or information chunks from a web search for an upcoming lesson. What is it like to organize and reorganize mobile pieces rather than trying to either compose content in a useful order or revise a document? Note that you can use cardstock as well for this process, but the plastic pieces allow you to revise and reuse with dry-erase fine-tip markers.

The Moveable Organizer Strategies

This section presents seven strategies for using moveable organizers: (1) Segmented Notes, (2) Personal Manipulatives, (3) Story Aids, (4) Card Sorts, (5) Concept Map Manipulatives, (6) Moveable Outlines, and (7) All-Class Brainstorming. As explained further in Why Moveable Organizers Work, each of these strategies is designed to expand student working memory, encourage revision, and take advantage of how visual representations in addition to oral and verbal content increase learning.

Segmented Notes

For segmented notes, students write chunks of information or ideas on separate cards, strips of paper, or other moveable surfaces so that they can easily reorder, insert, or delete chunks as they progress on a task. This strategy, which you saw an example of to start off this chapter, addresses two needs: (1) helping students stay organized and (2) helping students optimally organize information. For elementary school students, introduce it through the following steps. For middle and high school students who still struggle with gathering and organizing information, show them the strategy, provide the reasoning behind it, and ask them what parts of it might work for them and how they might modify it.

1. Students identify the topic they will research and the subtopics of most interest to them that will make up the body of their report. Some rather generic examples include the following.

    ‣ **Kenya:** History, governing philosophy, prominent citizens, wildlife conservation, geography

    ‣ **Mountain lions:** Habitat, diet, how pups are raised, family and pack structure and relationships, physiology

    ‣ **Maya Angelou:** Important life events, mentors, education, famous works, legacy

2. Students write each subtopic on the back of a separate envelope. Under the subtopic, they write the numbers *1, 2, 3, 4,* and *5*—or more, if they are

writing a longer report that requires more than five pieces of information per subtopic. They also label one more envelope *Sources* or *References*.

3. As students find information, they fill out a bibliography form for the source. Then, they write down the information on a piece of paper, name the source in the upper-left corner, place the paper in the appropriate envelope, and check off one of the numbers. Note that you may wish to create forms for students to fill out, both for writing the bibliography and for taking notes. The note-taking forms might be as simple as necessary to help students stay organized as they begin using this strategy. Figure 12.2 shows an example.

Figure 12.2: A note-card manipulative.

4. When students have gathered enough information, as indicated by having checked off the numbers on all the envelopes, they can work with the contents of each envelope separately, moving around the contents on a table to organize their thoughts. Then, they begin to write. They can place the sources in alphabetical order and add them to the report's reference section.

Ruby K. Payne (2013, 2019), author of *A Framework for Understanding Poverty*, and as previously illustrated in figure 12.1 (page 187), recommends stapling the outward-facing envelopes inside a manila folder—three letter-size envelopes fit easily on each side—so that the pieces of paper remain secure when the envelope flaps are tucked in.

You may be wondering, *Why not just have students take notes in separate sections of a digital file?* You'll find that your experience-and-movement learners especially appreciate this tactile approach to organizing information. And you'll find that all students who are still mastering report writing are more willing to consider the best order for presenting information if they can painlessly shift around the possibilities. Yes, high school students and experienced report writers of all ages might eventually shift to a digital format that encompasses some of this strategy's principles. Encourage them to create their own note-taking document that includes a way to ensure they capture their sources as they go.

Personal Manipulatives

Mathematics manipulatives are invaluable for helping students understand concepts. Fraction strips, counters, algebra tiles, and just about all other manipulatives are also mobile and can help students think. Here are two big ideas to convey to students about manipulatives.

1. **Manipulatives are for everyone:** Sometimes, both teachers and students compartmentalize the use of manipulatives as appropriate only for new concepts or for struggling students. If you have ever watched the television show *Numb3rs* (Heuton & Falacci, 2005), about a mathematician and his FBI agent brother, you've seen manipulatives in action. If you haven't, plenty of YouTube clips show the characters moving salt shakers about to explain escape-route probabilities, using balloons to explain surface tension, or pointing to how a sprinkler trajectory works to demonstrate how they can narrow down a criminal's location.

   Mathematicians use manipulatives to make abstract ideas concrete and easier to explain, but students can also explore ideas by playing with manipulatives, allowing them to extend their thinking about such concepts. This is especially true when students are working in groups because the visual representations make another student's reasoning easier to follow (Fernández & Yoshida, 2004).

2. **Manipulatives foster deep reasoning and justification:** Although this is true at all learning levels, this consideration is especially important if students are to go beyond calculation or recall to understanding and application of concepts. When using manipulatives becomes a norm, even the students who tend to declare, "I just know this is right and don't want to show my work," start to buy into the idea of using these tools to concretely express their abstract thoughts. They learn that sometimes a diagram is worth a thousand words.

This is another approach that benefits all learners. Experience-and-movement students actually think by touching, moving, and interacting with their environment. Structure-and-certainty students frequently have aha moments via manipulatives as they *see* how numbers relate to the reality of what the manipulatives show. Vision-and-interpretation and question-and-connection students benefit from learning to use manipulatives to explain their thinking; they have a concrete tool for forming a concrete explanation of where their answer came from.

Story Aids

Do you remember being in preschool and using one of those felt boards on which you can move around shapes and characters as you tell a story? Those boards and other story aids foster engagement, and there's a reason for that. Researchers Scott C. Marley and Zsuzsanna Szabo (2010) find that when students use manipulatives (as cued by the teacher) to act out what is happening in a story and then use their imaginations to recall the story, their comprehension and information retention are significantly greater than when students only listen to the story. These findings contain a mind-body connection that educators shouldn't ignore. When it comes to story aids, think simple—generic characters the students can create themselves out of wax craft sticks, or simple outlines of people and objects the students can cut out of card stock and keep for various stories.

Remember that your structure-and-certainty and experience-and-movement students gather information through their five senses; story aids add more visual information to the auditory story they hear so that two senses are now involved. One of my colleagues added aromas and textures to story time as well when she taught fifth grade, further engaging these students in ways that cemented knowledge of the story.

Card Sorts

Instead of using conventional worksheets, characterized by multiple questions with one right answer, make usable sets of cards or paper strips that provide practice in the concepts you are trying to teach. Here are some examples of ways to use this approach.

- **Sentence strips:** Type up the first paragraph or two of a story so that when you print off the document, you can cut each sentence into a separate strip of paper. Mix up the strips, and have a group of students use grammar clues to put the strips into the correct order. Make a rule that students cannot move a strip until they explain why they think it belongs in the spot to which they're moving it. Students have to apply what they know about verb tenses, possessives, pronouns, and other clues to get it right.

- **Information sorts:** Think of these as moveable matrices or matching tasks that students can use individually or collaboratively. Make card sets for students *or* have them create sets, perhaps with student groups each making sets with different information that the other groups will use in a jigsaw activity. Use the cards for any of the following purposes.

  ‣ *Knowledge*—Think of information students need to memorize regarding scientific elements, dates in history, mathematics facts, or other anchoring knowledge that enables automaticity for other tasks. For elements, picture rows of cards for the element name, symbol, number of electrons, fundamental state of matter, and so on. For dates, the rows might include the date, event, people involved, location, significance, and so on.

  ‣ *Patterning*—Use cards to help students recognize grammatical patterns and define a rule. For example, use the words *babies*, *candies*, *toys*, *boys*, and so on to help students begin to recognize how to form plurals for words ending with *y*. Or, have students sort families of mathematics facts (combinations of 10; equations that equal 5; mathematics triangles, such as $2 + 3$, $5 - 3$, and $5 - 2$; equations for which substituting simpler numbers facilitates easy mental mathematics; and so on).

▸ *Memorization*—Use cards as a manipulative students can use to memorize information. Flash cards fit in this category, as do sorting tasks for matching word definitions, dates and events, vocabulary, or other facts. Make things more fun via games, partner work, or planned movement (see chapter 13, page 201).

▸ *Sequencing*—Provide the events in a story on cards, and have students sort them into the right order. Or, have students work in groups to place each event significant to the storyline on a separate card. You'll find that they're more likely to add more events or change the sequence if they can insert cards and move them around instead of having to erase mistakes on paper.

All of these strategies use cards to extend student working memory, allowing students to work with patterns and concepts, thus increasing study time and enhancing long-term recall.

Concept Map Manipulatives

This approach separates the elements of a concept map into separate, moveable pieces so students can easily rearrange, change, or expand them. Remember from chapter 10 (page 159) that concept maps include hierarchical diagrams such as tree maps, graphic organizers, matrices, and more. Turning these into moveable organizers allows students to individually think and then collectively organize their thoughts. For example, students might work in a small group, with each person writing elements of a map on separate sticky notes. The group would then work to organize the information into a concept map. For success, look back at the suggestions for Group Work That Works (page 110).

All students benefit from how moveable concept maps facilitate collaboration, simplify revision, and allow for exploration of ideas. Experience-and-movement students often think best as they move and interact; even the simple act of rearranging sticky notes and then reviewing whether the new arrangement makes more sense can heighten their ability to analyze and synthesize.

Moveable Outlines

Instead of having students construct linear outlines in a document, moveable outlines capture the different topics and subtopics on separate cards or other tools they can sort and rearrange. You can also use this style to create a timeline of events in a story or period in history, allowing students to add more information or rearrange based on new thinking. They are useful in planning many forms of writing or for determining the steps in major projects. I often demonstrate their power in a lesson on writing personal narratives. You can adapt this approach for many forms of writing and use it across grade levels.

To get started, create a story yourself using the following process so that you have a great worked example to share as you explain the process to your students. You (and each student) will need at least five index cards. Or, cut copy paper into quarters, with each person receiving at least five quarters. Provide a paper clip, too, to hold the cards together in between writing sessions.

1. Choose a personal narrative topic. In workshops, I usually model this strategy with the prompt, "The first time I . . ." Choose something that you think you can turn into an interesting story.

2. On each of the cards (or strips), write a major event in the story, as shown in figure 12.3.

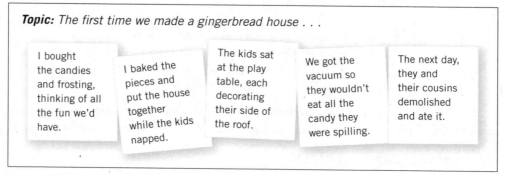

Topic: *The first time we made a gingerbread house . . .*

I bought the candies and frosting, thinking of all the fun we'd have.	I baked the pieces and put the house together while the kids napped.	The kids sat at the play table, each decorating their side of the roof.	We got the vacuum so they wouldn't eat all the candy they were spilling.	The next day, they and their cousins demolished and ate it.

Figure 12.3: *Cards for a mobile outline.*

3. Use the following cues to write some ideas on the cards about how you could expand your description of each event. The cards might each have three or four ideas.

   ‣ What did you think (thoughts) or feel (emotions)?

   This will be such fun, and we'll have a lovely table decoration for the family celebration tomorrow.

   ‣ What did you see? Hear? Taste? Touch? Smell?

   The aroma of spicy gingerbread. Crunches under my feet as I stepped on spilled sugars and chocolate candies. My fingers sticking in the roof icing, trying to apply it just as the kids needed it in a spot.

   ‣ What did you and others say?

   My husband as he took a video: "Hi, Mom. Tell us what's happening. . . . Are we all having fun?"

   ‣ What were you reminded of?

   My dad's tale of his men's club not being able to find the popcorn popper lid and deciding to pop the corn anyway to see how far it would fly . . .

4. Organize your ideas by labeling the cards as follows.

   ‣ Circle the ideas you brainstormed in step 3 that you think work the best.

   ‣ Put a *D* in the top-right corner of at least two cards—ones where you could write about events in dialogue form.

   ‣ Put an *S* on each card where you could describe the setting.

5. Add an introduction. Choose whether you will start with one of the following.

> ‣ *Dialogue—"Is today the day we make the gingerbread house, Mommy?"*

> ‣ *Startling statement—In less than twenty-four hours, we built a house and watched as it was completely destroyed.*

> ‣ *Setting description—There are a play table and two chairs in the middle of the kitchen; there is an unadorned gingerbread house at its center, surrounded by little bowls of peppermints, licorice, chocolate candies, pretzels, and other decorations.*

> ‣ *Emotion—I wasn't surprised when the first bowl of candy spilled. When the second one dumped on the floor, I started wishing I'd swept and scrubbed it thoroughly before we started. There was no way we could reuse that candy. When Dan's little elbow hit the third bowl, my husband turned on the video camera and asked, "Hi, Mom. How's the homebuilding?" I sound cheerful on that tape, but any close observer would notice my teeth were clenched.*

6. Rethink the cards. Do you have a good balance of the story elements? Do you need to describe more or fewer moments? Where might you insert something?

7. Write away!

Getting students to enrich their thinking means they will have less revision to do, whether it's connected to what they will write or the best way to create a project. Moveable outlines provide a structure for doing so because you are providing clear direction tied to success criteria (chapter 2, page 33) of the elements students can add, such as dialogue, sensory details, and so on. The flexible format motivates students to make changes before they write a first draft. Because students are deciding which events in a story will use dialogue or characterization, and so on, they'll move away from formulaic writing to making the piece their own. Further, vision-and-interpretation and question-and-connection students, who often have their big ideas in mind but struggle to include more specific details, will add those details from the start. Structure-and-certainty and experience-and-movement students who are good with detail will plan the flow of their story before they might accidentally bog down in description or in not knowing what to write about.

VIRTUAL CLASSROOMS

Note how easy adding this strategy is in a virtual environment. Students can engage using any paper they have. You can give an all-class instruction for a step in the process and use Think-Pair-Share by letting students brainstorm on their own, work in pairs in breakout rooms to try out their stories or sample dialogue, and so on and then come back together as a class to share.

All-Class Brainstorming

Moveable organizers help small groups, or the whole class, synthesize ideas after everyone has had a chance to reflect. Once again, the power is in their flexibility. Whereas summarizing student ideas on a whiteboard or electronic document adds a linear feel to the process, moveable organizers allow students to rearrange ideas as they emerge. Each student's idea can be added, moved, connected, or grouped with what is there. Adding wait time (chapter 4, page 63) by providing a couple of minutes for students to write their ideas on their own paper means that both introverts and extraverts will be included as the ideas come together. One example is using a moveable organizer to establish clear success criteria. These criteria enable students to monitor their own progress, which has an effect size of 0.88 (Corwin Visible Learning+, n.d.a).

Katie White (2019), author of *Unlocked: Assessment as the Key to Everyday Creativity in the Classroom*, urges teachers to involve students in setting success criteria for creative tasks:

> When teachers focus on inviting students to openly explore and pose questions, offering explicit goals and criteria at the outset might suppress students' intended progress during exploration.

> Even when the content is tied to prescribed learning goals and is non-negotiable, the processes by which students will explore this content will require *process* goals (for example, constructing a model that uses fractions, creating a three-dimensional representation of the water cycle, or engaging in a nature walk and photographing examples of patterns). (pp. 86–87)

All-Class Brainstorming with a moveable organizer can help students take this task seriously. Once students have spent time brainstorming their approach to an open question or another creative task, let them know they'll be helping you create a picture of what good work looks like on this particular task. Provide some prompts for each of them to reflect on.

- "What seems important to me in this task?"
- "What would a poor result look like?"
- "What would an excellent result look like?"
- "What would show that I've learned something through this task?"
- "Have I seen good examples of similar projects?"

White (2019) has additional ideas to prompt students to brainstorm success criteria.

As students propose ideas, ask them to capture their ideas on sheets of paper—scratch paper is fine, but ask them to write large enough for all to see. Have them use tape or magnets to affix their suggestions to the classroom whiteboard. The class can then look for categories and themes of the various criteria and use student-centered discussion techniques (chapter 7, page 101) to narrow down the possibilities. One or two students can be in charge of regrouping the papers as the class agrees on ideas. Alternatively, students might reflect individually, share in small groups, and then appoint a scribe to write their ideas on a classroom whiteboard—or in the chat feature in a virtual classroom.

Take advantage of students' different cognitive processes with this approach. While you might ask every student to contribute ideas, let experience-and-movement students be the runners, collecting and posting student work. Your question-and-connection students will be happy to help regroup and connect the various ideas. Don't be surprised if some of the more introverted students who are intrigued by a topic join in the movement, but this is primarily a strategy that lets extraverts use up some energy in a productive way that expands thinking for the whole class.

Two Big Success Essentials

Moveable organizers can engage students who prefer the experience-and-movement cognitive process, and increase student agility with explaining their thinking, the E and A in STEAM[2]. Yet, the tools need to match both task requirements and student needs to be effective. What follows are lessons learned and summaries of how to make moveable organizers work, from teachers who have successfully used them.

Choose Wisely

Manipulatives require teachers to make a lot of decisions. For example, should the paper strips students are working with be laminated so they can draft and then easily revise their ideas? Lamination is wonderful in a mathematics class, for example, when laminated graph paper frees students up to change the scales they've used to label a problem after they realize they're running out of space. As first mentioned in chapter 11 (page 175), note that several eco-friendly lamination products or reusable items, such as document sleeves, are available. Further, lamination saves paper in the long run.

The decisions continue. Have you thought about storage if future groups might use the same manipulatives? Consider color-coding, numbering, or changing the size or quality of the manipulatives to keep these tools organized. Is the font size big enough that students standing around a table can all read what is on the cards or strips? If not, a few students may take over the task. Does the tool you've chosen foster *metacognition*—students' thinking about their thinking? If a card sort is too easy, or if there's only one approach to a task that you've already taught, moveable organizers probably aren't a good use of time. Do students have sufficient fine motor skills to easily manipulate the tools you've chosen? As mentioned, I've seen fraction circles frustrate students who can't quite match up equivalent fraction pieces well enough to "see" the concepts.

Ultimately, you must ask the question, "Is it the best manipulative possible?" When Japanese teachers engage in lesson study to improve instruction, they discuss at length the right manipulative to use. Their criteria include the following (Fernández & Yoshida, 2004):

- It should help leave a record of the thought processes used by students to solve problems.
- Students should be able to readily understand its use.
- It should allow students to easily explain their solutions.
- It should be easy to put back into its original position or shape when the students need to reconsider their ideas. (p. 64)

I would add that students should receive a sufficient quantity so that they are able to compare at least two ways of thinking about the problem or task. This is especially true when students are thinking about mathematics. For example, being able to model two ways of using counters to explain a simple way to add 5 + 17 lets students compare the two methods directly, rather than having to remember one way while looking at the second way.

Teach Group Protocols

If groups are using moveable organizers, insist on a few key protocols. Your particular students might need slight variations on the following, depending on their ages and their mix of different cognitive processing styles.

- **Talk first, shift second:** Before students working in groups may shift around their manipulatives, they need to verbalize their reasoning and receive a nod from the group. Remind them that they're using a mobile organizer to make it easier to explain their thinking. Model this, for example, by demonstrating with story strips, "In this sentence, the girl's name is given—Sula. So we know that comes before this sentence, which just refers to *she*." Then move the strips. Remind students of discussion prompts such as, "I agree because . . ." and "I was wondering . . ." and "Who can explain . . . ?"

- **Reorder:** Picture five student groups all doing card sorts. You can add to the learning by having the groups each start with a different set of cards and rotate the supplies once the groups finish with their sets. Before the groups hand off the cards, make sure they reshuffle them into a random order or otherwise organize them the way you need them organized.

- **Record:** Remind students that they might want to capture their final mobile organization. This might involve summarizing the rules they've established for making plural forms of nouns, sketching the configuration of manipulatives that illustrates a good answer, or taking a photo of the correctly sorted knowledge cards from a card sort.

Common Concerns About Moveable Organizers

The following statements represent common concerns I hear from educators as they consider using moveable organizers. Beside each statement, you'll find text on how you might address any resistance you encounter (by yourself or with colleagues) because of such concerns.

- **"We strive to be a paperless school."** Make moveable organizers that you can use more than once—use card stock and laminate chart paper and cards so that you can write on them with dry-erase markers. Use plastic file folders—these, too, can be erased again and again. Groups can write ideas on individual whiteboards and share them at the center of a table, windowsill, or floor so that everyone can read them. Use scrap paper from the copy room, and remind people that virtual isn't the same as tactile involvement with objects, especially for the experience-and-movement students.

- **"Moveable organizers take time to create."** With your collaborative team, take inventory of what is lying around. What might you repurpose? Have students make the sets—give them word lists, and have groups each create one set that all the other groups will eventually use. Share sets from classroom to classroom. Once you've tried some of these strategies with your students, explore an education supply store or catalog, and think about what might be worth purchasing.

- **"How is this differentiation?"** Your structure-and-certainty and experience-and-movement students learn better when tactile activities are added to abstract concepts and tasks. Your vision-and-interpretation and question-and-connection students benefit from having access to tools to explain their thinking, stay flexible, and revise their ideas when better ones pop into their heads. Further, when you add the concrete to the abstract, you are providing more entry points for students with varying grasps of the ideas they're working with.

Why Moveable Organizers Work

Human brains and bodies are interconnected; thus, including the body in the learning process via objects that it can touch and manipulate improves cognition (Marley & Carbonneau, 2014). This is true for adults as well as for students. Try it, as suggested in this chapter's Doing Differentiation (page 189). For example, instead of making a list of priorities, cut up some scrap paper, and write each item on a separate piece of paper. Spread the pieces of paper out on a table in front of you. Move them around, group them, and try different criteria for deciding what to do first. Do you have concerns about the time commitment, how easy or hard a priority will be for you, or how to balance this with competing priorities? Most teachers I've worked with find that the papers on the table expand their working memory, allowing them to concentrate on the big ideas and develop a better list of priorities. The table lets people process more than the limited volume of information they can hold in their working memory.

Efficiency in Learning: Evidence-Based Guidelines to Manage Cognitive Load (Clark, Nguyen, & Sweller, 2005) summarizes multiple studies that indicate cognitive load affects students of novice understanding more than students at higher levels of proficiency. Instead of reserving manipulatives for younger students, expand their use for students facing new learning at any age. Further, researchers Emily R. Fyfe, Nicole M. McNeil, Ji Y. Son, and Robert L. Goldstone (2014) point out that starting with manipulatives can ground abstract concepts via concrete objects with which students are already familiar, thus activating prior knowledge. Finally, look back to the information in the section Graphic Recording (page 167); manipulatives often foster the same sorts of pictures in the brain. Students remember how they moved ideas into place in their maps, the way mathematical manipulatives illustrated a concept, and so on.

Reflection Activity

Consider the following actions and questions as you reflect on this chapter's content.

1. With your collaborative team, brainstorm how you can use Concept Map Manipulatives (page 193) to frame an enduring understanding and learning targets for a unit or lesson. Choose a state or provincial standard or curriculum goal. Have each team member record on paper or on an individual whiteboard (printing large enough so that words can be read at a distance) his or her phrasing of the big idea students are to retain. As a team, use student-centered discussion prompts (see Practice Prompts, page 103) to discuss similarities and differences, as well as to highlight phrasing that works. Move the papers or whiteboards around, regroup them, and circle common ideas. Then, split into two groups, and have each group draft a revised statement. Compare versions again, and then finalize the big idea's phrasing.

    Extending the task to set up the learning progression for the unit even more clearly illustrates the advantages of moveable organizers. Most groups find that they can easily add missing ideas and that they revise the order a few times before settling on the progression.

2. Write your own story using the Moveable Outlines approach (page 193). How does using the cards for planning differ from composing a story at a keyboard? How can you gain from the best of both?

3. Remember that one of the purposes of moveable organizers is to improve student flexibility in thinking, the *A* for agile in STEAM^2. You *want* students to rethink their conclusions, revise their arguments, make their stories come alive in a second or third draft, compare their conclusions with those of their classmates, and so on. Moveable organizers can help with all of these.

    Pose a reflection question to students as an exit ticket after they have worked with a strategy in this chapter. You might ask, "Did this strategy help you consider more than one idea or solution? If so, how many? Or, did you make changes in how you presented your ideas? If so, how? If not, look back at your product, and write about at least one way you might have changed something." What do you learn from students' reflections? What mindsets might need shifting? What skills need scaffolding?

CHAPTER 13

Planned Movement

In 2014, I conducted a professional development session in which I introduced middle school teachers to planned movement strategies. A week later, one of the teachers reported, "I tried the Treasure Hunt. It was so simple. I just posted the questions around the room instead of making a worksheet. Every student engaged the whole hour, with some returning to their desk to answer each question and others choosing to stand by the questions while they wrote. What an easy differentiation strategy to engage everyone!"

The simple takeaway of this is, if you don't plan for movement and interaction, some of your students will move and interact when you least want them to. If you've ever attended a daylong workshop for adults, you know participants need to get up and move. The same is true of students. That's why it's important that teachers incorporate strategies for movement that get students physically engaged in their learning. Planned movement differentiates by accommodating the needs of those who learn best through interaction with others and with their environment—your experience-and-movement and question-and-connection students. Planning for movement is one of the easiest ways to manage your classroom by including the active engagement these students crave.

In this chapter, you'll explore several strategies for including planned movement as part of classroom instruction. You'll also learn two big essentials for success with these strategies and answers to some common concerns teachers have about using them. As always, you can peruse the research base first (see Why Planned Movement Works, page 212) or choose one of the strategies and see what happens when your lessons include movement.

> **Planned Movement Strategies**
> *(From quickest to deepest)*
>
> ✓ Standing Room, Wiggle Room, page 202
> ✓ Forced Choice, page 203
> ✓ Question Hunts, page 204
> ✓ Task Fetch, page 204
> ✓ Knowledge Stations, page 206
> ✓ Pocket Problems, page 209

The Planned Movement Strategies

This section presents six strategies for facilitating planned movement in your classroom: (1) Standing Room, Wiggle Room, (2) Forced Choice, (3) Question Hunts,

(4) Task Fetch, (5) Knowledge Stations, and (6) Pocket Problems. Each of these strategies is designed to keep up the energy of extraverted learners during what can be long days of sitting at school. As you use the planned movement strategies in this section, ensure you don't inadvertently exclude students who require a wheelchair or who have other physical limitations from your use of movement strategies.

DOING DIFFERENTIATION

No matter your style, try the following with a task you usually find rather boring. Simply place your laptop or tablet on a standing desk–height surface. For example, you could use a bookshelf or a podium. I used a stack of big books atop my desk for a stand as I did the final edits on this book! Then, tap your feet or move a bit as you think. Give it a half hour or so. Are you more alert if you can move a bit?

Standing Room, Wiggle Room

Letting students stand in a spot where they can listen and observe while wiggling a bit to get their energy out is a simple way to keep them engaged. Whether I'm facilitating a site-based workshop or sessions at national conferences, a few educators always ask whether it would bother me if they stood for a while. Many, many students need the same chance to stretch and wiggle. Gary Anderson (2013), a high school English teacher, blogged about a situation that showed him the difference a little movement makes to his students:

> One day Calvin said, "I know I have more to say about this, but I just can't get the words out." I could tell he was being sincere. I looked at him, over six feet tall, scrunched in a hard plastic chair with a flip-up, auditorium-style desktop, and said, "Why don't you try standing up to write for a while? Just go over there and lean on the wall and see what happens." Calvin unfolded himself, went to the wall, and wrote and wrote and wrote.

How else might you incorporate standing or otherwise plan for movement? Might students work problems at a whiteboard, perhaps taking turns? Can they read at a windowsill or while leaning on a bookshelf? Or instead of standing, might they sit against a wall with their legs stretched out for a bit (possibly using a lapboard)?

Note classroom furniture is increasingly designed with movement in mind. Do a web search for desks with kick bars, supplemental kick bands, standing desks, and more. Some are very affordable and may fit within your school's budget. Many schools are experimenting with having students use therapy balls for chairs. If your classroom space is limited and you're wondering how to make room for students to stand and wiggle, try an all-class brainstorming session (page 196). What ideas do students have for where and with what they might stand or move? How would they ensure everyone can still learn? Experience-and-movement students may have ideas based on what past teachers have managed, and question-and-connection students excel at novel solutions. These two groups are most likely to benefit from this strategy.

If you aren't sure it will be worth the effort, review Why Planned Movement Works (page 212). Research backs up what the differentiation framework we're using has already told us: Plan for movement, or else students will move when you least want them to! This approach works with rather than against human nature.

Forced Choice

With forced choice, teachers pose a question, and students move as directed to indicate their choice of answer. The Forced Choice approach works well for reviewing true-or-false and right-or-wrong information. You can also use it as a preassessment, an energizer, or a quick survey tool. Here are two strategy variations.

1. **Lineup:** Have all students line up in a single-file line, facing you. (If, like me, you have students who are much taller than you, stand on a chair so they can all see you.) Let them know you're going to ask a question, and provide two alternatives. On your signal, they'll move left or right, depending on which answer they agree with. They can't stay in the middle. Tell them they need to be ready to justify their answer, so moving with their friends won't be helpful. Here are some examples.

   ▸ "Move left if you think three-fourths is greater than one-half." Point to your right, their left. "And move right if you think three-fourths is less than one-half." Point to your left. "Go—greater or less?" Point each way again. Then, call on a student to justify his or her answer. Ask students on both sides. Ask whether anyone wants to switch sides and why. Clarify if some students are still unsure of the correct answer. Then, begin again with another fraction.

   ▸ "Which of the two books we just read did you like better? If it was the first, move left. If it was the second, move right." Ask a few students why they liked their choice or what would have made the other book better.

   ▸ "Move left if you agree with Muhammad Ali's decision to report to the army after being drafted but to refuse to be inducted. Move right if you disagree." Then, ask for reasoning from both sides, repeating, "Who has something more to add?"

   ▸ "Move left if you think soap is an acid and right if you think it is a base." Again, ask a few students for justification, check if anyone wants to change their answer, have them reform the line, and ask another question.

   ▸ "Move left if you think the Black Sea is bigger than Lake Superior and right if you think Lake Superior is bigger. How do you know? Why do you think so?"

2. **Four corners:** This technique allows you to give four answer choices instead of just two. Designate four corners of the room as *A*, *B*, *C*, and *D*. Display a slide with a multiple-choice question, and ask students to move to the corner that reflects the correct answer. Make sure students know that you might call on anyone to explain their choice. This reduces copycat behavior.

This approach lets you continue to teach toward learning targets while quickly energizing the students who most need to move and interact. I've used them with groups ages 8 to 80, inside and outside, in classrooms, and in school hallways (if students promise to stay quiet). Remember, you're differentiating to keep the extraverted students engaged and also because experience-and-movement students truly learn by doing—their bodies help their brains remember what they are learning.

Question Hunts

Question hunts replace what would otherwise be a seatwork task with a chance for movement. Instead of handing out a worksheet, post a series of problems or questions around the room—on walls, on desks, anywhere. Number them. Then, have students record their answers in their notebooks or on their mobile devices. If the tasks can be done in any order, have students choose where they'll start, and then ask them to complete the problems in any order, without crowding, as the tasks become available. If the tasks need to be done in a certain order, you might group them by colors and ask different student groups to start with different colors.

This strategy both allows for movement and adds the same kind of novelty curiosity creators activate by grabbing students' attention (see Why Curiosity Creators Work, page 135). Observe your students as they engage with this. What choices do they make? Do some of the more introverted students move less, heading next to a close task while more extraverted students avail themselves of the opportunity to move all the way across the room? Do some stand and work? Do others head to their seats? Who interacts? As long as norms around respecting space and using inside voices are in place, this is a strategy that students can adjust on their own to meet their needs.

Task Fetch

Instead of handing out all activities at the start of a lesson, Task Fetch allows students to leave their seats to retrieve tasks. If you have window or whiteboard ledges, bookshelves, or a surface large enough to hold a few baskets, you can quickly arrange a lesson around this strategy. Instead of handing out worksheets or constructing formal stations or group tasks, create a series of tasks connected to a single lesson, and let students self-organize. Students then each fetch a task from a ledge, shelf, or basket; complete the task at their desk; return it to its spot; and collect another. The ongoing rhythm of work and movement keeps students engaged. It allows you to make fewer sets of materials, take advantage of library resources, provide practice with manipulatives—your imagination is the limit.

For mathematics, try one of the following.

- Place together in a bag a task card and manipulatives that provide different opportunities to practice strategies and apply concepts. Or, set up tasks based on resources like *About Teaching Mathematics* by Marilyn Burns (2015): Place a geoboard (a geometry manipulative that lets students stretch rubber bands around evenly spaced pegs to explore shapes and angles), rubber bands, and a task card in a bag. Bundle up fraction tiles with a sequence of tasks, perhaps placing a stack of graph paper that features one-inch squares underneath the bundle so students can grab a sheet and record their answers. Your school's curriculum may also have supplemental materials that lend themselves to this approach.

- Arrange tasks so students gain practice with set, area, and distance models for fractions. You might use problems straight out of students' workbooks, but set them up with manipulatives. Or, select related tasks from a book in another textbook series (What's in your teacher resource room or another classroom?) that may extend thinking, provide needed practice, or model a different approach to a concept. Consider having students use the book itself. Make bookmarks that serve as task cards to identify page numbers and problems.

- Print off a problem from https://nrich.maths.org, or designate a classroom computer for one task at that website. The website's interactive games and tasks work well, requiring application of mathematical ideas.

In other content areas, the Task Fetch strategy allows you to maximize use of materials from the library and the internet in the following ways.

- Print off one copy of an article from the web, place it in a plastic sleeve, and include a couple of guiding questions on a task card.

- Place a bookmark with a task on it in a book from the school or public library; the bookmark should appear alongside pages relevant to the task. This is an excellent way to engage students with photographs, short excerpts from primary sources, or maps, or to engage students in comparing how multiple sources reported on the same event.

- Use a collection of tasks to help students identify a topic for a science project, identify the topic they'll research to add to class knowledge about a historical event, or practice drawing techniques—perhaps even some from the Graphic Recording section (page 167).

- Include tasks that allow for creative thinking. Perhaps use a task prompt for examining a photo, such as, "Choose a person in this photo. Jot down what that person might be thinking or feeling," or "Write a note to a person in the photo. What would you ask this person? What might you tell him or her about what happened after this moment in history?" Review the Visual Entry Points strategy (page 127) for creating curiosity.

- Tasks might also include making moveable organizers or working with open questions provided on a task card.

Assemble a few more options than you have students so that no one is without some-thing to do. Note that you might create enough options by having duplicate sets of some tasks. Number every task, and designate spaces for the materials for each task. You might color-code tasks students can do with a partner so that students also have chances to interact.

In addition to adding physical movement to classroom activities, most teachers find that because Task Fetch strategies permit most students to self-direct their learning, the strategies give teachers more time to help specific students who have individual questions or who need a bit more direction.

Knowledge Stations

Knowledge stations have activities that build or activate prior knowledge students need. Knowledge stations allow for movement if students rotate among them or have the choice to sit at or to lean over a table while working. Even personalized learning at a computer can serve as a station *if* other stations allow for more movement. Think about locating one or two stations at standing desks or a higher surface such as the top of a bookshelf. Or, might one station allow students to sprawl out a bit on the classroom car-pet, or with carpet squares, just for a change?

Knowledge stations are particularly useful in building prior (foundational) knowledge for new learning. Activating the knowledge students already have, or frontloading what they need to know, increases learning success (Bråten, Johansen, & Strømsø, 2017).

However, activating or providing the knowledge students need to succeed with new content can be tricky. For example, a teacher might be planning a unit on *All Quiet on the Western Front* (Remarque, 1982), *The Book Thief* (Zusak, 2006), or *The Watsons Go to Birmingham—1963* (Curtis, 1995) but realizes students don't know enough about the topic to get through the first chapter. In these examples, the respective topics are World War I, the capitulation of France during World War II, and conditions in Alabama in the 1960s. What *doesn't* work is lecturing or interrupting frequently to explain terms and events. Instead, try front-loading prior knowledge through a series of stations by having students engage in reading and writing as they draw information from pictures, primary sources, nonfiction texts, maps, websites, and other sources.

Students enjoy the autonomy this approach offers. In one group of sixth-grade students I worked with, 73 percent gave the activity an 8, 9, or 10 out of 10 as a way to learn; 30 percent gave it a perfect 10. It's also adaptable for any grade level or content area. For example, teachers can use knowledge stations to build prior knowledge about science lab techniques and various mathematics concepts (ideas include stations with examples of fair and unfair games, or with different geometric figures for analysis of properties), as well as to introduce unit concepts through various modalities or with materials with different reading levels.

The stations may be actual places in the room or materials students pick up and com-plete at their desk, similar to the Task Fetch strategy (page 204). Sometimes, students who have completed a station can help others get started on it.

If you are using knowledge stations for the first time, know that students may not naturally use their time wisely in the beginning. Your investment in guiding them to monitor their progress and manage their time will pay off as students develop the exact skills they need to conduct independent research. They can set goals, assess quality, journal on what helps them do their best work, and more. This makes Knowledge Stations well suited for increasing student maturity, the *M* in STEAM^2. Here's how to move from chaos to student-centered control as quickly as possible.

- Rate the stations based on how long you anticipate it will take students to complete them. Mark them with stars rather than minutes so that you have one-, two-, and three-star stations. This helps students manage their time since they can grab a quick one-star station toward the end of class rather than quit working because they aren't sure they have time for another.

- Provide students with a station guide. Depending on the activities you select, the station guides might include all the directions students need *or* blank pages that students label, one for each station. Because the activities are varied, students soon catch on that this guide isn't a typical worksheet packet.

- Once or twice during the stations unit, ask students to reflect on their work habits and what they could do differently to improve their performance.

- Post a Completed Stations chart, listing student names down the side and stations across the top. When students complete a station, they check it off on the chart. *Many* students I've used these charts with report they speed up as they see how many stations others are completing. Further, you can see at a glance how to help an idle student get busy, perhaps selecting a station you believe would engage the student. Emphasize self-monitoring and quality, not competition.

- Have students turn Wait-Go Cards (page 67) to the Wait side if they need help.

Consider the opportunities for differentiation this approach offers each of your four learner types (figure 1.1, page 18).

- You can design sample stations with different cognitive processing styles in mind. For example, figure 13.1 (page 208) offers a series of activities to match each style related to background knowledge about Martin Luther King Jr.'s most famous speech, and it supports students in completing both comfortable and stretch activities.

- Note that solo and partner tasks involve different parts of the brain. For some stations, students can choose whether to work alone or with a partner, meeting the needs of extraverted and introverted students.

- Students can do many tasks on their own, providing more time for teachers to scaffold in the moment with prompts, clarifications, or other assistance when a student needs help.

- You can easily direct struggling students to stations they will be able to complete independently until you have time to help them with ones they are stuck on.

Structure and Certainty (Let Me Know What to Do) Stations

1. You have been given a map of the United States. Use the atlas provided to locate and label the places mentioned in Dr. King's speech.

2. Watch the first seven minutes of Dr. King's speech. You'll also find the transcript at this station. Make a list of things you notice about people in the crowd. An example would be that many are carrying signs. Challenge yourself to make as long of a list as you can. Underline the phrases that people in the crowd respond to. When do they cheer? What do they say? What phrase do you hear Dr. King repeat several times?

Vision and Interpretation (Let Me Follow My Own Lead) Stations

3. Here are pictures of the crowd gathered at the Lincoln Memorial during the March on Washington. Choose one person, and pretend you are that person. Write a letter to a friend about what you experienced during that day. What did you see, hear, and feel? What did you talk about with others? These are just a few ideas. Your letter should be a page long. Make sure you describe the person you chose and which photo he or she is in.

4. *Anaphora* is using a repeated phrase for emphasis. Here are three famous uses of anaphora. Read these and then write an example of your own. (The station includes examples coming from the likes of President Obama, Shirley Chisholm, and Charles Dickens.)

Experience and Movement (Let Me Do Something) Stations

5. These pictures show the way African Americans were treated before the Civil Rights Act of 1964 was passed. For each picture, figure out the civil right that African American people did not have. You may work alone or with a partner.

6. The envelope at this station has cards that show significant events in the civil rights movement. Put the events in the order they happened. Then review each event. In your notebook, write a sentence about how each event is related to the 1963 March on Washington.

Question and Connection (Let Me Lead as I Learn) Stations

7. This station has information on President Lincoln and Dr. Martin Luther King Jr. Work with a partner to complete the chart that shows five similarities and five differences between the two men. An example of each is given.

8. The following are several people who attended the March on Washington. With a partner, choose one of these people. Together, imagine and write out an interview dialogue, and prepare to read it for the class, with one of you being the interviewer and the other being the person who attended the march. Write at least five questions and the person's responses.

- Wilt Chamberlain, America's top basketball star in 1963
- A. Philip Randolph, the African American leader who organized the march
- James Smith, a sixteen-year-old from New York who walked seven hundred miles with two friends to participate in the march
- Joan Baez, a famous singer who began the program at the Lincoln Memorial with the song "Oh, Freedom"
- Rosa Parks, the activist who began the Montgomery Bus Boycott in 1955
- Sidney Poitier, the most famous African American movie star at that time
- Dorie Ladner, a leader of the Student Nonviolent Coordinating Committee (SNCC)
- John Lewis, a speaker that day who became a member of Congress

Figure 13.1: Knowledge stations divided by preferred cognitive processing style.

Note that an approach like the one illustrated in figure 13.1 offers endless opportunities for differentiation. I developed this particular set as a demonstration for teachers in Saudi Arabia, who then collaborated on stations for the last speech of the Prophet Muhammad. My colleague Fatmah Alhawasi used the stations with one of her classes and taught the speech the traditional way (without stations) with another class. She reported that assessment scores were significantly higher for the class that used the stations. Those students enjoyed them and found memorizing the speech (one of the learning objectives) easier than the students who didn't do the stations.

Pocket Problems

Pocket problems are a much more structured version of Task Fetch (page 204), designed for small groups. They add movement in two ways: group members need to fetch the problems and, to compare work, groups move to converse with other groups. Prepare twenty-six problems, and place two copies of each, labeled with the letters A–Z, into a board outfitted with pockets labeled A–Z. Students work in groups of four, each assuming one of the following roles.

1. **Messenger:** This student goes to the pocket problem board and selects group problems.

2. **Reader:** This student reads a problem aloud, then places it where everyone can review it.

3. **Organizer:** For mathematics, this student operates the group's calculator. For language arts or social studies, this student might be in charge of texts or web searches.

4. **Writer:** This student records the group's solution.

To increase efficiency with this approach, consider using Wait-Go Cards (page 67) so that everyone has a chance to think about the problem before the group members begin working together to solve it. A group can put a problem back if no one knows how to solve it. Once group members agree on a solution, the writer records it on the back of the pocket card. The messenger then returns it to the pocket board, clipping it facedown to the outside of the pocket. When two groups have completed a problem, the second messenger checks to see whether the answers are the same. If not, the groups conference to determine who is right. The teacher then checks the cards to see whether the solutions are correct.

Sometimes, classes are motivated by setting goals for how many total problems they can solve correctly during class time. Some teachers help involve all students by designating who will explain a correct answer. Asking students who struggle with a concept to explain it ensures that the group works to help every student understand.

This strategy combines many elements we have discussed. With students conferring to justify their answers, the emphasis is on reasoning rather than on looking only for correct answers. Opportunities for movement engage experience-and-movement students, while question-and-connection students enjoy the collaboration and the bit of competition in the air. Finally, because the tasks need to be groupworthy, vision-and-interpretation students benefit from being able to think through multiple approaches or ways to illustrate group thinking.

Two Big Success Essentials

Planned movement definitely increases engagement, the E in STEAM[2] for many extraverted students. However, it's easy to overlook details that help these activities go well and that make them comfortable for more introverted students. What follows are lessons learned and summaries of how to make planned movement work, from teachers who have successfully used these strategies.

Set Norms

To ensure that planned movement strategies are comfortable for all students and result in the intended learning goals, set norms for movement in your classroom and establish consensus on students' rights and responsibilities regarding movement. Note that rights and responsibilities are interdependent, with each value incomplete without the other; only by taking responsibility for actions do students (or adults) ensure that others' rights are honored. Perhaps you, too, were raised with the parental admonition, "Your rights stop where your siblings' rights start." As a teacher, think of how you look out for the rights of each student in your classroom while also looking out for the welfare of the whole class as a learning community. Over-focus on one or the other, and you end up with problems.

When setting norms, model what a couple of these interdependencies around rights and responsibilities might look like, such as the following examples.

- *I have a right to move during this activity.*

  I have a responsibility to not interfere with others' learning as I move.

- *I have a right to stretch and wiggle.*

  I have a responsibility to respect others' personal space as I stretch and wiggle.

- *I have a right to leave my seat during this activity.*

  I have a responsibility to return to my seat as instructed.

Post one of these examples, or one of your own devising that fits your students. Have students brainstorm what they might add. To facilitate this activity, you might let students engage in Think-Pair-Share. Or, have students reflect with exit tickets, letting them know that it's OK if they can only think of a right or a responsibility; a classroom discussion might fill in the rest.

Prepare Task Cards

Think of task cards (refer to Task Fetch, page 204) as your insurance for many of the planned movement strategies in this chapter. By numbering them, color-coding them, showing worked examples where appropriate, or providing vocabulary words or other needed scaffolding, you'll increase students' capacity to succeed, thrive, engage, be agile, and mature in their ability to direct their own learning.

Common Concerns About Planned Movement

The following statements represent common concerns I hear from educators as they consider using planned movement strategies. Beside each statement, you'll find text on how you might address any resistance you encounter (by yourself or with colleagues) because of such concerns.

- **"It'll be chaos."** If tasks are engaging, there is less need to manage student behavior. Also, allowing students to move acknowledges that people need to move. Remember that many disciplinary battles arise because students—and adults—aren't naturally wired to sit still and listen.

  To avoid chaos, plan ahead. Which strategies might be easiest for your students to start with? Might you model Forced Choice (page 203) with a half-dozen students? I once used it first with students who joined me for an extra mathematics tutorial session, and they were happy to demonstrate it for the rest of the class. Might you have half the students work with Task Fetch while the others work in small groups for thirty minutes or so, and then have them switch for the next thirty minutes, so that only half as many students are moving about at one time? Brainstorm with your collaborative team new ideas to balance movement with learning.

- **"A few students might ruin it for all."** Although this is a possibility, consider that many students whom teachers already consider a challenge might benefit most from being able to get up and move around. For students who struggle to stay on task during learning that involves planned movement, perhaps have them work a little closer to you. Or, work with them to develop their own plan to engage in a task.

- **"I don't have enough space."** Look back to the opening example in this chapter of the boy who just needed to stand to re-engage and excel at a writing task. You might ask secondary students to offer ideas that help support movement within a confined space, such as just letting students stand, lean, or wiggle. Don't be surprised if they come up with some creative solutions and thus have ownership in making them work.

- **"This is a lecture class."** Even within the framework of a lecture, you can permit students to lean on a ledge and take notes. If you have a whiteboard, let them take notes on it and later capture an image of the board on their mobile device. You can also review content using the four corners approach from Forced Choice. Or, have everyone stand. Read a statement and ask them to sit down if they disagree. Get some oxygen flowing to their brains so they can pay attention more easily!

- **"My students aren't mature enough."** The youngest students need the most movement. Think about this: Students who struggle to sit still (because of age, attention difficulties, a feeling that they are too big for their desk, or even boredom) will often do things, even misbehave, to get out of an uncomfortable situation. It might not be mature, but it's rather intelligent.

  Again, start small. Maybe you begin with a question hunt that involves only five questions—and you repeat the questions on five sets of color-coded cards so that a few students are moving to the red ones, a few to the blue ones, and so on. Perhaps the activity lasts only ten minutes. You don't have to let students move every second of the day. You're helping them self-regulate, and you're helping yourself by letting them get the wiggles out while class moves ahead.

Why Planned Movement Works

Multiple studies show the positive impact of movement on student academics (Donnelly et al., 2009; Hollar et al., 2010; Kercood & Banda, 2012). Physical education class and recess are also important, but the strategies in this chapter help ensure that instruction also accommodates students' varied needs for movement. Researchers Suneeta Kercood and Devender R. Banda (2012) find that allowing students to sit on therapy balls or to doodle increases their performance on listening and comprehension tasks, whether or not they have been diagnosed with attention problems. They also cite multiple studies showing the positive effects on academic performance of allowing students to move:

> Paying attention and listening during lectures or meetings or conversations can be challenging at times for all of us. When placed in such listening situations for extended time periods, most of us tend to keep ourselves occupied by doodling, moving around in our seats, tapping our finger/hands or legs, sometimes talking out of turn, making shopping or to-do lists in our note pads, or twirling strings in our clothing, etc. Listening can also be challenging for all children, who during school hours are required to listen to verbally presented educational materials such as lectures, or lessons and stories, and have to answer comprehension questions based on the content. This can be especially challenging for students who already have attention problems, and are expected to listen without moving or fidgeting. (Kercood & Banda, 2012, p. 19)

David A. Sousa and Carol Ann Tomlinson (2018) place students' needs for sound and movement on continua. Some students need to move more than others, and some work better in noisier environments than others. The strategies in this chapter for structuring and planning for movement will help ensure that all students feel comfortable.

VIRTUAL CLASSROOMS

The term *zoned out* aptly applies to all of us if we spend too much time in front of screens for any purpose. Certainly, *zoomed out* has entered the vocabulary of many educators and students who use Zoom to connect! Here are some strategies I saw my doctoral students use to stay engaged during virtual instruction in 2020. Note how contrary the following strategies (which worked!) may be to common advice parents give to their children, such as, "Create a quiet place to study."

- Using standing or walking desks and treadmills
- Connecting out of doors on a balcony or deck
- Standing while taking notes on a whiteboard that they later used in a virtual class presentation
- Using a Graphic Recording approach (page 167) for a presentation, drawing on a sidewalk with chalk, and submitting a video of their explanation as they moved around their diagrams
- Donning simple costume elements (hats, glasses, and so on) for case-study presentations, complete with gestures
- Taking advantage of asynchronous portions of class (Many students watched the recorded lecture at the crack of dawn, went for a walk or run, and returned in time for the live portion of class.)
- Using manipulatives to model and explain situations or problems in breakout rooms

How might you encourage your students to move and interact with their environment in productive ways while online?

Reflection Activity

Consider the following actions and questions as you reflect on this chapter's content.

1. Reflect on your own learning experiences.

    ‣ How long could you sit still as a child? If you have children, is it easy or difficult for them to sit still? What were they like when they were the age of your students? Do these experiences have any influence on your classroom expectations?

    ‣ How long can the adults around you sit still for professional learning?

2. If you already run a rather extraverted classroom, with lots of student movement and interaction, discuss with a more introverted colleague how you might help your more introverted students remain energized. Remember, this isn't about who is shy; it's about how everyone can stay energized to do their best work.

3. If you run a rather introverted classroom, strategize with one or two of your introverted colleagues. What strategies help each of you gain back energy through the course of the school day? How can you keep up your own energy with more "chaos" in your class? Brainstorm strategies for the following concerns and others you identify.

   ‣ Making space for movement

   ‣ Using effective signals for a student or a group to calm down a bit without creating a discipline issue

   ‣ Setting classroom norms to promote both the privilege and the responsibilities of planned movement

CHAPTER 14

Talking to Write

While writing is often a solo effort, talking through ideas for essays, stories, persuasive arguments, and other forms of writing differentiates learning by expanding and enriching the thoughts of all students before they work to formalize them in writing. Remember that students who prefer extraversion think out loud; they get their best thoughts as they voice ideas and hear the reactions of others. Thus, talking prepares them for the introverted task of writing. Further, students who prefer introversion also benefit from discussing ideas as voicing their thoughts activates more regions of their brains. Best-selling author Ann Patchett talks to write and has spoken openly about tossing out her first manuscript of *The Dutch House* (Patchett, 2019)—and deleting all files—just a month before the book was due:

> It was getting to the end of 2018. Patchett had just a few months left before her no-going-back deadline, and like an unruly toddler, the book would not behave. She pulled it together with help from a number of friends, all writers themselves.
>
> From Barbara Kingsolver, Patchett got the idea to change what happens to the children's mother. From Nell Freudenberger, she got the recommendation to read the works of Kate DiCamillo, author of *Because of Winn-Dixie*, with whom she began an email friendship—and who then suggested a new ending.
>
> And from Jane Hamilton, to whom she always reads drafts of her books aloud (and vice versa), she received the gift of tough love. "She said, 'I really like it, but the whole third section is trash,'" Patchett recalls. "Well, not trash, but she said there were major problems. So I had to rethink a lot of stuff." (as cited in Lyall, 2019)

If a well-regarded author benefits from talking to write, might your students? Like Ann's writing, students will gain insights into what they might write, where their writing is effectively communicating, and how they might improve it as they talk it through with others.

This chapter's strategies help students clarify their ideas, expand their viewpoints, learn from the opinions

Talking to Write Strategies
(From quickest to deepest)

- ✓ Talk-Pair-Write, page 216
- ✓ Essential Question Priming, page 217
- ✓ Yes-And Improvisation, page 218
- ✓ Imaginative Dialogue Pairs, page 219
- ✓ All-Class Priming, page 220
- ✓ Simulations and Role Plays, page 223

of others, and, thus, draft a better product. In addition to these strategies, you'll learn two big essentials for success with these approaches and answers to some common concerns teachers have about using them. If you prefer to start with the research that underpins these strategies, see Why Talking to Write Works (page 226).

DOING DIFFERENTIATION

As if you were preparing to write a blog entry, consider how doable differentiation around talking before writing supports helping students mature, the *M* in the STEAM² framework.

With a colleague, discuss the essential question, "What are immature behaviors in our students versus behaviors we should expect of this age group?" To facilitate this conversation, consider using a big notes strategy (page 176), such as organizing your ideas on a whiteboard. Then, examine figure 1.1 (page 18) and figure 1.5 (page 28). Together, discuss whether any of your ideas about maturity and immaturity might be biased against students with one or more of the cognitive processes. Finally, reflect individually and in writing. What doable differentiation strategies might best help you adjust your classroom for students whose behavior isn't always mature? What might help them grow? And, which strategies might help you avoid putting some students at a disadvantage because of how they naturally process information or are energized? As a reflection activity, consider how your discussion of the essential question has expanded your thinking on this topic. Consider drafting a blog with your thoughts.

The Talking to Write Strategies

This section presents six strategies for talking to write: (1) Talk-Pair-Write, (2) Essential Question Priming, (3) Yes-And Improvisation, (4) Imaginative Dialogue Pairs, (5) All-Class Priming, and (6) Simulations and Role Plays. Each of these strategies is designed to expand student perspectives and ideas and to energize more extraverted students for the introverted task of writing.

Think of how students in your classroom struggle to express themselves and how talking to write might help. For mathematics, might students be able to better explain a solution if they first explained it to a classmate? In science, how might All-Class Priming (page 220) set up secondary students to draft an idea for a nature restoration project somewhere in their own community? In social studies, how might a simulation prime students for a persuasive essay? Talking to write is viable for all content areas and all age groups.

Talk-Pair-Write

Letting students talk before they write simply lets them try out ideas orally. Start with a group overview of the topic or task, let students then pair up to narrow down their ideas, and then ask them to write. This strategy reverses the solo-pair-group pattern of

Retrieve-Pair-Share (page 66) and is useful for any writing that requires reasoning, synthesizing ideas, or justifying one's ideas. Here are the steps.

1. **Talk:** Provide students with an overview of the upcoming writing task so that they understand the goal of their conversation. The writing might be as short as their conclusion about a topic, or a journal entry, or as long as a formal paper. Then, use a student-centered discussion strategy (page 103). This could be an all-class or small-group discussion.

2. **Pair:** Ask students to pair up with a partner to discuss the main ideas covered in the discussion and what they might write about. (A group of three will work as well if there is an odd number of students.) These can be teacher-assigned pairs or student choice, depending on classroom dynamics. Or, consider using four corners (page 204) with students pairing up with others who've moved to their corner, showing similar positions on the topic. For example, if you were discussing courageous characters from literature, you might list four characters, attribute them to a corner of your room, and ask students to move to the corner for the one they believe showed the most courage.

3. **Write:** Ask students to work individually on the writing assignment.

Note that this approach takes little planning, helps expand student thinking on a topic, meets extraverted students' needs before they write (both experience-and-movement and question-and-connection), and still allows for individual composition.

Essential Question Priming

Essential questions provide avenues for inquiry that go beyond a lesson. Authors and educational consultants Douglas Fisher, Nancy Frey, and Diane Lapp (2012) suggest providing literature circles with an essential question such as the following.

- What makes a true friend?

- What do heroes do?

- What is justice?

- When is following the rules not OK?

Note that these questions have meaning beyond the specific text students are studying, connect to their lives, and will surface again in other content areas as well as in life outside of school. Essential questions such as these take students beyond the simple concepts of who, what, and why to the big ideas a text is exploring. After the discussion, students write their own essays to address the essential question, with evidence from the text. Note that only a small percentage of writing assignments asks students to write more than a paragraph (Santelises & Dabrowski, 2015). These kinds of discussions prompt longer essays and lend themselves to productive peer review if the success criteria are clear.

This strategy is especially helpful for structure-and-certainty and experience-and-movement students, who often gain the certainty they desire by exploring with someone else as they move from the facts about a text or story to the big ideas they will be writing about.

Yes-And Improvisation

Yes-And Improvisation is a standard improvisational technique that students can use to expand how they're thinking about a topic. Teaching improvisation skills to students has been shown to increase agility and maturity (Flanagan, 2015). For writing, this simple technique boosts student creativity before they begin writing. One student states an idea or provides an opening line of dialogue for a scene. The next student says, "Yes, and . . . .", adding another idea or line of dialogue that builds on what the first student said. Back and forth they go, adding, "Yes, and . . . ."

For example, in a literature study, have students pair up and predict what a character might do next. Ask a student to share a prediction and why he or she thinks it might happen. Then, ask other classmates to add on more reasons. The goal is for peers not to contradict a student's answer but to help build the argument in favor of it. For example, students reading *Harry Potter and the Prisoner of Azkaban* (Rowling, 1999) might have the following improvisation.

> *Student A: I think Ron is going to betray Harry in a later book because Ron's envy of Harry is growing. Ron's only got hand-me-down everything, and Harry gets a Firebolt broomstick.*
>
> *Student B: Yes, and Ron was really upset about that incident with Scabbers and never talked it through with Harry. Bottling things up leads to anger and bad thinking.*
>
> *Student C: Yes, and it seems as if Harry is siding with Hermione a lot, and so Ron feels betrayed by that. What comes around might go around?*

This round might conclude after two or three more ideas are added. Then, a new round might start with another prediction.

Other possible discussions could involve how friends might support a character, what a character's motivations are, how the setting does or doesn't support the story, and so on. This strategy is meant to help students learn to listen to each other as they also expand ideas for writing.

In any subject, students might combine Yes-And Improvisation with concept maps (chapter 10, page 159) so they have a record from which to build their written response. Think of how you might use this approach with topics such as the following.

- What is true about having a growth mindset?

- What do we need to remember about Bloody Sunday in Selma, Alabama?

- What are some practical uses for your new knowledge about right triangles?

- How is the history of the suffrage movement relevant to us today?

- How can we effectively educate others about the differences between and relationships between weather patterns and climate change?

Yes-And Improvisation plays to the strengths of your question-and-connection students. Norming the use of wait time in between responses will also allow the pause your vision-and-interpretation students need to come up with an idea. Experience-and-movement students often enjoy this chance to talk before writing and think best out loud. Finally, structure-and-certainty students may feel that Yes-And Improvisation is a stretch. Try scaffolding strategies such as providing wait time, having them watch demonstrations by other students, or pairing them with another structure-and-certainty student so they can encourage each other and work at their own pace, building their confidence.

Imaginative Dialogue Pairs

The name of the strategy says it all: pair students up to dialogue, using their imaginations, to prepare for writing. In these dialogues, students step into the shoes of objects or characters, assume a stakeholder position on an issue, or otherwise engage their imaginations to go beyond the texts and other information they have studied to enrich their ideas for writing. When students take seriously the idea that they are activating their ability to empathize by taking on these roles for the dialogue, they can expand their understanding of motivations, emotions, dilemmas, and other ways in which the person or object they are portraying may think differently. During discussion, students might take notes in a graphic organizer that allows for comparing and contrasting or for filling in the five Ws either during or after the conversation; choose the tool that readies them for the assigned form of writing. Here are some examples of ways to use this strategy.

- **Point-of-view or setting change:** With the goal of having students rewrite a story from a different point of view or in a different setting, pair students up, and ask them to form a what-if question based on a fiction text they're reading. Have them dialogue with each other as if they were two characters in the story to help them form ideas about what they might write. For instance, you might share examples that tell stories from unusual points of view such as *The True Story of the 3 Little Pigs! By A. Wolf* (Scieszka, 1989) or short selections from *Ender's Game* (Card, 1985), where events are conveyed through the eyes of the boy Ender, and *Ender's Shadow* (Card, 1999), where the same events are conveyed through the eyes of his friend Bean.

- **Persuasive writing:** Have students pair up and dialogue as if they hold opposite points of view on an issue. If the topic is something they feel strongly about, they can focus on forming a good argument. The topic might be something they'd like to see change at school, it might involve organized sports, or it might be anything else about which they have firsthand knowledge. One student presents his or her reasoning to the other, who responds as if he or she were the authority hearing the argument—the principal, the coach, the head of food services, the city council, and so on.

- **Narrative:** Let students dialogue with each other before writing dialogue. Students take turns explaining a scene in a story they're writing. They then work together to imagine what the characters might naturally say in the situation.

- **Compare and contrast:** Have students dialogue as if they were two historical figures—for example, the antiseptic medicine pioneers Joseph Lister and Ignaz Semmelweis discussing resistance to their lifesaving recommendations;

Frederick Douglass and Martin Luther King Jr. discussing where and how they chose to take their next stands; or Susan B. Anthony and Gloria Steinem discussing leadership and women's rights. The possibilities are endless. Students need background knowledge first (see Knowledge Stations, page 206), but the imaginative dialogue may help them organize their thoughts.

As part of this exercise, students might journal about writing imaginative dialogue on their own versus talking it through with a partner. How do they get their best ideas? They might also try a legitimate form of talking to themselves: dialoguing with a pet, a favorite toy, an airplane, a tree, or anything else that might give them ideas for enriching a narrative or other piece of writing.

The aim of all of these imaginative writing exercises is to give your more extraverted students the chance to talk and to stimulate more ideas for your structure-and-certainty and experience-and-movement students, who often need scaffolding as they move from simple to more complex forms of writing such as persuasion or short stories.

All-Class Priming

To get an old-fashioned water pump flowing, you often have to prime it, adding a little water to get the juices flowing. In this strategy, the teacher plans an all-class activity that similarly gets students' creative juices flowing for the writing activity ahead. This strategy is ideal when all students are examining the same issue. For example, adults and students alike struggle to talk and write about race, class, gender, and other areas of diversity and equity. All-class priming helps them process how they might approach the topic.

This strategy prepares students to write a persuasive argument, but teachers might also use it for opinion pieces, narrative writing, and other types of writing. A teacher might help the whole class prepare to discuss and write about the issue by having the class engage with the following steps.

1. **Introduce the topic:** Display at the front of the room a *guiding question*, which is a question that encompasses the fundamental query students will be answering. Examples for diversity and equity include the following. (Note that the first question in each pair is meant for grades K–3 students.)

   ‣ What can we do every day to help classmates know they are part of our classroom family? What actions show that honoring diversity is part of a culture?

   ‣ What does kindness look like to each of us? What do we need to learn and do to treat others as they wish to be treated?

   ‣ How is each of us special, and what can we learn from each other? How can students honor diversity and work for equity in our class, in our school, and in our community?

2. **Introduce the essential question:** To set students' focus, use a short reading such as a poem, an anchor text, a picture book, or a film or film clip to establish an essential question. Let the students know the nature of the

writing assignment they will work on following the all-class discussion. These discussions are often most productive if the reading introduces a dilemma.

3. **Seek opinions:** Use Forced Choice (page 203) to have students declare their opinion on the essential question posed in the introductory text or film. Or, if the text introduces an unsolved problem, you might use a big notes moveable concept map (page 179) to capture student ideas about possible solutions. A third alternative is to use the Retrieve-Pair-Share strategy (page 66) with the whole class (or perhaps discuss in small groups) to access students' ideas. Whatever you choose, capture student ideas so the class can refer back to them as the students organize their writing.

4. **Move from talking to writing:** Provide any additional assignment instructions at this point in the lesson, and direct students to begin writing.

Let's look at primary-grade and secondary-grade examples for using this strategy, particularly how you might determine essential questions.

Primary-Grade Example

Sulwe, a picture book by Lupita Nyong'o (2019), tells the story of a little girl whose skin is darker than that of anyone in her family or anyone at school. She longs to have skin that is light and bright like her mother's; that is, until a magical dream helps her look at skin color in a beautiful way. Essential questions might include the following.

• How am I the same as other people? How am I different?

• How can we show we value everyone just as they are?

• What does our class look like when we respect everyone?

For the youngest students (K–2), the writing assignment might consist of cartoon panels illustrating their answers. They might write a letter to you about how they plan to show respect for classmates. Or, they could write a descriptive piece about the look and sound of your classroom if everyone is showing respect.

Secondary-Grade Example

New Kid by Jerry Craft (2019), the Newbery Medal–winning graphic novel, follows Jordan Banks, a seventh-grade student new to a pricey private school. He'd rather attend an art school. The book takes many twists and turns as Jordan discovers who his real friends are and how to handle stereotypes and slurs toward himself and others. It also tackles messes created by adults who stumble among being politically correct, courageous, and clueless. The occasional insertion of two-page spreads from Jordan's sketchbook provides windows into Jordan's thoughts, reactions, and questions.

New Kid (Craft, 2019) is a quick read, but you could also focus the class on a particular scene or dialogue. Read aloud, displaying the accompanying pictures via a document camera. Plenty of images from the book are also on the internet, including a trailer from the author. Here is a sample passage from the book, which features the characters as illustrations talking in word bubbles:

Drew: So what's up with Ms. Rawle always calling me Deandre?

Jordan: I know, right? Some kids even called me Maury a few times.

Drew: See? Those are the things that bother me. Like whenever a class talks about slavery or civil rights—

Jordan: Everyone stares at you, right? And financial aid!

Drew: I even got stared at when we talked about *minority* partnerships in business.

Jordan: Ugh! So do you ever tell your parents how you feel?

Drew: It's just me and my grandmother. And I don't wanna worry her. You know that generation doesn't like to complain.

Jordan: For real! My gran'pa *never* complains.

Drew: She says that in order to become successful one day, I need to get used to being a "fly in the buttermilk"!

Jordan: A fly in the . . . wow! I never heard that before.

Drew: If we weren't smart, we couldn't have gotten into this school in the first place, right?

Jordan: Right.

Drew: Then why do they make it so tough for us? (Craft, 2019, pp. 87–89)

You might begin a discussion of this passage by having students name the stereotypes Drew and Jordan point out, as well as describe others they have experienced. Perhaps continue with a Retrieve-Pair-Share on what needs to change or what students might constructively do if they encounter one of the stereotypes. This grounding in the text and their own experience primes the pump for potential essential questions such as the following.

- "How can we interrupt stereotypes?"
- "How might 'good' stereotypes still be harmful?"
- "How can we help others reexamine and dismiss stereotypes?"
- "What role can cultural archetypes play without involving stereotyping?"

After the discussion, students might write an imaginary letter to someone in the story or a real letter to someone in your school or community with an idea that would address issues involved in one of the essential questions. They could also write persuasive papers that discuss a solution or personal narratives that relate to the essential question.

All-class priming accomplishes so many things. You're energizing extraverted students for the introverted task of writing. You're helping introverted students by having them entertain more points of view before they begin to write. Pressure-prompted students not only get a chance to explore ideas but also a mechanism (through a Forced Choice or similar activity) to settle on a position for their writing. Structure-and-certainty students receive information they know they can use. Experience-and-movement students see the connections to real life and have the chance to talk and move. Question-and-connection students no doubt enjoy expressing opinions and seeing connections among issues. And vision-and-interpretation students, their ideas expanded by input from others, can turn to their inner world for writing with more possibilities for a unique approach. Through this approach, students are truly ready for the hard work of producing high-quality writing.

VIRTUAL CLASSROOMS

All-Class Priming lends itself well to virtual environments and to flipped instruction, where students engage with materials outside of the virtual classroom to acquire basic knowledge, leaving more class time for student-centered discussions (chapter 7, page 101). Consider sharing the essential question via the flipped video, text, or another device during asynchronous instruction time, saving all-class sessions for discussion in large and small groups.

Note that role plays, the next section's topic, are also effective in virtual classrooms. Use a fishbowl discussion (Discussion Protocols, page 108) with as many as seven or eight students engaged in any one role play. Consider having only the currently-participating students have their cameras on so that it is easier for the observers to follow what they are saying. Have observers decide in advance what kind of graphic organizer they can use to capture viewpoints.

Simulations and Role Plays

In simulations and role plays, students step into the roles of people involved in a story or a historical event, or they take the viewpoint of people who hold different opinions on an issue. There are other possibilities, such as viewing an essential question through the eyes of various historical figures. Research supports simulations and role playing for both effectively engaging students and for retention of the knowledge they acquire (Stevens, 2015). Well-constructed simulations result in deep understanding of core content by engaging students in using the information they are learning as they play out their roles. Note that for simulations and role plays to help students master success criteria, they take planning and preparation. Either the teacher needs to provide the background information students need to accurately portray their assumed role, or the teacher should provide students with clear expectations for the research and information gathering they will engage in to obtain that information. Note the actual simulation requires structure and focus.

Before creating a simulation from scratch, examine or use an existing one. Many generous teachers have shared excellent designs on the internet. A place to start searching is the Zinn Education Project (www.zinnedproject.org). Under the Teaching Materials tab, you'll find complete lesson plans, searchable by topic and grade level. You might also begin by browsing the list of Teaching Activity PDFs (also under the Teaching Materials tab) for examples that connect to your history, science, and literature curricula.

For role plays, students still adopt a particular point of view and engage as if that view were theirs. However, many views they espouse will still be based on their current knowledge, life experience, or the information they are currently learning. For example, students might role play being students at a basketball game to explore sportsmanship—this needs little preparation. Or, they might role play American abolitionist Sojourner Truth in conversation with Vice President Kamala Harris, requiring quite a bit of preparation. A web search for *role-play lesson plans* generates dozens of useful links for all subject areas, such as Learning for Justice (https://learningforjustice.org) and Theatre Dance (https://bit.ly/37Q0Rx9). If you find these plans helpful in stimulating excellent writing, collaborate with other teachers to develop one that custom-fits your needs.

Think of simulations as in-depth all-class priming, and role plays as a quicker version. They differentiate in the same ways, deepening content knowledge, expanding ideas, narrowing options, and fostering the crucial skill of being able to understand and evaluate multiple points of view.

Two Big Success Essentials

Talking to write brings more student success with the difficult work of expressing ideas through writing, thriving as their communication improves, and staying engaged through the introverted portion of the tasks since their energy is up—the S, T, and E in the STEAM[2] framework. What follows are lessons learned and summaries of how to make talking to write work from teachers who have successfully used these strategies.

Organize for Moving From Talking to Writing

By planning in advance to capture students' thoughts, you'll make the most of student discussion time as they shift into writing. Which method fits best with what the students will be writing and how they'll be interacting?

For an all-class discussion, you might appoint a few students as recorders who take notes (displayed at the front of the room) for everyone. This works especially well for All-Class Priming (page 220). One student might list pros and the other cons for an argument. Or, several students might capture information as the class looks at an event or issue from multiple points of view. Think of how a class might explore the tensions around building new pipelines, opening a mine, removing a dam, and more to understand the competing interest groups and stakeholders.

Or, students might capture their thoughts, especially if you use a small group talking-to-write strategy. Help students choose the graphic organizer that will set them up for the writing task, looking back at ideas in chapter 10 (page 159) and chapter 11 (page 175). Ensuring that students understand the form their writing will take helps them take the right notes as they move from talking to writing. For example, tell students, "You'll be analyzing this character's actions from the point of view of a different character," "You'll be writing a persuasive argument to influence a policy decision," "You'll be writing a critical essay," or "You'll be comparing and contrasting the leadership styles of two figures in the ongoing struggle for the endangered coral reefs of our oceans."

Prime the Excellent Writers

Some students, especially those inclined toward vision and interpretation, will object to some of the simpler strategies, saying they'd rather just get to writing. Emphasize that *even* professional writers benefit from another writer or an editor or a critique group. Share Ann Patchett's process from the beginning of this chapter (page 215). Let them know that by using this strategy, they will learn to expand what they might write about before they narrow down and begin. See Why Talking to Write Works (page 226) to understand the crucial role interaction plays in forming students' ability to function as mature people.

Common Concerns About Talking to Write

The following statements represent common concerns I hear from educators as they consider using talking-to-write strategies. Beside each statement, you'll find text on how you might address any resistance you encounter (by yourself or with colleagues) because of such concerns.

- **"Students will copy each other's ideas."** By talking to write, students are *expanding and clarifying* their own thinking by listening to others. Even if they agree, resulting in their writing assignments having similar content, they'll be writing on their own. They won't be copying structure, reasoning, punctuation, and so on.

- **"Writing is individual expression."** Yes, and students will still be writing on their own. Look back to this chapter's opening story. That is how real writers work—they get input, hone their ideas, and check their thinking. Was Ann Patchett (2019) cheating when she used an idea from Kate DiCamillo to polish the ending of *The Dutch House*? Am I cheating when I get on Zoom with another educator to talk through the best way to approach a book outline or the best example to use in a chapter opening?

  Interaction keeps students from falling victim to their own blind spots. It clarifies the path for writing, leading to less revision. Talking to write introduces students to a key process that professional writers benefit from day in and day out.

- **"Students can't talk with others before formal writing assessments."** This is true, but the groundwork for high achievement in formal writing assignments is laid through the collaborative work that this chapter outlines. Hopefully, through this work, students will have had deep practice with multiple forms of writing since you've been separating content and process. If you or a colleague are concerned about preparing students for formal writing assignments, try having them practice with the Imaginative Dialogue Pairs strategy (page 219) on their own for some assignments so that they have it as a strategy for formal assessment. They don't have to write complete sentences. They could even add some graphic recording elements (page 167) as they plan for writing.

Why Talking to Write Works

Carl Jung's (1921/1923) framework of psychological type, which I related to differentiation in chapter 1 (page 15), also outlines each person's optimal pathway for development and maturity. By definition, children aren't mature, but type provides a language for understanding the process of maturing (Hodgson, 2012; Murphy, 2013). Consider that the essence of type represents students' preferences for the following.

- Taking in information through sensing or intuition (see Sensing and Intuition, page 23)

- Making decisions through one of the following cognitive processes

  ‣ *Sensing*—A person first employs logical criteria—if-then considerations, pro-con considerations, considerations of precedents being set, and so on.

  ‣ *Intuition*—A person first employs values-centered criteria, such as, How might a decision affect each person or stakeholder group? What values might be upheld or violated? and Are there extenuating circumstances that warrant bending the rules or showing mercy?

Note that chapter 1 doesn't discuss the preferences for thinking and feeling, but understanding these differences in approaches to decisions can be helpful in building relationships with students and in motivating them. They're important, but they are not as crucial to instruction as sensing and intuition. Figure 14.1 clarifies these preferences.

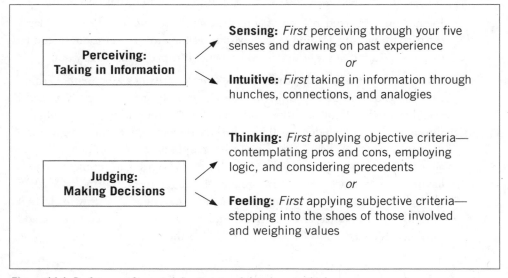

Figure 14.1: Preferences for remaining open and drawing conclusions.

Jung (1921/1923, 1921/1971) also notes that people use these processes—taking in information or making decisions—in different worlds. They use one in the external world of taking action and interacting with others and the other in the internal world when alone, reflecting and pondering. The charts in figure 14.2 illustrate *psychological balance*, which is when people spend enough (not necessarily equal) time in these two worlds so they can sufficiently explore information and come to closure. You've seen the impact on students—and adults—of a lack of balance: either they rush to conclusions, or they can't make up their minds! Everyone has a need for information and a need to make decisions, just as they must cope with being with people and with being alone.

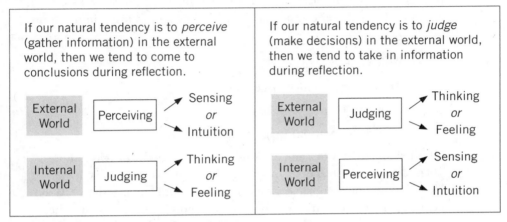

Figure 14.2: Psychological balance when judging and perceiving.

Thus, whether people lean toward extraversion or introversion, they need to access both the external and internal worlds to adequately take in information and make decisions. When people lack any of these, they become stymied in the process of maturing. Think about it: How do we describe immature people?

- They rush to a decision (they don't take in enough information).
- They can't seem to make a decision (they take in too much information).

Either behavior results in an unbalanced, immature approach to life and indicates that the individual hasn't learned to access the correct cognitive processes in the inner and outer worlds for his or her most natural path to maturity.

It is absolutely normal for students not to have developed their psychological preferences. They do not yet have conscious control (Murphy, 2013). Many strategies in this book are designed to help students spend plenty of time in their natural soil for growth while supporting them to stretch and develop the other processes that pave the path to maturity. Yes, successful, thriving, engaged, agile, *and* maturing.

With this explanation in mind, can you see how talking to write enriches and deepens students' thoughts? Can you see how this strategy gives them access to both their judging and perceiving pathways?

Reflection Activity

Consider the following actions and questions as you reflect on this chapter's content.

1. Experiment with the quality of your own writing. Does talking to write help, or are you better off writing and then talking through revisions? How does your own style color your education beliefs?

2. Students of all ages can explore the concepts of extraversion and introversion. Introduce the definitions from the Extraversion and Introversion section in chapter 1 (page 20) after using any of the following strategies in this book.

   ‣ Retrieve-Pair-Share (page 66)

   ‣ Wait-Go Cards (page 67)

   ‣ Anticipation Guides (page 123)

   ‣ Question Hunts (page 204)

   ‣ Knowledge Stations (page 206)

   Or, show the definitions and ask students to sit quietly for two minutes. Then, discuss their reactions to sitting still. How easy was it for them? How draining or energizing? Emphasize that your chosen activity is about being energized. Introverts can be just as friendly as extraverts, and they can definitely have friends. They just need time for themselves to recharge. Extraverts may not be show-offs or love to go to parties. They just get tired if they're sitting too long with no one to talk to. Use the rights and responsibilities interdependencies in Set Norms (page 210) to explore how students can honor both styles in the classroom.

3. Explore the interdependency between the sensing and intuitive preferences with your collaborative team. In a nutshell, can you imagine life (or the classroom) if you only saw the trees (sensing detail) or the forest (intuitive big picture)? People need both! For example, teams often feel empowered after a good conversation that balances reality (sensing) with vision (intuitive) as they think about employing a new strategy or initiative. You might prime the pump with a story such as *Charlotte's Web* (White, 1980) as a starting place. In *Charlotte's Web* (White, 1980), you step into a barn where the animals can talk to each other. When Wilbur the little piglet learns the fate of all little piglets on the farm, Charlotte the spider promises to save his life. Write each question from figure 14.3 on a separate sheet of chart paper. Work as a group to generate three to five answers for each. Then, arrange them as shown, with either sample response given for each; or write responses on a class whiteboard, arranged in the same way.

What are Charlotte's realities? What positive results flow from her focus on her realities?	What is Charlotte's vision? What positive results flow from her focus on her vision?
• She spins fabulous webs.	• She can save Wilbur's life.
What might happen if Charlotte overfocuses on her realities, losing sight of her vision? • She'll give up because of all the limitations of being a tiny spider.	What might happen if Charlotte overfocuses on her vision, losing sight of her realities? • She might forget to note the strengths of the friends that can help her.

Figure 14.3: *Yes-And Improvisation used to foster teacher discussion.*

Then, discuss how reality and vision relate to your team goals for students. What realities, such as time and resources, must team members keep in mind? What is the team's audacious vision for its students? How do team members find the right balance to avoid the downsides? Where do they go deep? Where might their energy go first?

PART 3

LESSON PLANNING

CHAPTER 15

Two-Step Differentiation

Doable differentiation flows from ensuring that over the course of a day, a unit, or a longer lesson, no students are constantly at a disadvantage because of their natural approach to learning. Throughout these pages, I've emphasized numerous strategies teachers can easily add to existing lessons and unit plans, such as Task Order (page 48), Anticipation Guides (page 123), and Spiderweb Discussions (page 146). Others, such as Posthole Questions (page 143), Moveable Outlines (page 193), or Knowledge Stations (page 206), might form the basis for an entire lesson or unit. Rather than present a series of strategies on a specific theme, this chapter adds one more tool to your toolkit for using the twelve strategy groups in this book: differentiating whole lessons or units so that all students are successful, thriving, engaged, agile, and maturing, our STEAM[2].

Start with any lesson or unit you'd like to differentiate—one you or a colleague created or one from your curriculum. As a prestep, apply the knowledge you gained from chapter 2 (page 33) by identifying clear goals and expectations. As this is critical, review chapter 2 if you have *any* questions about ensuring your goals and expectations are clear. In particular, make sure you have detailed learning progressions that will aid students in reaching your goals and expectations for them. From there, differentiation is a simple two-step process that depends on understanding the cognitive processing styles detailed in chapter 1 (page 15).

1. Identify the cognitive process *fit*.

2. Identify what you can change to *teach around* the cognitive processes.

That's it. To amplify how to do the two steps, first, use figure 1.1 (page 18) and figure 1.5 (page 28) to consider, "Whose needs are naturally met via this original lesson plan?" Second, use the same figures to consider what you might add to the lesson or unit to teach around the cognitive processes so that, over the course of an hour, a day, or a unit, all learners experience something that meets their style.

As you plan, remember the following.

- You don't have to differentiate every minute of every day. *But* these two steps ensure that none of your students are at a constant disadvantage.

- You might differentiate over the course of a unit or, in elementary classrooms, over the course of a day by giving choices or by assessing for learning in a differentiated way. *But* these two steps ensure that every student is naturally motivated.

- You might continue to teach many of your favorite units as in the past. *But* these two steps ensure that you're inviting along students who don't learn the way you do.

Once you recognize your own blind spots, it's far easier to know when to adjust your approach for students who just don't think like you. In this chapter, you'll first review a differentiated lesson plan geared toward adult learning that uses this chapter's two-step process. By looking at an example for adult professional development, you can think about your reactions when your style is and isn't honored. From there, you'll review a primary-grade example and a secondary-grade example. Each of these illustrates how this simple two-step process can help you achieve differentiation in your classroom using the other strategies you've read about throughout this book.

DOING DIFFERENTIATION

Consider figure 1.1 (page 18), concentrating on the cognitive process that is opposite your own. Note that structure and certainty, which fits the needs of introverted and sensing students, is opposite question and connection, which fits the needs of extraverted and intuitive students. Similarly, experience and movement, which fits the needs of extraverted and sensing students, is opposite to vision and interpretation, which meets the needs of introverted and intuitive students.

As you look at the content and processes that fit the style opposite your own, bring to mind your own school experiences. Can you think of a few assignments or courses with which you struggled? Were any of those a good fit for the style opposite your own? Now, look at the doable differentiation strategies listed for your own cognitive processing style. How might it have benefitted you had your teachers sometimes added a few of these approaches to increase your engagement?

A Differentiated Lesson Plan for Adults

In 2008, Beth Russell and I conducted a professional development workshop exercise where we categorized task descriptions (student assignments) using a rubric that listed task characteristics at various levels. Here's how we applied two-step differentiation as we planned for this workshop at the school where Beth was principal.

Our prestep involved setting the following clear goals and expectations for this activity.

1. Help collaborative teams establish common definitions of high-level and low-level student tasks.

2. Foster an understanding of how implementation of a task and not just the task itself is central to providing high-level student tasks.

3. Demonstrate differentiation strategies to meet the needs of all four cognitive processing styles.

With this essential foundation established, we could focus on executing the two-step process as detailed in the following sections.

Step 1: Identify the Cognitive Process Fit

Beth and I started with a general plan based on a workshop we'd experienced together and analyzed which cognitive processing styles it addressed. Figure 15.1 shows how you might use a graphic organizer to list the fit for each learning activity or step to visualize a lesson plan. This example shows how our original workshop experience, consisting of four steps, fits into the four cognitive processing styles.

Structure and Certainty (Let Me Know What to Do)	Vision and Interpretation (Let Me Follow My Own Lead)
	1. On their own, teachers read each of the twelve task cards and use the information provided to rank them as high level or low level.
Experience and Movement (Let Me Do Something)	**Question and Connection (Let Me Lead as I Learn)**
4. Facilitate a discussion to summarize how the lesson did and did not meet differentiation goals.	2. In groups, teachers compare their ratings and discuss why they rated each task as they did. 3. Each group comes to a unanimous agreement on each task rating.

Figure 15.1: Original task rigor lesson plan.

Visit **go.SolutionTree.com/instruction** *for a free reproducible version of this figure.*

Can you see the imbalances in this lesson plan? Unsurprisingly, my default tendency is vision and interpretation, and Beth's is question and connection. Is it any wonder we decided to bring this activity back to her staff? Yet we knew we needed to change it. We'd been using the cognitive processes framework at Beth's school for seven years, and every teacher and every student knew his or her preferred style. The majority of Beth's teachers preferred structure and certainty, and nothing in our lesson plan appealed to that group of teachers.

Step 2: Identify What You Can Change to Teach Around the Cognitive Processes

Even though the original approach wasn't balanced across the four styles, note that we didn't toss out this activity. Rather, we differentiated it so that we taught *around* the four cognitive processes. In making changes, we didn't try to meet everyone's needs every second, but we made it a priority to ensure we included one activity for every style during the session. This required some changes and expansion of our steps to ensure that discussions and summarizations met the first two learning targets and to meet our third learning target: demonstrate differentiation for the four cognitive processing styles.

With a focus established, we developed a new, revised lesson plan. Note in table 15.1 (page 236) that the "What Is Rigor?" reading and task cards for primary and secondary learning tasks referred to here are available at the Solution Tree website (visit www .SolutionTree.com/free-resources/plcatwork/cacc).

Table 15.1: *Comparing Original and Revised Lesson Plans*

Original Lesson Plan	Revised Lesson Plan
1. On their own, teachers read each of the twelve task cards and use the information provided to rank them as high level or low level.	1. Begin with an all-group discussion using a big notes moveable concept map on a whiteboard. Write *Rigor* in the middle, and circle it. Ask teachers to write what comes to mind when they hear *rigor* directly on the board or on strips of paper that they tape to the board.
2. In groups, teachers compare their ratings and discuss why they rated each task as they did.	2. Distribute copies of "What Is Rigor?" (Kise & Russell, 2010, pp. 190–193). To set clear expectations, let teachers know that after the reading, they'll be working together to rate tasks for their content areas as high level or low level. Then, have them work in small groups to read the text using the discussion protocol, read and say something.
	3. When small groups have finished the reading, have them make a moveable concept map (using a tree map) with statements that describe high-level and low-level tasks.
	4. To demonstrate using task cards, hold an all-group discussion, having teachers rate two tasks individually as high level and low level and then come to an agreement. 5. Provide a set of task cards to each teacher, and have the teachers sort the task cards into two piles: (1) high level and (2) low level.

3. Each group comes to a unanimous agreement on each task rating.	6. Display a sample chart for capturing individual ratings for each task, and give instructions that groups are to use student-centered discussions as they discuss and come to unanimous agreement on each task's rating. Have them hold the discussions.
	7. Have each group revise its tree map defining high-level and low-level tasks.
	8. Hold an all-group discussion as to what each group learned about rigor. Ensure that the following two huge ideas surface.
	    a. How a task is implemented can increase or decrease rigor.
	    b. Where a task is placed within a unit may increase or decrease rigor.

4. Facilitate a discussion to summarize how the lesson did and did not meet differentiation goals.	9. Use Retrieve-Pair-Share to discuss differentiation and cognitive processes.
	10. Remind teachers that instruction requires a mix of high-level and low-level tasks; ask them to bring two sample tasks from their own lessons to the next collaborative meeting. The groups will again work together to rate the tasks.

Figure 15.2 shows how the revised activities fit within the graphic organizer for the four cognitive processing styles.

Structure and Certainty (Let Me Know What to Do)	Vision and Interpretation (Let Me Follow My Own Lead)
4. To demonstrate using the task cards, hold an all-group discussion, having teachers rate two tasks individually as high level and low level and then come to an agreement. 6. Display a sample chart for capturing individual ratings for each task, and give instructions that groups are to use student-centered discussions as they discuss and come to unanimous agreement on each task's rating. Have them hold the discussions.	5. Provide a set of task cards to each teacher, and have the teachers sort the task cards into two piles: (1) high level and (2) low level. 9. Use Retrieve-Pair-Share to discuss differentiation and cognitive processes.
Experience and Movement (Let Me Do Something)	**Question and Connection (Let Me Lead as I Learn)**

1. Begin with an all-group discussion using a big notes moveable concept map on a whiteboard. Write *Rigor* in the middle, and circle it. Ask teachers to write what comes to mind when they hear *rigor* directly on the board or on strips of paper that they tape to the board.
2. Distribute copies of "What Is Rigor?" (Kise & Russell, 2010, pp. 190–193). To set clear expectations, let teachers know that after the reading, they'll be working together to rate tasks for their content areas as high level or low level. Then, have them work in small groups to read the text using the discussion protocol, read and say something.
10. Remind teachers that instruction requires a mix of high-level and low-level tasks; ask them to bring two sample tasks from their own lessons to the next collaborative meeting. The groups will again work together to rate the tasks.
	3. When small groups have finished the reading, have them make a moveable concept map (using a tree map) with statements that describe high-level and low-level tasks.
	7. Have each group revise its tree map defining high-level and low-level tasks.
	8. Hold an all-group discussion as to what each group learned about rigor. Ensure that the following two huge ideas surface.
	    a. How a task is implemented can increase or decrease rigor.
	    b. Where a task is placed within a unit may increase or decrease rigor.

Figure 15.2: *Differentiated task rigor lesson plan.*

Note that we *didn't* change the lesson to spend equal time using each of the cognitive processes. Instead, we adjusted the activities to allow some space for those who prefer introversion while taking advantage of an in-person workshop format. We also added structuring elements so that those with the cognitive processes on the left-hand side of figure 15.2 (page 237) could engage in the activities without distraction from procedural questions.

Now, the lesson has clear goals, activities to build an understanding of rigor, and differentiated adjustments to ensure everyone feels successful and stays engaged.

A Primary-Grade Example

Let's look at what differentiation might look like for an ecology unit for grades K–2. Note that for the purposes of this example, I found standards that are similar across the three grades and then provided a basic plan, adjusted for each grade level. I'll explain how I moved from the prestep of clear goals and expectations to the differentiated lesson plans.

To establish clear goals and expectations, I drew from the Minnesota Department of Education's (2019) state science standards for the following examples, which reflect a kindergarten standard, a first-grade standard, and a second-grade standard related to habitats:

> OL.3.1.1.1 Develop a simple model to represent the relationship between the needs of different plants and animals (including humans) and the places they live. (P: 2, CC: 4, CI: LS2) *Examples of relationships may include that deer eat buds and leaves, therefore, they usually live in forested areas; and grasses need sunlight, so they often grow in meadows. Examples of models may include food chains, collages, and/or sorting activities.* (p. 8)
>
> 1L.3.2.2.2 Plan and design a solution to a human problem by mimicking how plants and/or animals use their external parts to help them survive, grow, and meet their needs.* (P: 6, CC: 6, CI: LS1, ETS2) *Examples of human problems that can be solved by mimicking plant or animal solutions may include designing clothing or equipment to protect bicyclists by mimicking turtle shells, acorn shells, and animal scales; stabilizing structures by mimicking animal tails and roots on plants; keeping out intruders by mimicking thorns on branches and animal quills, and detecting intruders by mimicking eyes and ears.* (p. 11)
>
> 2L.4.1.1.1 Construct an argument with evidence that evaluates how in a particular habitat some organisms can survive well, some survive less well, and some cannot survive at all. (P: 7, CC: 2, CI: LS4, ETS2) *Emphasis is on the interdependence of parts of a system (organisms and their habitat). Examples of habitats should include those found in Minnesota, such as a wetland, prairie, or garden. Examples of evidence may include needs and characteristics of the organisms and habitats involved.* (p. 14)

Note that these standards have clear verbs (*model, plan,* and *construct*) that are helpful in moving from the standards to clear goals and expectations for students. While there are lots of possibilities, let's work with the following three tasks for the purpose of this example.

- **Kindergarten:** Students will do a card sort, showing that they can match plants and animals, and the food and shelter the animals need, to the habitats: prairie, boreal forest, and peat bog.

- **Grade 1:** Students will show how the function of an external animal or plant part can be mimicked to solve a human problem by drawing a representation of their solution and writing an accompanying explanation.

- **Grade 2:** In small groups, students will present arguments, with evidence, that support why each of three animals would thrive, survive less well, or not survive in the habitat assigned to their group.

The essential questions and learning tasks for the unit would then ensure students have the knowledge they need to meet these clear goals. Obviously, kindergartners aren't going to learn about every kind of habitat in the world; planning becomes easier when parameters are set. The second-grade standard mentions Minnesota habitats specifically; for simplicity, I've limited the expectations to Minnesota organisms and habitats for all three grades. Further, since Minnesota sprawls over almost 100,000 square miles with numerous ecosystems, I've focused students on just three ecosystems to establish necessary clarity for workable success criteria: (1) southwest prairie, (2) northeast boreal forest, and (3) the peat bogs of the northwest part of the state.

Step 1: Identify the Cognitive Process Fit

Start by looking at where the final projects or tasks fit within the cognitive processes, as shown in figure 15.3. Figure 1.1 (page 18) becomes a handy resource in deciding fit.

Structure and Certainty (Let Me Know What to Do)	Vision and Interpretation (Let Me Follow My Own Lead)
Kindergarten: Modeling (using food chains, collages, or card sorts); *this task involves working with facts and can be highly structured.*	First grade: Problem solving (designing equipment that mimics plants or animals to solve a human problem) where each student does a solo project; *this task allows students to follow their own curiosity and use their imaginations.*
Experience and Movement (Let Me Do Something)	**Question and Connection (Let Me Lead as I Learn)**
	Second grade: Argumentation (constructing arguments on how organisms might die out, survive, or thrive in the same habitat); *this task lets students tell about what they have learned and work with the big picture of survival, drawing on facts rather than memorizing facts being the goal.*

Figure 15.3: *Process for establishing fit for grades K–2 lesson goals.*

The keys to establishing fit are the specific task and success criteria you created in the prestep; this is why clear goals and expectations are essential to differentiation. For example, if a teaching team decides that the second-grade product would be individual persuasive essays rather than presentations or oral discussions, then it would fit better for the more introverted vision-and-interpretation students. If kindergarten teachers decided to have students work in groups to create different habitats in the classroom, with paper grasses and trees, and then act as tour guides to other groups, the task would better fit experience-and-movement students. For this step, concentrate on how you, or your team, plan to structure a task and then identify the best fit.

Let's go a little deeper into the initial plan for all three grade levels and assume that all teachers will begin the unit by reading *Creekfinding: A True Story* by Jacqueline Briggs Martin (2017). It recounts how scientist and leading epidemiologist Mike Osterholm learned of a long-buried creek under cornfields in Iowa (identical to the cornfields in southern Minnesota!) and how he undertook a years-long process to restore it to its original course and condition. This picture book contains plenty to spark students' thinking about how animals disappeared and reappeared as the habitat changed, laying a foundation for all three tasks.

Now, it's time to differentiate so that all students can succeed, thrive as part of the classroom community, engage with the fascinating ideas about habitat and survival, develop agility with tasks that are a bit of a stretch, and mature. Think of how different points of emphasis might support students maturing in different ways; for example, you might provide chances to collaborate or work alone, self-monitor progress, and more.

Step 2: Identify What You Can Change to Teach Around the Cognitive Processes

As before, now that you've identified the cognitive process that will most naturally engage with the final learning tasks for meeting the chosen standards, it's time to plan so that, over the course of the unit, all students have chances to engage through their own styles. Use a graphic organizer similar to the example in figure 15.4 to brainstorm ideas for each of the cognitive processes.

With a list of ideas aligned to each cognitive process, make a chart similar to figure 15.5 (page 242) to plan the flow of the unit, ensuring that at least one of the activities you identified for each cognitive process is included. The specific example in this figure shows what a differentiated lesson might look like for each grade level (K–2) so that you have three examples of teaching around cognitive processes. The chart you make need only reflect one grade level.

Through this work, you have clear goals, clear learning targets, and a plan for teaching around the cognitive processes. Once you select activities, you can finish up by preparing the rubrics, worked examples, and instructions students would need to be successful.

	Structure and Certainty (Let Me Know What to Do)	Vision and Interpretation (Let Me Follow My Own Lead)
Traits of This Cognitive Processing Style	At their best, these students seek clarity on what is to be learned and the best way to learn it. Their motivation may be efficiency ("Let's not waste time guessing if there's a good way to do it"), a desire to please adults, or a healthy love of getting the right answer.	At their best, these students seek to answer their own questions, use their imaginations, and express what they have learned. Their motivation may be curiosity, a desire to solve a problem, or a desire to follow up on connections, imaginings, and hunches their brains create.
Favorite Doable Differentiation Strategies for This Style	Direct Instruction Thinking Maps Learning Progression Study Guides Worked Examples Discussion Protocols	Student-Generated Open Questions Catalysts Knowledge Stations Open Questions for Text Reading Materials
Notes		
	Experience and Movement (Let Me Do Something)	**Question and Connection (Let Me Lead as I Learn)**
Traits of This Cognitive Processing Style	At their best, these students use acute observations of the real world to solve problems. They think by touching, manipulating, and experimenting, often through purposeful trial and error. Their motivations involve making, solving, or fixing things, often to help others one on one.	At their best, these students move quickly from what is taught to what could be. They think by collaborating, discussing, or debating to generate ideas or plans that get others excited. Their motivations include influencing others and using theoretical or imaginative approaches to create new ideas.
Favorite Doable Differentiation Strategies for This Style	Standing Room, Wiggle Room Group Whiteboards Manipulatives Talking to write strategies Question Hunts	Anticipation Guides Posthole Questions All-Class Brainstorming Multiple Right Answers Concept Map Manipulatives
Notes		

Figure 15.4: Planning template for teaching around the cognitive processes.
Visit go.SolutionTree.com/instruction for a free reproducible version of this figure.

	Kindergarten	First Grade	Second Grade
Cognitive Processes and Strategy	For all listed grade levels, provide a learning map that shows the topics to be covered. Also, preview the final assignment, showing either a worked example from a previous class or one that you make.		
Activity 1: Experience and movement. Planned movement—Students move from posted picture to posted picture in small groups, talking about the guiding questions.	Set up a poster walk of five or six creek images. (Search for web images of creeks, city creeks, underground creeks, polluted creeks, and buried creeks.) Students do the walk in small groups, discussing the guiding questions: How are these creeks similar and different? What may have happened to make these differences?	Provide a picture gallery of creek life. (Search for web images of plants, mammals, birds, reptiles, and amphibians mentioned in *Creekfinding*.) Students do the walk in small groups, discussing the guiding questions: What do you notice about these living things? What features do they have that humans don't have? What do these features do?	Provide a picture gallery of creek life. (Search for web images of plants, mammals, birds, reptiles, and amphibians mentioned in *Creekfinding*.) Students do the walk in small groups, discussing the guiding questions: What do you know about this living thing? What does it need in its habitat to thrive?
Activity 2: Structure and certainty. Big notes chart paper or group whiteboard	Provide groups with a big notes chart paper or group whiteboard to capture their answers to the guiding questions. Encourage the use of both words and images so that students with all levels of writing skills can add to the organizer.	Have each group choose two or three of the living things in the pictures to concentrate on. Provide a big notes laminated tool of a graphic organizer, such as a matrix, to capture their answers to the guiding questions.	Color-code the living things in the pictures into three groups. 1. Those that emerged first as the creek was reestablished 2. Those that emerged in the middle of the restoration 3. Those that appeared toward the end of *Creekfinding* Have each student group choose one living thing from each group. Groups can use the triangle notes version of the four corners graphic organizer to record information. Let them decide what will be important information for the final project. Let them know that they will later be able to fill in things they don't know.

Activity 3: Vision and interpretation. Read aloud with questions that emphasize making inferences and drawing conclusions.	Post and explain the question, "What can we learn from *Creekfinding* about what plants and animals need in an environment to thrive?" Read *Creekfinding* to the class. Using Wait-Go Cards or another wait time strategy, have each student comment on the text as you read. All cards start on the Go side. When students have made a comment, they turn their card to Wait until all have contributed. Post the following discussion prompt reminders to help them remember what to say. ? I have a question. ⇔ I'd like to make a connection with our poster walk. ● I'd like to make a connection with something else I know.	Post and explain the question, "Not all living things can thrive in the creek we'll be reading about as it evolves. Which ones interest you the most? What about their features helps them find food, protect themselves, and thrive in other ways? As I read, note on your individual whiteboards which animals interest you. Afterward, we'll talk about what we've noticed about these animals." Read *Creekfinding* to the class.	Post and explain the question, "The characteristics of the creek as an ecosystem change throughout this story. What happens to the creek that lets your living things thrive? What do they need?" Read *Creekfinding* aloud. Or, have enough copies for one group to read it independently while other groups work on other knowledge stations related to ecosystems.
Activity 4: Question and connection: Group project	Use Visual Representations for Group Summaries (page 180). (Each group chooses one living thing shown in *Creekfinding*, a nonlinguistic representation.) Students work together to illustrate what that living thing needs to thrive. Have copies of the book available so they can revisit illustrations.	Have groups brainstorm using bubble maps. The task itself, designing equipment based on an animal characteristic that solves a human problem, is a posthole question. Using a separate bubble map for each characteristic, they review their matrix and brainstorm what human problems this characteristic might solve. They can then, for example, draw their idea, craft with art supplies, or model it with clay, and explain their invention to the class.	Provide each group with one more living thing that lives in Iowa creeks but isn't depicted in the story. Each group is to design a poster (chart paper that reflects a graphic or freeform organizer) to answer, "When in the creek restoration process could this living thing be introduced and thrive? What needs to be present in the habitat? What are your evidence and reasoning?"
Unit Continuation	Provide additional activities for background knowledge on the other two habitats the unit will cover: boreal forests and peat bogs. Then, students can complete learning tasks to demonstrate their mastery of the standard.		

Figure 15.5: Lesson plan for teaching around cognitive processes—*Primary-grade example.*

Visit go.SolutionTree.com/instruction for a free reproducible version of this figure.

A Secondary-Grade Example

Here's an example based on a lesson from a secondary science teacher for a three-week unit on energy transformations. He developed the original concept early on in a multi-year professional development effort on differentiation that I facilitated at his school. I revisited this lesson in light of the proposed Minnesota state science standards, in which *energy* is one of four core disciplinary ideas that run throughout the standards (Minnesota Department of Education, 2019). However, the standards assume prior knowledge about forms of energy to meet learning targets (Minnesota Department of Education, 2019):

> 7L.3.1.1.3 Develop and use a model to describe the cycling of matter and flow of energy among living and nonliving parts of an ecosystem. (P: 2, CC: 5, CI: LS2) *Emphasis is on describing the conservation of matter and flow of energy into and out of various ecosystems.* (p. 30)
>
> 8P.2.1.1.2 Construct and interpret graphical displays of data to describe the relationship of kinetic energy to the mass and speed of an object. (P: 4, CC: 3, CI: PS3) *Emphasis is on descriptive relationships between kinetic energy and mass separately from kinetic energy and speed. Examples may include riding a bicycle at different speeds, rolling different sizes of rocks downhill, and getting hit by a Wiffle ball versus a tennis ball.* (p. 35)

Therefore, I kept an introductory energy unit with the following learning targets.

1.   Understand the seven forms of energy and how energy gets transformed from one form to another.

2.   See that energy is neither created nor destroyed.

3.   Appreciate alternative methods for making electricity.

In this case, examining the standards revealed a gap in the knowledge students would need to succeed with upcoming units based on the actual standards. The original lesson fit well with STEAM[2] as well; if students are going to learn about various energy concepts via different standards at nearly every grade level, teachers not only want them to be successful but engaged with the material as well as increasingly agile with various approaches to science and learning that the standards require.

Step 1: Identify the Cognitive Process Fit

In working on the original lesson plan, the teacher realized the class textbook took an approach most suitable for learners who prefer structure and certainty, with descriptions of the seven forms of energy and several objective questions at the end of the chapter, the majority of which involve reviewing and recalling the information. Figure 15.6 illustrates how this mapped onto the four cognitive processing styles.

The teacher's cognitive processing preference orients toward the question-and-connection style, so he was eager to differentiate.

Structure and Certainty (Let Me Know What to Do)	Vision and Interpretation (Let Me Follow My Own Lead)
Original textbook approach to material: Direct instruction through lecture and textbook reading. Students demonstrate mastery of knowledge of seven forms of energy, conservation of energy, and alternative methods for making electricity by answering fact-based questions.	
Experience and Movement (Let Me Do Something)	**Question and Connection** (Let Me Lead as I Learn)

Figure 15.6: *Process for establishing fit for secondary-level learning tasks.*

Step 2: Identify What You Can Change to Teach Around the Cognitive Processes

With the textbook materials so clearly meeting the needs of only the cognitive process that the teacher least preferred, his first idea for differentiating was a group project that would engage students with his question-and-connection style. You'll see it as the final step (step 7) of his final lesson plan.

Sometimes, all you need to do is start with the existing materials and adjust for the opposite by adding one activity. Why? Remember from chapter 1 (page 15) that structure and certainty honors introversion and sensing. Question and connection honors extraversion and intuition. When lessons include activities from diagonal quadrants (as in figure 15.7, page 246) no student is completely left out. In this case, though, the teacher knew he needed more activities to help students gain the knowledge they required to be successful with the final group project, so he added other learning tasks, teaching around the styles to more fully engage all students. Figure 15.7 contains the revised, differentiated unit lessons.

I cannot firmly enough emphasize that teachers need not (and should not attempt to) differentiate every moment of every day. However, over the course of the unit, every student will have moments of learning in his or her own style and moments where he or she is required to stretch.

Structure and Certainty (Let Me Know What to Do)	Vision and Interpretation (Let Me Follow My Own Lead)
1. Introduce a learning map. Provide direct instruction regarding the seven forms of energy. Students then discuss examples in the room or in their lives of these forms of energy. 2. Show a film that introduces the topic. Students use a graphic organizer for notes and a vocabulary sheet.	6. Engage students in independent research as background for a final group project.
Experience and Movement (Let Me Do Something)	**Question and Connection (Let Me Lead as I Learn)**
3. Set up an energy walking tour. Students work together to see different forms of energy in their environment, inside and outside, keeping a log. 5. Assign structured experiments for different forms of energy (making batteries, using motors and generators, and so on).	4. Assign a picture portfolio project in which students illustrate each of the energy transformations. 7. Engage students in a group project, making a model of an alternative energy source (wind, solar, hydro, and so on) and presenting to "sell" their alternative energy idea.

Figure 15.7: *Lesson plan for teaching around cognitive processes—Secondary-grade example.*

Not all the details are here. Picture the teacher providing students with a graphic organizer for the direct instruction that guides students in gathering the factual information but doesn't simply tell them the facts. Know that there are clear instructions for the laboratory experiments. Students see models from past classes of alternative-energy projects before engaging in their research. The final project also has a detailed rubric so that students understand the project requirements and scoring criteria. The teacher or teacher team puts all those details together after the main structure of the lesson is in place so that bridges are built for learning back and forth between the students who live on the left side of figure 1.1 (page 18) and those who live on the right side of it.

Try it. Pull out a plan you've used but would love to improve. Use figure 1.1 along with the graphic organizer in figure 15.1 (page 235) to revise, and see more students succeed, thrive, engage, demonstrate agility, and mature—the STEAM² goal for educating the whole child.

Reflection Activity

Consider the following actions and questions as you reflect on this chapter's content.

1. The best way to reflect on this chapter is to apply the two-step differentiation process to one of your lessons or units. If you're unsure whether you're

differentiating enough, show the lesson or unit to a colleague who doesn't think like you. What might he or she add or subtract?

2. The two-step differentiation process shown in this chapter assumes that all students will be working with the same content and creating the same products. Note that several strategies, such as strategies for providing choices (chapter 3, page 47), Layered Curriculum (Assignment Menus, page 55), and Knowledge Stations (page 206), as well as other doable differentiation strategies, allow for differentiation of content and product. Reflect on the following on your own, or discuss the following with your collaborative team.

   ‣ When do you need to differentiate content so that, for example, tasks match a student's current capacity for comprehending text or working with mathematical concepts?

   ‣ When does differentiating for content become an equity issue, preventing some students from working with higher-level content?

   ‣ When is differentiating to give all students access to the same high-level content an equity strategy?

   ‣ When does differentiating to give all students access to the same high-level content become an equity issue because of difficulties providing the time and support some students need to succeed?

   To prime the discussion, look back to the example of the goals of reading *Hamlet* (chapter 2, page 33). Differentiating content and products is an issue that can't really be solved once and for all but that needs consideration each time your team engages in differentiation.

3. Take a hard look at your curriculum (alone or with your team), using figure 15.4 (page 241) to list lessons you plan to use. Is there any bias? Are some students at an advantage because it favors their cognitive process? How can you brainstorm to incorporate doable differentiation strategies to increase equity through this lens?

Epilogue

Consider the following scene: a third-floor dimly lit hallway at an urban high school, where I'm in the midst of facilitating a year-long professional development effort on differentiated instruction for grades 7–12 teachers. I've just left a meeting with content-team leaders when another teacher catches me in the hallway. The following describes the ensuing discussion.

Teacher: Can I ask you about something from my class today?

Jane: Sure.

Teacher: I was demonstrating a mathematics problem at the whiteboard, and one of my more vocal students said, "That doesn't really make sense. I could explain it better than you."

[The teacher hesitates.]

I handed him the marker. Was that the right thing to do?

Jane: Well, how did it go?

Teacher: You know, he did a really good job. And the other students paid attention to what he was saying like you wouldn't believe. I let him do another one the next day. Now other students want to try "being teacher," as they call it.

Jane: So, what are you thinking?

Teacher: It's planned movement, isn't it? And a bit of choice. And big notes.

Jane: [Nods]

Teacher: I'm thinking I give a couple of students a day a chance to do this. But we probably need to discuss a few norms around respect for my instruction and the reasons for that. Maybe I'll use those discussion prompts?

Jane: That sounds great! Have you thought about demonstrating how the class can handle and learn from a mistake?

Teacher: Yeah, I like that idea. You know, I'm pretty sure the vocal student is a let me lead as I learn type [question and connection], which is kind of my opposite. What a difference in behavior when he got to put it to use! That two-step differentiation worked. Thanks; I really get it now.

[The teacher turns and skips down the hall back to his classroom.]

Yes, a tenth-grade mathematics teacher literally skipped down the hall following this conversation. While you don't necessarily need to skip, that sense of *Yes!* is what I hope these pages will do for you.

Much as doable differentiation is, of course, about the students—instilling STEAM^2 by bringing both a whole-child approach and embedding social and emotional learning in academic learning—I also want all of the adults in a learning community to experience success, thrive in their chosen roles, engage fully in their work, move with agility when the inevitable unexpected happens, and continue maturing in wisdom via more and more experiences with student success.

As a consultant, my mission is to partner with educators to co-create environments where everyone wants to be. In a school, I want everyone—students, teachers, administrators, support staff, families, coaches—to feel not just welcome but successful, thriving, engaged, agile, and maturing through lifelong learning.

One teacher can delve into the four cognitive processes, begin reframing students who simply think differently, and try out this book's twelve strategies to bring STEAM^2 to his or her classroom. I've seen over and over, just like in my little story of the mathematics teacher, how this understanding bolsters teacher confidence, adds immediately useful tools to their teaching repertoire, and increases their ability to both build relationships with students and scaffold for success. Another favorite moment of mine occurred when a teacher, again, hurrying to catch me in a hallway, said, "The students—they understand me so much better now. Teaching is *easier!*"

If you are an administrator, teacher leader, or in a district office role, imagine being able to talk with teachers less about what is right or wrong with instruction but about teacher and student strengths, how teachers might best present content, and how just one extra differentiating step to ensure no one is left out makes a world of difference.

It's a given that the twelve strategies don't solve everything in a mixed-ability classroom. But if you've been trying the strategies, you've no doubt seen that students who are engaged with content can work at a higher cognitive level than if they aren't engaged. You've seen that as students develop more agility among learning tasks that draw on different cognitive processes, the "I can't" changes to, "Oh, this is out of my style, and I need a different strategy." You've seen students mature as they listen to each other, build on ideas, justify their conclusions, and respectfully examine mistakes.

These factors lead to more intrinsic motivation; more students engage in the tasks before them, letting you concentrate on those who need more support or extension. I've seen it over and over in classrooms around the world. Remember the following.

- You don't have to differentiate every moment.
- You can still use favorite lessons, adjusting via the two-step process.
- You don't have to know every student's style; you've got them all!
- You *do* need to have clear goals, understand your own approach, and adjust for students who don't think like you.

I hope that as you delve into the recipes in this cookbook of strategies, you will also find, "Yes, this is doable!"

References and Resources

Adams, J. L. (2019). *Conceptual blockbusting: A guide to better ideas* (5th ed.). New York: Basic Books.

Agarwal, P. K. (2020). Powerful learning is all about retrieval. *Education Update, 62*(3), 1–4.

Agee, J. (2018). *The wall in the middle of the book.* New York: Dial Books.

Allen-Lyall, B., & Davis, V. (2020). Empowering students to make their own reading choices: A teaching framework. *Reading Improvement, 57*(1), 1–10.

Almarode, J., Fisher, D., & Frey, N. (2019). Bringing clarity to science instruction. *Science Teacher, 87*(3), 19–23.

Anderson, G. (2013, July 28). What I learned in summer school. *What's Not Wrong?* Accessed at https://whatsnotwrong.wordpress.com/2013/07/28/what-i-learned-in-summer-school on August 25, 2020.

Anderson, L. W., & Krathwohl, D. R. (Eds.). (2001). *A taxonomy for learning, teaching, and assessing: A revision of Bloom's taxonomy of educational objectives.* New York: Longman.

Angeli, C., & Valanides, N. (2013). Using educational data mining methods to assess field-dependent and field-independent learners' complex problem solving. *Educational Technology Research and Development, 61*(3), 521–548.

Arain, M., Haque, M., Johal, L., Mathur, P., Nel, W., Rais, A., et al. (2013). Maturation of the adolescent brain. *Neuropsychiatric Disease and Treatment, 9,* 449–461.

Audusseau, J., & Juhel, J. (2015). Working memory in children predicts performance on a gambling task. *Journal of Genetic Psychology, 176*(1), 38–54.

Austen, J. (2003). *Pride and prejudice.* New York: Penguin. (Original work published 1813)

Averette, P. (n.d.). *Save the last word for me.* Accessed at www.nsrfharmony.org/wp-content/uploads/2017/10/save_last_word_0.pdf on February 25, 2021.

AVID Center. (2017). *Making the note-taking process more accessible: What educators can do.* Accessed at www.avid.org/cms/lib/CA02000374/Centricity/Domain/35/Making%20the%20Note-Taking%20Process%20More%20Accessible.pdf on March 3, 2020.

Bal, A. P. (2016). The effect of the differentiated teaching approach in the algebraic learning field on students' academic achievements. *Eurasian Journal of Educational Research, 63,* 185–204.

Beers, K. (2003). *When kids can't read: What teachers can do—Guide for teachers 6–12.* Portsmouth, NH: Heinemann.

Berk, L. E., & Meyers, A. B. (2013). The role of make-believe play in the development of executive function status of research and future directions. *American Journal of Play, 6*(1), 98–110. Accessed at https://files.eric.ed.gov/fulltext/EJ1016170.pdf on August 25, 2020.

Beymer, P. N., & Thomson, M. M. (2015). The effects of choice in the classroom: Is there too little or too much choice? *Support for Learning, 30*(2), 105–120.

Blair, S., & Sutherland, M. A. (2018). *The learning puzzle: Linking personality and learning.* Auckland, New Zealand: Personality Dynamics. Accessed at www.personalitypuzzles.com /wp-content/uploads/2018/08/The-Learning-Puzzle-Guidebook.pdf on February 28, 2021.

Boaler, J., & Zoido, P. (2016). Why math education in the U.S. doesn't add up. *Scientific American Mind, 27*(6), 18–19. Accessed at www.scientificamerican.com/article/why-math -education-in-the-u-s-doesn-t-add-up on April 30, 2018.

Bråten, I., Johansen, R.-P., & Strømsø, H. I. (2017). Effects of different ways of introducing a reading task on intrinsic motivation and comprehension. *Journal of Research in Reading, 40*(1), 17–36.

Bridges, R. (2009). *Ruby Bridges goes to school: My true story.* New York: Cartwheel Books.

Burke, J. (2002). *Tools for thought: Graphic organizers for your classroom.* Portsmouth, NH: Heinemann.

Burns, M. (2015). *About teaching mathematics: A K–8 resource* (4th ed.). Sausalito, CA: Math Solutions.

Card, O. S. (1985). *Ender's game.* New York: Tor Books.

Card, O. S. (1999). *Ender's shadow.* New York: Tor Books.

Cavendish, M. (Ed.), & Clark, A. (n.d.). *Singapore math: A visual approach to word problems.* Singapore: Times Publishing Group. Accessed at www.hmhco.com/~/media/sites/home /education/global/pdf/white-papers/mathematics/elementary/math-in-focus/mif_model _drawing_lr.pdf on February 4, 2021.

Chamine, S. (2012). *Positive intelligence: Why only 20% of teams and individuals achieve their true potential and how you can achieve yours.* Austin, TX: Greenleaf Book Group Press.

Clark, R., Nguyen, F., & Sweller, J. (2005). *Efficiency in learning: Evidence-based guidelines to manage cognitive load.* San Francisco: Wiley.

Cohen, E. G., & Lotan, R. A. (2014). *Designing groupwork: Strategies for the heterogeneous classroom* (3rd ed.). New York: Teachers College Press.

Collaborative for Academic, Social, and Emotional Learning. (n.d.). *SEL is . . .* Accessed at https://casel.org/what-is-sel on December 4, 2020.

Cornell University. (n.d.). *The Cornell note taking system.* Accessed at http://lsc.cornell.edu /study-skills/cornell-note-taking-system on March 3, 2020.

Corwin Visible Learning+. (n.d.a). *Global research database.* Accessed at www.visiblelearningmetax .com/Influences on November 3, 2019.

Corwin Visible Learning+. (n.d.b). *Self-reported grades.* Accessed at www.visiblelearningmetax.com /Influences/View/self-reported_grades on November 3, 2019.

Costa, A. L. (n.d.). *What are habits of mind?* Accessed at www.habitsofmindinstitute.org/what -are-habits-of-mind on November 17, 2020.

Costa, A. L., & Kallick, B. (2015). Five strategies for questioning with intention. *Educational Leadership, 73*(1), 66–69.

Craft, J. (2019). *New kid.* New York: Quill Tree Books.

Crichton, H., & McDaid, A. (2016). Learning intentions and success criteria: Learners' and teachers' views. *Curriculum Journal, 27*(2), 190–203.

Curtis, C. P. (1995). *The Watsons go to Birmingham—1963.* New York: Random House.

Dabrowski, J., & Marshall, T. R. (2018). *Motivation and engagement in student assignments: The role of choice and relevancy.* Washington, DC: The Education Trust. Accessed at https://edtrust.org /resource/motivation-and-engagement-in-student-assignments on August 26, 2020.

Dali, S. (1939). *The enigma of Hitler.* Accessed at www.museoreinasofia.es/en/collection/artwork /enigma-hitler on February 28, 2021.

Dali, S. (1958). *The discovery of America by Christopher Columbus.* Accessed at https://archive .thedali.org/mwebcgi/mweb.exe?request=record;id=1506;type=101 on February 28, 2021.

Davidow, J. Y., Sheridan, M. A., Van Dijk, K. R. A., Santillana, R. M., Snyder, J., Bustamante, C. M. V., et al. (2019). Development of prefrontal cortical connectivity and the enduring effect of learned value on cognitive control. *Journal of Cognitive Neuroscience, 31*(1), 64–77.

Daywalt, D. (2013). *The day the crayons quit.* New York: Philomel Books.

Dejarnette, N. K. (2018). Early childhood steam: Reflections from a year of steam initiatives implemented in a high-needs primary school. *Education, 139*(2), 96–110.

Delisle, J. R. (2015). Differentiation doesn't work. *Education Week, 34*(15), 28, 36. Accessed at www.edweek.org/ew/articles/2015/01/07/differentiation-doesnt-work.html on March 30, 2019.

Dickens, C. (2014). *Oliver Twist.* New York: Shine Classics. (Original work published 1838)

Donnelly, J. E., Greene, J. L., Gibson, C. A., Smith, B. K., Washburn, R. A., Sullivan, D. K., et al. (2009). Physical activity across the curriculum (PAAC): A randomized controlled trial to promote physical activity and diminish overweight and obesity in elementary school children. *Preventive Medicine, 49*(4), 336–341.

Dr. Seuss. (1997). *A hatful of Seuss: Five favorite Dr. Seuss stories.* New York: Random House.

Duckworth, A. (2016). *Grit: The power of passion and perseverance.* New York: Scribner.

DuFour, R., DuFour, R., Eaker, R., Many, T., & Mattos, M. (2016). *Learning by doing: A handbook for Professional Learning Communities at Work* (3rd ed.). Bloomington, IN: Solution Tree Press.

Dunn, K., & Darlington, E. (2016). GCSE Geography teachers' experiences of differentiation in the classroom. *International Research in Geographical and Environmental Education, 25*(4), 344–357.

Dweck, C. S. (2016). *Mindset: The new psychology of success* (Updated ed.). New York: Ballantine Books.

Eggers, D. (2017). *Her right foot.* San Francisco: Chronicle Books.

Ellis, D. (2000). *The breadwinner: An Afghan child in a war torn land.* Toronto, Ontario, Canada: Douglas & McIntyre.

Einstein, G., & May, C. (2019). The art of memory: Drawing can improve memory. *Observer, 32*(4), 38–39. Accessed at www.psychologicalscience.org/redesign/wp-content/uploads /2019/04/April_OBS_2019-Online.pdf on February 28, 2021.

Ewoldt, K. B., & Morgan, J. J. (2017). Color-coded graphic organizers for teaching writing to students with learning disabilities. *Teaching Exceptional Children, 49*(3), 175–184.

Felder, R. M., & Brent, R. (2005). Understanding student differences. *Journal of Engineering Education, 94*(1), 57–72.

Fernández, C., & Yoshida, M. (2004). *Lesson study: A Japanese approach to improving mathematics teaching and learning.* Mahwah, NJ: Erlbaum.

Fisher, D., & Frey, N. (2014). *Better learning through structured teaching: A framework for the gradual release of responsibility* (2nd ed.). Alexandria, VA: Association for Supervision and Curriculum Development.

Fisher, D., Frey, N., & Almarode, J. (2019). 5 questions PLCs should ask to promote equity. *Learning Forward, 40*(5), 44–47.

Fisher, D., Frey, N., Amador, O., & Assof, J. (2019). *The teacher clarity playbook: A hands-on guide to creating learning intentions and success criteria for organized, effective instruction.* Thousand Oaks, CA: Corwin Press.

Fisher, D., Frey, N., & Lapp, D. (2012). *Teaching students to read like detectives: Comprehending, analyzing, and discussing text.* Bloomington, IN: Solution Tree Press.

Flanagan, L. (2015, February 25). How improv can open up the mind to learning in the classroom and beyond [Blog post]. Accessed at www.kqed.org/mindshift/39108/how-improv -can-open-up-the-mind-to-learning-in-the-classroom-and-beyond on February 28, 2021.

Froiland, J. M., & Worrell, F. C. (2016). Intrinsic motivation, learning goals, engagement, and achievement in a diverse high school. *Psychology in the Schools, 53*(3), 321–336.

Frey, N., Fisher, D., & Everlove, S. (2009). *Productive group work: How to engage students, build teamwork, and promote understanding.* Alexandria, VA: Association for Supervision and Curriculum Development.

Fuller, A., & Fuller, L. (2021). *Neurodevelopmental differentiation: Optimizing brain systems to maximize learning.* Bloomington, IN: Solution Tree Press.

Fyfe, E. R., McNeil, N. M., Son, J. Y., & Goldstone, R. L. (2014). Concreteness fading in mathematics and science instruction: A systematic review. *Educational Psychology Review*, *26*(1), 9–25.

Gillies, R. M., Nichols, K., & Khan, A. (2015). The effects of scientific representations on primary students' development of scientific discourse and conceptual understandings during cooperative contemporary inquiry-science. *Cambridge Journal of Education*, *45*(4), 427–449.

Goulis, L. (2019, November 14). *How Play-Doh's makers got themselves out of a sticky situation.* Accessed at www.kidsnews.com.au/just-for-fun/how-playdohs-makers-got-themselves-out-of-a-sticky-situation/news-story/04e0d3503318243ab5fcd31a6e81eee7 on January 4, 2021.

Grift, G., & Major, C. (2020). *Teachers as architects of learning: Twelve constructs to design and configure successful learning experiences* (2nd ed.). Bloomington, IN: Solution Tree Press.

Gunderson, S., Jones, R., & Scanland, K. (2004). *The jobs revolution: Changing how America works.* Chicago: Copywriters Inc.

Hall, K. (2019). *Stories that stick: How storytelling can captivate customers, influence audiences, and transform your business.* New York: HarperCollins.

Hammond, Z. (2015). *Culturally responsive teaching and the brain: Promoting authentic engagement and rigor among culturally and linguistically diverse students.* Thousand Oaks, CA: Corwin Press.

Hammond, Z. (2020). The power of protocols for equity. *Educational Leadership*, *77*(7), 45–50.

Hanewicz, C., Platt, A., & Arendt, A. (2017). Creating a learner-centered teaching environment using student choice in assignments. *Distance Education*, *38*(3), 273–287.

Hardy, I., Kloetzer, B., Moeller, K., & Sodian, B. (2010). The analysis of classroom discourse: Elementary school science curricula advancing reasoning with evidence. *Educational Assessment*, *15*(3–4), 197–221.

Hattie, J. (2012). *Visible learning for teachers: Maximizing impact on learning.* New York: Routledge.

Heath, C., & Heath, D. (2007). *Made to stick: Why some ideas survive and others die.* New York: Random House.

Heuton, C., & Falacci, N. (Producers). (2005). *Numb3rs* [Television series]. New York: CBS.

Hodgson, D. (2012). *Personality in the classroom: Motivating and inspiring every teacher and student.* Bethel, CT: Crown House.

Hodgson, D. (2018). The elephant in the classroom. *TypeFace*, *29*(4), 18–19.

Hollar, D., Messiah, S. E., Lopez-Mitnik, G., Hollar, T. L., Almon, M., & Agatston, A. S. (2010). Effect of a two-year obesity prevention intervention on percentile changes in body mass index and academic performance in low-income elementary school children. *American Journal of Public Health*, *100*(4), 646–653.

Humphrey, S. L., & Feez, S. (2016). Direct instruction fit for purpose: Applying a metalinguistic toolkit to enhance creative writing in the early secondary years. *Australian Journal of Language & Literacy*, *39*(3), 207–219.

Hyerle, D. N., & Alper, L. (Eds.). (2011). *Student successes with Thinking Maps: School-based research, results, and models for achievement using visual tools* (2nd ed.). Thousand Oaks, CA: Corwin Press.

Hyerle, D. N., & Alper, L. (Eds.). (2014). *Pathways to thinking schools*. Thousand Oaks, CA: Corwin Press.

Ingram, J., & Elliott, V. (2016). A critical analysis of the role of wait time in classroom interactions and the effects on student and teacher interactional behaviours. *Cambridge Journal of Education, 46*(1), 37–53.

Jarosz, A. F., Colflesh, G. J. H., & Wiley, J. (2012). Uncorking the muse: Alcohol intoxication facilitates creative problem solving. *Consciousness and Cognition, 21*(1), 487–493.

Jung, C. G. (1923). General description of the types. In *Psychological Types* (H. G. Bayes, Trans.). Accessed at https://psychclassics.yorku.ca/Jung/types.htm on February 28, 2021. (Original work published 1921)

Jung, C. G. (1971). Psychological types (Vol. 6). In G. Adler & R. F. C. Hull (Eds. & Trans.), *The collected works of C. G. Jung*. Princeton, NJ: Princeton University Press. (Original work published 1921)

Kaddoura, M. (2013). Think Pair Share: A teaching learning strategy to enhance students' critical thinking. *Educational Research Quarterly, 36*(4), 3–24.

Kashdan, T. B., & Steger, M. F. (2007). Curiosity and pathways to well-being and meaning in life: Traits, states, and everyday behaviors. *Motivation and Emotion, 31*(3), 159–173.

Kercood, S., & Banda, D. R. (2012). The effects of added physical activity on performance during a listening comprehension task for students with and without attention problems. *International Journal of Applied Educational Studies, 13*(1), 19–32.

Keys, D. (2000). *Catastrophe: An investigation into the origins of the modern world*. New York: Ballantine Books.

Kise, J. A. G. (2007). *Differentiation through personality types: A framework for instruction, assessment, and classroom management*. Thousand Oaks, CA: Corwin Press.

Kise, J. A. G. (2009, August 5). *Type tips for memorization*. Presented at the Association for Psychological Type International Conference, Dallas, TX.

Kise, J. A. G. (2010). *Type, learning styles and memorization*. Unpublished manuscript.

Kise, J. A. G. (2014). *Unleashing the positive power of differences: Polarity thinking in our schools*. Thousand Oaks, CA: Corwin Press.

Kise, J. A. G. (2017). *Differentiated coaching: A framework for helping educators change* (2nd ed.). Thousand Oaks, CA: Corwin Press.

Kise, J. A. G. (2019). *Holistic leadership, thriving schools: Twelve lenses to balance priorities and serve the whole student*. Bloomington, IN: Solution Tree Press.

Kise, J. A. G., & Russell, B. (2010). *Creating a coaching culture for professional learning communities*. Bloomington, IN: Solution Tree Press.

Knight, J. (2013). *High-impact instruction: A framework for great teaching.* Thousand Oaks, CA: Corwin Press.

Lai, C.-P., Zhang, W., & Chang, Y.-L. (2020). Differentiated instruction enhances sixth-grade students' mathematics self-efficacy, learning motives, and problem-solving skills. *Social Behavior & Personality: An International Journal, 48*(6).

Lai, H., Wang, S., Zhao, Y., Zhang, L., Yang, C., & Gong, Q. (2019). Brain gray matter correlates of extraversion: A systematic review and meta-analysis of voxel-based morphometry studies. *Human Brain Mapping, 40*(14), 4038–4657.

Lespiau, F., & Tricot, A. (2019). Using primary knowledge: An efficient way to motivate students and promote the learning of formal reasoning. *Educational Psychology Review, 31*(2), 915–938.

Lieberman, M. D. (2013). *Social: Why our brains are wired to connect.* New York: Crown.

Little, C. A., McCoach, D. B., & Reis, S. M. (2014). Effects of differentiated reading instruction on student achievement in middle school. *Journal of Advanced Academics, 25*(4), 384–402.

Learning for Justice. (n.d.a). *Teaching strategy: Say something.* Accessed at www.learningforjustice .org/classroom-resources/teaching-strategies/community-inquiry/say-something on February 25, 2021.

Learning for Justice. (n.d.b). *Teaching strategy: Text-based fishbowl.* Accessed at www .learningforjustice.org/classroom-resources/teaching-strategies/community-inquiry /textbased-fishbowlon February 25, 2021.

Levine, K. (2002). *Hana's suitcase: The quest to solve a Holocaust mystery.* New York: Random House.

Lubin, J., & Polloway, E. A. (2016). Mnemonic instruction in science and social studies for students with learning problems: A review. *Learning Disabilities: A Contemporary Journal, 14*(2), 207–224.

Lyall, S. (2019, September 18). Ann Patchett will eventually discuss her book. *The New York Times.* Accessed at www.nytimes.com/2019/09/18/books/ann-patchett-dutch-house.html on March 15, 2020.

Ma, L. (1999). *Knowing and teaching elementary mathematics: Teachers' understanding of fundamental mathematics in China and the United States.* Mahwah, NJ: Erlbaum.

Ma, L. (2020). *Knowing and teaching elementary mathematics: Teachers' understanding of fundamental mathematics in China and the United States* (20th anniversary ed.). New York: Routledge.

Macdaid, G. P., McCaulley, M. H., & Kainz, R. I. (1987). *Myers-Briggs Type Indicator atlas of type tables.* Gainesville, FL: Center for Applications of Psychological Type.

Main, S., Blackhouse, M., Jackson, R., & Hill, S. (2020). Mitigating reading failure in adolescents: Outcomes of a direct instruction reading program in one secondary school. *Australian Journal of Language and Literacy, 43*(2), 152–166.

Majors, M. (2016). Looking back to Jung: The 8-process scores on the majors type assessments. *TypeFace, 27*(1), 20–21.

Marley, S. C., & Carbonneau, K. J. (2014). Future directions for theory and research with instructional manipulatives: Commentary on the special issue papers. *Educational Psychology Review, 26*(1), 91–100.

Marley, S. C., & Szabo, Z. (2010). Improving children's listening comprehension with a manipulation strategy. *Journal of Educational Research, 103*(4), 227–238.

Martin, J. B. (2017). *Creekfinding: A true story.* Minneapolis, MN: University of Minnesota Press.

Marzano, R. J. (2011–2012). Art and science of teaching: It's how you use a strategy. *Educational Leadership, 69*(4), 88–89.

Massey, S. R. (2015). The multidimensionality of children's picture books for upper grades. *English Journal, 104*(5), 45–58.

McGrath, J. (2013, January 22). *Civil rights—Ruby Bridges* [Video file]. Accessed at www.youtube.com/watch?v=ecBORXfap9A on November 19, 2020.

McMahon, W. (2019). *Differentiation is hard but necessary. (Don't worry, there's help.).* Accessed at www.edsurge.com/news/2019-09-03-differentiation-is-hard-but-necessary-don-t-worry-there-s-help on January 26, 2021.

McPeek, R. W., Breiner, J., Murphy, E., Brock, C., Grossman, L., Loeb, M., et al. (2013). Student type, teacher type, and type training: CAPT type and education research 2008–2011 project summary. *Journal of Psychological Type, 73*(3), 21–54.

McTighe, J., & Curtis, G. (2019). *Leading modern learning: A blueprint for vision-driven schools* (2nd ed.). Bloomington, IN: Solution Tree Press.

McTighe, J., & Wiggins, G. (2013). *Essential questions: Opening doors to student understanding.* Alexandria, VA: Association for Supervision and Curriculum Development.

Meyer, D. (n.d.a). *3 acts real world math tasks.* Accessed at https://tapintoteenminds.com/3acts-by-author/danmeyer on February 25, 2021.

Meyer, D. (n.d.b). *Bucky the badger* [Blog post]. Accessed at https://mrmeyer.com/threeacts/buckythebadger on December 9, 2020.

Meyer, D. (2010, March). *Math class needs a makeover* [Video file]. Accessed at www.ted.com/talks/dan_meyer_math_class_needs_a_makeover on November 18, 2020.

Meyer, D. (2011, May 11). *The three acts of a mathematical story* [Blog post]. Accessed at https://blog.mrmeyer.com/2011/the-three-acts-of-a-mathematical-story on February 25, 2021.

Michigan Medicine. (2018, April 30). *Study explores link between curiosity and school achievement.* Accessed at www.sciencedaily.com/releases/2018/04/180430075616.htm on April 24, 2020.

Mielke, P., & Frontier, T. (2012). Keeping improvement in mind. *Educational Leadership, 70*(3), 10–13.

Mikles, C. (2002). *Making mathematics more visual using algebra tiles.* Sacramento, CA: CPM Education Program.

Mills, M., Monk, S., Keddie, A., Renshaw, P., Christie, P., Geelan, D., & Gowlett, C. (2014). Differentiated learning: From policy to classroom. *Oxford Review of Education, 40*(3), 331–348.

Miller, D. (2009). *The book whisperer: Awakening the inner reader in every child.* San Francisco: Jossey-Bass.

Miller, D. (2013). *Reading in the wild: The book whisperer's keys to cultivating lifelong reading habits.* San Francisco: Jossey-Bass.

Miller, M. (2018). Let them write plays! *Educational Leadership, 75*(7), 38–42.

Minnesota Department of Education. (2019). *Minnesota K–12 academic standards in science —2019* [Commissioner-approved draft]. Roseville, MN: Author. Accessed at https://education.mn.gov/mdeprod/idcplg?IdcService=GET_FILE&dDocName=MDE086711&RevisionSelectionMethod=latestReleased&Rendition=primary on April 20, 2020.

Mooney, M. (1988). *Developing life-long readers.* Katonah, NY: Owen.

Morehead, K., Dunlosky, J., & Rawson, K. A. (2019). How much mightier is the pen than the keyboard for note-taking? A replication and extension of Mueller and Oppenheimer (2014). *Educational Psychology Review, 31*(3), 753–780.

Muhammad, G. (2020). *Cultivating genius: An equity framework for culturally and historically responsive literacy.* New York: Scholastic.

Murphy, E. (1992). *The developing child: Using Jungian type to understand children.* Boston: Brealey.

Murphy, E. (2013). *The developing child: Using Jungian type to understand children.* Gainesville, FL: Center for Applications of Psychological Type.

Myers, I. B., McCaulley, M. H., Quenk, N. L., & Hammer, A. L. (1998). *MBTI manual: A guide to the development and use of the Myers-Briggs Type Indicator* (3rd ed.). Palo Alto, CA: Consulting Psychologists Press.

Myers, I. B., McCaulley, M. H., Quenk, N. L., & Hammer, A. L. (2018). *MBTI manual for the Global Step I and Step II assessments* (4th ed.). Sunnyvale, CA: The Myers-Briggs Company.

Myers, I. B., & Myers, P. B. (1995). *Gifts differing: Understanding personality type* (2nd ed.). Mountain View, CA: Consulting Psychologists Press.

Nardi, D. (2011). *Neuroscience of personality: Brain savvy insights for all types of people.* Los Angeles: Radiance House.

Nardi, D. (2020). *The magic diamond: Jung's 8 paths for self-coaching.* Cheyenne, WY: Radiance House.

National Governors Association Center for Best Practices & Council of Chief State School Officers. (2010). *Common Core State Standards for English language arts and literacy in history/social studies, science, and technical subjects.* Washington, DC: Authors. Accessed at www.corestandards.org/assets/CCSSI_ELA%20Standards.pdf on November 17, 2020.

National Urban Alliance. (2005). *Most essential strategies* [Workshop materials]. New York: Author.

Nunley, K. F. (2006). *Differentiating the high school classroom: Solution strategies for 18 common obstacles*. Thousand Oaks, CA: Corwin Press.

Nunley, K. F. (2014). *An overview of Dr. Kathy Nunley's layered curriculum*. Accessed at https://help4teachers.com/how.htm on February 9, 2021.

Nyong'o, L. (2019). *Sulwe*. New York: Simon & Schuster.

Park, L. S. (2019). *Nya's long walk: A step at a time*. Boston: Houghton Mifflin Harcourt.

Parrish, S. (2010). *Number talks: Helping children build mental math and computation strategies, grades K–5*. Sausalito, CA: Math Solutions.

Patall, E. A., Cooper, H., & Robinson, J. C. (2008). The effects of choice on intrinsic motivation and related outcomes: A meta-analysis of research findings. *Psychological Bulletin, 134*(2), 270–300.

Patchett, A. (2019). *The Dutch house*. New York: HarperCollins.

Payne, D., & VanSant, S. (2009). *Great minds don't think alike: Success for students through the application of psychological type in schools*. Gainesville, FL: Center for Applications of Psychological Type.

Payne, R. K. (2013). *A framework for understanding poverty: A cognitive approach* (5th ed.). Highlands, TX: aha! Process.

Payne, R. K. (2019). *A framework for understanding poverty: A cognitive approach* (6th ed.). Highlands, TX: aha! Process.

Peterson, D. S., & Taylor, B. M. (2012). Using higher order questioning to accelerate students' growth in reading. *The Reading Teacher, 65*(5), 295–304.

Petrilli, M. J. (2011). All together now? Educating high and low achievers in the same classroom. *Education Next, 11*(1). Accessed at www.educationnext.org/all-together-now on March 30, 2019.

Petruța, G.-P. (2017). The possibility of combining some interactive methods for stimulating multiple intelligences in students within biology lessons. *Scientific Papers Agronomy Series, 60*(2), 268–273.

Pink, D. H. (2009). *Drive: The surprising truth about what motivates us*. New York: Riverhead Books.

Pluck, G., & Johnson, H. (2011). Stimulating curiosity to enhance learning. *GESJ: Education Science and Psychology, 2*(19), 24–31.

Popham, W. J. (2011). *Transformative assessment in action: An inside look at applying the process*. Alexandria, VA: Association for Supervision and Curriculum Development.

Powers, R. (2018). *The overstory*. New York: Norton.

Quammen, D. (2008). *Natural acts: A sidelong view of science and nature* (Revised and expanded ed.). New York: Norton. (Original work published 1985)

Rea, D. W., & Zinskie, C. D. (2017). Educating students in poverty: Building equity and capacity with a holistic framework and community school model. *National Youth-at-Risk Journal, 2*(2), 1–24.

Remarque, E. M. (1982). *All quiet on the western front* (A. W. Wheen, Trans.). New York: Ballantine Books.

Ritchhart, R. (2002). *Intellectual character: What it is, why it matters, and how to get it.* San Francisco: Jossey-Bass.

Rohde, M. (2013). *The sketchnote handbook: The illustrated guide to visual note taking.* San Francisco: Peachpit Press.

Rowe, M. B. (1974a). Pausing phenomena: Influence on the quality of instruction. *Journal of Psycholinguistic Research, 3*(3), 203–224.

Rowe, M. B. (1974b). Wait-time and rewards as instructional variables, their influence on language, logic and fate control: Part one—Wait-time. *Journal of Research in Science Teaching, 11*(2), 81–94.

Rowling, J. K. (1997). *Harry Potter and the Sorcerer's Stone.* New York: Scholastic.

Rowling, J. K. (1999). *Harry Potter and the prisoner of Azkaban.* New York: Scholastic.

Santelises, S. B., & Dabrowski, J. (2015). *Checking in: Do classroom assignments reflect today's higher standards?* Washington, DC: The Education Trust. Accessed at https://edtrust.org /wp-content/uploads/2014/09/CheckingIn_TheEducationTrust_Sept20152.pdf on August 26, 2020.

Schmoker, M. (2010). When pedagogic fads trump priorities. *Education Week, 30*(5), 22–23. Accessed at www.edweek.org/ew/articles/2010/09/29/05schmoker.h30.html on August 28, 2020.

Schroeder, N. L., Nesbit, J. C., Anguiano, C. J., & Adesope, O. O. (2018). Studying and constructing concept maps: A meta-analysis. *Educational Psychology Review, 30*(2), 431–455.

Schulze, S., Lüke, T., & Kuhl, J. (2020). Working memory sensitive math intervention for primary school students: A multiple baseline design study. *Learning Disabilities—A Contemporary Journal, 18*(2), 213–240.

Schuster, L., & Anderson, N. C. (2005). *Good questions for math teaching: Why ask them and what to ask, grades 5–8.* Sausalito, CA: Math Solutions.

Schuster, L., & Anderson, N. C. (2020). *Good questions for math teaching: Why ask them and what to ask, grades 5–8* (2nd ed.). Sausalito, CA: Math Solutions.

Scieszka, J. (1989). *The true story of the 3 little pigs! By A. Wolf.* New York: Puffin Books.

Sendova, E., & Boytchev, P. (2019). Keeping the children as question marks: Educational attempts to tap curiosity and the drive for challenge. *Constructivist Foundations, 14*(3), 331–334.

Shakespeare, W. (2019). *Hamlet* (2nd Norton Critical ed.; R. S. Miola, Ed.). New York: Norton. (Original work published 1603)

Shellenbarger, S. (2014, July 29). The power of the doodle: Improve your focus and memory. *The Wall Street Journal*. Accessed at www.wsj.com/articles/the-power-of-the-doodle -improve-your-focus-and-memory-1406675744 on August 28, 2020.

Shure, M. B. (2001). *I can problem solve: An interpersonal cognitive problem-solving program— Preschool* (2nd ed.). Champaign, IL: Research Press.

Sinclair, U. (2001). *The jungle*. Mineola, NY: Dover. (Original work published 1906)

Solnit, R. (2019). *Cinderella liberator*. Chicago: Haymarket Books.

Sousa, D. A., & Tomlinson, C. A. (2018). *Differentiation and the brain: How neuroscience supports the learner-friendly classroom* (2nd ed.). Bloomington, IN: Solution Tree Press.

Spencer, C. (Producer), Johnston, P. (Director), & Moore, R. (Director). (2018). *Ralph breaks the internet* [Motion picture]. United States: Disney Animation Studios.

Spires, A. (2014). *The most magnificent thing*. New York: Hachette.

Spiegelman, A. (2011). *The complete Maus: A survivor's tale* (25th anniversary ed.). New York: Penguin Books.

Starko, A. J. (2005). *Creativity in the classroom: Schools of curious delight* (3rd ed.). Mahwah, NJ: Erlbaum.

Starko, A. J. (2018). *Creativity in the classroom: Schools of curious delight* (6th ed.). New York: Routledge.

Stein, M. K., Smith, M. S., Henningsen, M., & Silver, E. A. (2009). *Implementing standards- based mathematics instruction: A casebook for professional development* (2nd ed.). New York: Teachers College Press.

Stevens, R. (2015). Role-play and student engagement: Reflections from the classroom. *Teaching in Higher Education, 20*(5), 481–492.

Stowe, H. B. (2005). *Uncle Tom's cabin*. West Berlin, NJ: Townsend Press. (Original work published 1852)

Sullivan, P., Bobis, J., Downton, A., Feng, M., Livy, S., Hughes, S., et al. (2020). Characteristics of learning environments in which students are open to risk taking and mistake-making. *Australian Primary Mathematics Classroom Journal, 25*(2), 3–8.

Sullivan, P., & Lilburn, P. (2002). *Good questions for math teaching: Why ask them and what to ask, K–6*. Sausalito, CA: Math Solutions.

Sutherland, M. (2014, May 29–31). *An ISFP speaks: Time to design education to honour all personality types*. Presented at the British Association for Psychological Type Conference, Greenwich, England.

Swaby, R. (2015). *Headstrong: 52 women who changed science—and the world*. New York: Broadway Books.

Tallie, M. E. (2019). *Layla's happiness*. New York: Enchanted Lion Books.

Tan, C. (2017). Teaching critical thinking: Cultural challenges and strategies in Singapore. *British Educational Research Journal, 43*(5), 988–1002.

Tasimi, A., & Wynn, K. (2016). Costly rejection of wrongdoers by infants and children. *Cognition, 151,* 76–79.

Thomas B. Fordham Institute. (2008). *High-achieving students in the era of NCLB.* Washington, DC: Author. Accessed at http://edex.s3-us-west-2.amazonaws.com/publication/pdfs/20080618_high_achievers_7.pdf on March 30, 2019.

Tienken, C. H., Goldberg, S., & DiRocco, D. (2010). Questioning the questions. *Education Digest, 75*(9), 28–32.

Tomlinson, C. A. (2017). *How to differentiate instruction in academically diverse classrooms* (3rd ed.). Alexandria, VA: Association for Supervision and Curriculum Development.

Tomlinson, C. A., & Imbeau, M. B. (2010). *Leading and managing a differentiated classroom.* Alexandria, VA: Association for Supervision and Curriculum Development.

Tovani, C. (2015). Let's switch questioning around. *Educational Leadership, 73*(1), 30–35.

Townsley, M., & Wear, N. L. (2020). *Making grades matter: Standards-based grading in a secondary PLC at Work.* Bloomington, IN: Solution Tree Press.

Ulstad, S. O., Halvari, H., Sørebø, Ø., & Deci, E. L. (2018). Motivational predictors of learning strategies, participation, exertion, and performance in physical education: A randomized controlled trial. *Motivation and Emotion, 42*(4), 497–512.

Vilen, A., & Berger, R. (2020). Courageous conversations for equity and agency. *Educational Leadership, 77*(7), 39–44.

Vîrgă, D., Curşeu, P. L., Maricuţoiu, L., Sava, F. A., Macsinga, I., & Măgurean, S. (2014). Personality, relationship conflict, and teamwork-related mental models. *PLOS ONE, 9*(12), 1–9.

Virginia Board of Education. (2008). *History and social science standards of learning for Virginia public schools.* Richmond, VA: Author. Accessed at www.doe.virginia.gov/testing/sol/standards_docs/history_socialscience/next_version/stds_all_history.pdf on March 8, 2020.

Wallace, T. L., & Sung, H. C. (2017). Student perceptions of autonomy-supportive instructional interactions in the middle grades. *Journal of Experimental Education, 85*(3), 425–449.

Wallis, C., & Dell, K. (2004, May 10). What makes teens tick. *TIME.* Accessed at http://content.time.com/time/magazine/article/0,9171,994126,00.html on December 8, 2020.

Wallmark, L. (2019). *Hedy Lamarr's double life: Hollywood legend and brilliant inventor.* New York: Sterling Children's Books.

Warner, J. (2018). *Why they can't write: Killing the five-paragraph essay and other necessities.* Baltimore, MD: Johns Hopkins Press.

Webb, N. L. (2002, March 28). *Depth-of-knowledge levels for four content areas.* Accessed at www.acpsd.net/cms/lib/SC02209457/Centricity/Domain/74/DOK%20Four%20Content%20Areas%20Webb.pdf on November 19, 2020.

White, E. B. (1980). *Charlotte's web.* New York: HarperCollins.

White, K. (2019). *Unlocked: Assessment as the key to everyday creativity in the classroom.* Bloomington, IN: Solution Tree Press.

Wiggins, A. (2017). *The best class you never taught: How spider web discussion can turn students into learning leaders.* Alexandria, VA: Association for Supervision and Curriculum Development.

Wiggins, A. (2020). A better way to assess discussions. *Educational Leadership, 77*(7), 34–38.

Wiggins, G., & McTighe, J. (2005). *Understanding by design* (Expanded 2nd ed.). Alexandria, VA: Association for Supervision and Curriculum Development.

Wiliam, D. (2011). *Embedded formative assessment.* Bloomington, IN: Solution Tree Press.

Wiliam, D. (2018). *Embedded formative assessment* (2nd ed.). Bloomington, IN: Solution Tree Press.

Winter, J. (2017). *The world is not a rectangle: A portrait of architect Zaha Hadid.* New York: Beach Lane Books.

Wolf, M. (2018). *Reader, come home: The reading brain in a digital world.* New York: HarperCollins.

Yousafzai, M. (2017). *Malala's magic pencil.* New York: Little, Brown.

Zusak, M. (2006). *The book thief.* New York: Knopf.

Index

Holistic Leadership, Thriving Schools
Jane A. G. Kise
Build a school where students flourish academically while getting their needs met socially, physically, and emotionally. With this practical guide, school leaders will discover a toolkit of strategies for navigating competing priorities and uniting their school communities around one common purpose: supporting the whole child.
BKF821

Neurodevelopmental Differentiation
Andrew Fuller and Lucy Fuller
Imagine schools where everyone learns at high levels. Not just some students. Every student. Backed by both scientific and educational research, this resource aims to help educators bring these schools to life through the power of neurodevelopmental differentiation.
BKB015

Step In, Step Up
Jane A. G. Kise and Barbara K. Watterston
Step In, Step Up guides current and aspiring women leaders in education through a twelve-week development journey. An assortment of activities, reflection prompts, and stories empowers readers to overcome gender barriers and engage in opportunities to learn, grow, and lead within their school communities.
BKF827

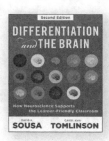

Differentiation and the Brain, Second Edition
David A. Sousa and Carol Ann Tomlinson
The second edition of this best-selling resource will help you create truly effective, brain-friendly classrooms for all learners. The authors share an array of updated examples, scenarios, and exercises, as well as the latest research from cognitive psychology, neuroscience, and pedagogy.
BKF804

Solution Tree | Press

a division of
Solution Tree

Visit SolutionTree.com or call 800.733.6786 to order.